Series 99
Operations Professional Qualification Examination

License Exam Manual

KAPLAN FINANCIAL EDUCATION

At press time, this edition contains the most complete and accurate information currently available. Owing to the nature of license examinations, however, information may have been added recently to the actual test that does not appear in this edition. Please contact the publisher to verify that you have the most current edition.

This publication is designed to provide accurate and authoritative information in regard to the subject matter covered. It is sold with the understanding that the publisher is not engaged in rendering legal, accounting, or other professional services. If legal advice or other expert assistance is required, the services of a competent professional should be sought.

SERIES 99 OPERATIONS PROFESSIONAL QUALIFICATION EXAMINATION LICENSE EXAM MANUAL
©2011 Kaplan, Inc.

If you find imperfections or incorrect information in this product, please visit www.kfeducation.com and submit an errata report.

Published in November 2011 by Kaplan Financial Education.

Printed in the United States of America.

ISBN: 978-1-4277-3884-4 / 1-4277-3884-X

PPN: 3200-2099

Contents

2   Broker-Dealer Operations   45

Introduction

Welcome to the Series 99 License Exam Manual. Thank you for choosing this exam preparation system for your educational needs. This manual has applied adult learning principles to give you the tools you'll need to pass your exam on the first attempt.

Some of these special features include:

- exam-focused questions and content to maximize exam preparation;
- an interactive design that integrates content with questions to increase retention;
- integrated SecuritiesPro™ QBank exam preparation tools to sharpen test-taking skills; and
- exam-tips blog, updates, and addenda.

Securities licensing exams are now known as FINRA exams. Exam questions may include reference to the FINRA organization when speaking of the industry's self-regulator. However, you will continue to see exam questions refer to either NASD or NYSE, particularly when specific rules are referenced. It is expected this will continue until all the individual rules of NASD and NYSE have been consolidated after each rule has been approved by the SEC.

Why Do I Need to Pass the Series 99 Exam?

The Series 99 examination is designed to prove minimum competency of entry-level investment bankers. This examination is intended in part to protect investors by measuring the degree to which each representative has the ability to perform the major functions of an entry-level investment banker.

Exception to the Series 99 Examination Requirement

Certain registration categories will permit registration as an Operations Professional without passing the Series 99 examination.

Anyone holding the following registration categories within the two years immediately prior to registering as an Operations Professional may qualify as an Operations Professional without taking the Series 99 examination:

- Registered Options Principal (Series 4)
- Investment Company Products/Variable Contracts Representative (Series 6)
- General Securities Representative (Series 7)
- General Securities Sales Supervisor (Series 9/10)
- Compliance Officer (Series 14)
- Supervisory Analyst (Series 16)
- United Kingdom Securities Representative (Series 17)
- General Securities Principal (Series 24)

- Investment Company Products/Variable Products Principal (Series 26)
- Financial and Operations Principal (Series 27)
- Introducing Broker-Dealer Financial and Operations Principal (Series 28)
- Canada Securities Representative (Series 37 or 38)
- Municipal Fund Securities Limited Principal (Series 51)
- Municipal Securities Principal (Series 53)

Are There Any Prerequisites?

You must be associated with a member firm.

What Is the Series 99 Exam Like?

The Series 99 is a 2 1/2-hour, 100-question exam administered by FINRA. It is offered as a computer-based exam at Prometric or Pearson VUE testing centers around the country.

What Score Must I Achieve to Pass?

The passing score for the Series 99 examination is NOT necessarily 70% because multiple forms of the examination are administered. Passing scores will fluctuate moderately from examination to examination. One individual may pass with a 71% while another may fail with a 72%, depending on the weighting of each exam question.

What Topics Will I See on the Exam?

The questions you will see on the Series 99 exam do not appear in any particular order. The computer is programmed to select a new, random set of questions for each exam taker according to the preset topic weighting of the exam. Each Series 99 candidate will see the same number of questions on each topic but will see a different mix of questions.

The Series 99 exam is divided into three critical function areas.

Content Area	Number of Questions
1. Basic Knowledge Associated with the Securities Industry	32
2. Basic Knowledge Associated with Broker-Dealer Operations	48
3. Professional Conduct and Ethical Considerations	20
	100

PREPARING FOR THE EXAM

How Is the License Exam Manual Organized?

The License Exam Manual consists of units and Unit Tests. In addition to the regular text, each unit has some unique features designed to help you with quick understanding of the material. When an additional point will be valuable to your comprehension, special notes are embedded in the text. Examples of these are included in the following.

TAKE NOTE

These highlight special or unusual information and amplify important points.

TEST TOPIC ALERT

Each Test Topic Alert! highlights content that is likely to appear on the exam.

EXAMPLE

These give practical examples and numerical instances of the material just covered and convert theory into practice.

You will also see Quick Quizzes, which will help ensure that you understand and retain the material covered in that particular section. Quick Quizzes are a quick interactive review of what you just read.

The book is made up of units organized to explain the material that FINRA has outlined for the exam.

The SecuritiesPro™ QBank contains a large bank of questions that are similar in style and content to those you will encounter on the exam. You may use it to generate tests by a specific topic or create exams that are similar in difficulty and proportionate mixture to the exam.

Your study packet also includes Mastery Exams. These are designed to closely simulate the true exam center experience in degree of difficulty and topic coverage and are an exceptional indicator of future actual exam score as well as areas of strength and weakness. When you have completed these exams, you will receive a detailed breakdown by topic of performance. This diagnostic breakdown will alert you to precisely where you need to concentrate further exam practice.

What Topics Are Covered in the Course?

The License Exam Manual consists of three units, each devoted to a particular area of study that you will need to know to pass the Series 99. Each unit is divided into study sections devoted to more specific areas with which you need to become familiar.

How Much Time Should I Spend Studying?

Plan to spend approximately 30–40 hours reading the material and carefully answering the questions. Spread your study time over the 2–3 weeks before the date on which you are scheduled to take the Series 99 exam. Your actual time may vary depending on your reading rate, comprehension, professional background, and study environment.

What Is the Best Way to Structure My Study Time?

The following schedule is suggested to help you obtain maximum retention from your study efforts. Remember, this is a guideline only because each individual may require more or less time to complete the steps included.

Step 1. Read a unit and complete the Unit Test. Review rationales for all questions whether you got them right or wrong (2–3 hours per unit).

Step 2. On the SecuritiesPro™ QBank, create and complete a test for each topic included under that unit heading. For best results, select the maximum number of questions within each topic. Carefully review all rationales. Do an additional test on any topic on which you score under 60%. After completion of all topic tests, create a 25-question test comprising all unit topics. Repeat this 25-question test until you score at least 70% (4–6 hours).

TAKE NOTE
Do not be overly concerned with your score on the first attempt at any of these tests. Instead, take the opportunity to learn from your mistakes and increase your knowledge.

Step 3. When you have finished the units and their Unit Tests on the QBank, then complete at least four of the 100-question exams. Complete as many as necessary to achieve a score of at least 80–90%. Create and complete additional topic tests as necessary to correct problem areas.

Step 4. Each Online Practice Final mirrors the actual test in number of questions and subject matter coverage. Questions included in these exams are unique from all other question bank products, so you will see only new questions. Like the actual exam, you will not see the answer key and rationale, but the detailed diagnostic breakdown will provide you with clear guidance on areas where further study is required (2–3 hours per exam).

How Well Can I Expect to Do?

The exams administered by FINRA are not easy. You must display considerable understanding and knowledge of the topics presented in this course to pass the exam and qualify for registration.

If you study diligently, complete all sections of the course, and consistently score at least 85% on the tests, you should be well prepared to pass the exam. However, it is important for you to realize that merely knowing the answers to our questions will not enable you to pass unless you understand the essence of the information behind the question.

Successful Test-Taking Tips

Passing the exam depends not only on how well you learn the subject matter but also on how well you take exams. You can develop your test-taking skills—and improve your score—by learning the following test-taking techniques:

■ Read the full question

■ Avoid jumping to conclusions—watch for hedge clauses

■ Interpret the unfamiliar question

■ Look for key words and phrases

■ Identify the intent of the question

■ Memorize key points

■ Use a calculator

■ Avoid changing answers

■ Pace yourself

Each of these pointers is explained in the following, including examples that show how to use them to improve your performance on the exam.

Read the Full Question

You cannot expect to answer a question correctly if you do not know what it is asking. If you see a question that seems familiar and easy, you might anticipate the answer, mark it, and move on before you finish reading it. This is a serious mistake. Be sure to read the full question before answering it—questions are often written to trap people who assume too much.

Avoid Jumping to Conclusions—Watch for Hedge Clauses

The questions on FINRA exams are often embellished with deceptive distractors as choices. To avoid being misled by seemingly obvious answers, make it a practice to read each question and each answer twice before selecting your choice. Doing so will provide you with a much better chance of doing well on the exam.

Watch out for hedge clauses embedded in the question. (Examples of hedge clauses include the terms if, not, all, none, and except.) In the case of if statements, the question can be answered correctly only by taking into account the qualifier. If you ignore the qualifier, you will not answer correctly.

Qualifiers are sometimes combined in a question. Some that you will frequently see together are all with except and none with except. In general, when a question starts with all or none and ends with except, you are looking for an answer that is opposite to what the question appears to be asking.

Interpret the Unfamiliar Question

Do not be surprised if some questions on the exam seem unfamiliar at first. If you have studied your material, you will have the information to answer all of the questions correctly. The challenge may be a matter of understanding what the question is asking.

Very often, questions present information indirectly. You may have to interpret the meaning of certain elements before you can answer the question. Be aware that the exam will approach a concept from different angles.

Look for Key Words and Phrases

Look for words that are tip-offs to the situation presented. For example, if you see the word prospectus in the question, you know the question is about a new issue. Sometimes a question will even supply you with the answer if you can recognize the key words it contains. Few questions provide blatant clues, but many do offer key words that can guide you to selecting the correct answer if you pay attention. Be sure to read all instructional phrases carefully.

Take time to identify the key words to answer this type of question correctly.

Identify the Intent of the Question

Many questions on FINRA exams supply so much information that you lose track of what is being asked. This is often the case in story problems. Learn to separate the story from the question.

Take the time to identify what the question is asking. Of course, your ability to do so assumes you have studied sufficiently. There is no method for correctly answering questions if you don't know the material.

Memorize Key Points

Reasoning and logic will help you answer many questions, but you will have to memorize a good deal of information.

Check the Exam-Tips Blog

On the Kaplan Series 99 Website, there are a number of important tools to keep you current. The *Exam-tips Blog*, *Updates/Addenda*, and *Corrections* links are valuable assets that should be checked often.

Use a Calculator

It is unlikely that the Series 99 will require the use of a calculator. However, if you have become accustomed to using a calculator for math (if any), you will be provided with one by the testing center staff.

Avoid Changing Answers

If you are unsure of an answer, your first hunch is the one most likely to be correct. Do not change answers on the exam without good reason. In general, change an answer only if you:

- discover that you did not read the question correctly; or
- find new or additional helpful information in another question.

Pace Yourself

Some people will finish the exam early and some do not have time to finish all of the questions. Watch the time carefully (your time remaining will be displayed on your computer screen) and pace yourself throughout the exam.

Do not waste time by dwelling on a question if you simply do not know the answer. Make the best guess you can, mark the question for Record for Review, and return to the question if time allows. Make sure that you have time to read all of the questions so that you can record the answers you do know.

THE EXAM

How Do I Enroll in the Exam?

To obtain an admission ticket to a FINRA exam, your firm must file an application form and processing fees with FINRA. To take the exam, you should make an appointment with a Prometric Testing Center as far in advance as possible of the date on which you would like to take the exam.

You may schedule your appointment at Prometric, 24 hours a day, seven days a week, on the secure Prometric Website at www.prometric.com or Pearson VUE at www.vue.com/finra. You may also use these sites to reschedule or cancel your exam, locate a test center, and get a printed confirmation of your appointment. To speak with a Prometric representative by phone, please contact the Prometric Contact Center at 1-800-578-6273 or Pearson VUE at 1-866-396-6273. You must have your Central Registration Depository (CRD) number available when scheduling an exam. This unique personal identification number should be provided to you by your member firm.

What Should I Take to the Exam?

Take one form of personal identification with your signature and photograph as issued by a government agency. You cannot take reference materials or anything else into the testing area. Basic calculators, along with scratch paper and pencils, will be provided by the testing center proctors, although you cannot take them with you when you leave.

Additional Trial Questions

During your exam, you will see extra trial questions. These are potential exam-bank questions being tested during the course of the exam. These questions are not included in your final score and you will be given extra time to answer them.

Exam Results and Reports

At the end of the exam, your score will be displayed, indicating whether you passed. The next business day after your exam, your results will be emailed to your firm and to the self-regulatory organization and state securities commission specified on your application.

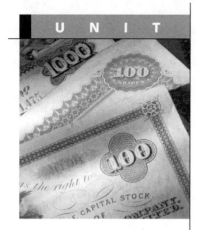

1

Securities Industry

T he securities industry is the marketplace where companies can raise capital to fund operations, and the investing public may invest in the companies. The financial instruments used to fund these operations come in two forms: equity (ownership) and debt. This unit will review the basic structure of financial markets and the various securities offered therein.

This unit will cover information that will account for 32 questions on the Series 99 exam.

When you have completed this unit, you should be able to:

■ **describe** the different markets and functions of SROs;

■ **describe** clearing and depository facilities;

■ **contrast** public and private offerings;

■ **contrast** SIPC and the FDIC;

■ **list** and **describe** the various types of securities;

■ **explain** and **contrast** the roles of broker/dealers and registered investment advisors;

■ **list** and **describe** a broker/dealer's net capital requirements and reporting methods;

■ **list** and **contrast** the types of broker/dealers;

■ **explain** commissions and markups; and

■ **describe** institutional clearings and settlement arrangements.

1. 1 THE COMPANY

Whenever a group of people work together to provide a product or service to customers, they form a unit in the foundation of business: a company. Whether it is a two-person partnership or a corporation of thousands of employees, they are all seeking to do the same thing: generate profits to employ workers and compensate owners.

There are many forms a company may take, each with their own advantages and disadvantages. In order to understand the company's operations, it is important to understand the framework it works under, as well as the risks associated with ownership in the company.

1. 1. 1   CORPORATIONS

A corporation is a legal entity that has been created by the laws of the state in which it is incorporated. Upon creation, a corporation becomes a person, with many of the same legal characteristics of a natural person (an individual).

Unlike natural persons, however, a corporation is immortal. While companies that are formed as a partnership cease with the death or retirement of a partner, a corporation will continue to exist unless it is dissolved through liquidation.

This status as a separate legal entity from its owners (shareholders) provides benefits to its owners. Specifically, it provides the owners with a limited liability, allowing them to not be held responsible for the liability of the corporation.

Corporations are organized under a board structure, where a board of directors represents the shareholders and oversees and appoints the firm's management. Taxation of a corporation varies depending on which subchapter of Chapter 1 of the Internal Revenue Code it elects to be taxed under.

1. 1. 2   REAL ESTATE INVESTMENT TRUSTS (REITs)

A real estate investment trust (REIT) is a company that manages a portfolio of real estate investments in order to earn profits for shareholders. REITs may be traded publicly and serve as a source of long-term financing for real estate projects. A REIT pools capital in a manner similar to an investment company, and shareholders receive dividends from investment income or capital gains distributions.

REITs are organized as trusts where investors buy shares or certificates of beneficial interest either on stock exchanges or in the OTC market. Under the guidelines of Subchapter M of the Internal Revenue Code, a REIT can avoid being taxed as a corporation by having at least 75% of total investment assets in real estate, deriving at least 75% of gross income from rents or mortgage interest, and distributing 90% or more of its net investment income to its shareholders.

1. 2 EQUITY SECURITIES

When individual investors become owners of a corporation by purchasing stock in that company, they can participate in the company's prosperity by sharing in earnings through the receipt of dividends (distributed profits) and, particularly in the case of common stock, benefit from an increase in the price of the shares.

1. 2. 1   COMMON STOCK

Common stock represents equity ownership in a corporation. A company issues stock to raise business capital, and investors who buy the stock also buy a share of ownership in the company's net worth. Whatever a business owns (its assets) less its creditors' claims (its liabilities) belongs to the businessowners (its stockholders).

Each share of stock entitles its owner to a portion of the company's earnings and dividends and a proportionate vote in major management decisions. Most corporations are organized in such a way that their stockholders regularly vote for and elect a few individuals to a board of directors to oversee company business. By electing a board of directors, stockholders have a say in the company's management but are not involved in the day-to-day details of its operations.

EXAMPLE

If a corporation issues 100 shares of stock, each share represents an identical 1/100—or 1%—ownership position in the company. An investor who owns 10 shares of stock would own 10% of the company; an investor who owns 50 shares of stock would own 50% of the company.

Corporations may issue two types of stock: common and preferred. When speaking of stocks, people generally mean common stock. Preferred stock also represents equity ownership in a corporation but usually does not have the same voting rights or appreciation potential as common stock. Preferred stock normally pays a fixed quarterly dividend and has priority claims over common stock; that is, the preferred is paid first if a company goes bankrupt, and common stockholders will never receive a dividend until the preferred shareholders have been paid theirs.

Sample Stock Certificate

1. 2. 1. 1 Benefits of Owning Common Stock

1. 2. 1. 1. 1 Growth (Capital Gains)

An increase in the market price of securities is capital appreciation. Historically, owning common stock has provided investors with returns in excess of the inflation rate. For this reason, most investors with a long-term investment horizon have included common stock in their portfolios as a hedge against inflation. Of course, it must be mentioned that stock prices can decline, particularly over the short run.

EXAMPLE An investor buys shares of RST for $60 per share on January 1, 2012. On December 31, 2012, the shares are worth $90, an increase of 50% in the market price.

1. 2. 1. 1. 2 Income

Many corporations pay regular quarterly cash dividends to stockholders. A company's dividends may increase over time as profitability increases. Dividends, which can be a significant source of income for investors, are a major reason many people invest in stocks.

Issuers may also pay stock dividends (additional shares in the issuing company) or property dividends (shares in a subsidiary company or a product sample).

EXAMPLE RST paid a dividend of $2 per share during 2011, which provided the investor with a dividend yield of 3.3% ($2 ÷ $60 = 3.33%) in addition to the price appreciation.

TAKE NOTE The increase in the price of RST stock in the previous example is an unrealized gain until the stock is sold; when it is sold, it becomes a realized gain. Capital gains are not taxed until they are realized.

1. 2. 1. 1. 3 Rights of Stockholders

Common stockholders have the right to vote for corporate directors. Frequently, it is not possible for the stockholder to attend the stockholder's meetings to personally cast his vote. An absentee ballot, known as a **proxy**, is made available for those shareholders who vote by mail. They have the right to sell or give away their shares without permission of the corporation. Common stock is freely transferable to anyone who wants to buy it or receive it as a gift. Without this feature, there would be no stock markets. Common stockholders have a right to limited access to the corporation's books.

For the most part, common stockholders have the right to examine the minutes of meetings of the board of directors and the right to examine the list of the stockholders. Usually, this right is not exercised unless the performance of the corporation's management declines seriously. They also have the right to receive an audited set of financial statements of the company's performance each year (annual reports).

Common stockholders usually have the preemptive right to maintain their proportionate share of ownership in the corporation. The word *preempt* means to put oneself in front of another.

1. 2. 1. 1. 4 Limited Liability

One of the most important features of equity ownership (common stock or preferred stock) is limited liability. In the event of a corporation's bankruptcy, when corporate assets are not adequate to meet corporate obligations, personal assets are not at risk. One cannot be forced to sell any personal assets to help pay the debts of the business.

If an individual invests $5,000 in the stock of a corporation that goes bankrupt, he may lose his entire $5,000 if the company is not salvaged, but he will not be forced to pay out any more monies to take care of additional debts. He is personally at risk only for the amount he has invested. A partner or sole proprietor risks not only the amount he has personally invested in his business, but also his personal assets should the business not be able to pay off its obligations.

1. 2. 1. 2 Risks of Owning Common Stock

Regardless of their expectations, investors have no assurances that they will receive the returns they expect from their investments.

1. 2. 1. 2. 1 Market Risk

The chance that a stock will decline in price is one risk of owning common stock (known as market risk). A stock's price fluctuates daily as perceptions of the company's business prospects change and influence the actions of buyers and sellers. Investors have no assurance whatsoever that they will be able to recoup the investment in a stock at any time.

1. 2. 1. 2. 2 Decreased or No Income

A risk of stock ownership is the possibility of dividend income decreasing or ceasing entirely if the company loses money.

1. 2. 1. 2. 3 Low Priority at Dissolution

If a company enters bankruptcy, the holders of its bonds and preferred stock have priority over common stockholders. A company's debt and preferred shares are considered senior securities. Common stockholders have residual rights to corporate assets upon dissolution.

TAKE NOTE

In owning common equity, the investor stands to lose current income through dividend reduction or suspension, as well as capital loss, should the market price decline. In return, however, the shareholder has limited liability; that is, the liability is limited to the amount invested.

In summation, why would you include common stock in a client's portfolio?

- Potential capital appreciation
- Income from dividends
- Hedge against inflation

In doing so, the client would be incurring the following risks:

- Market
- Business difficulties leading to possible reduction or elimination of the dividend and even bankruptcy leading to loss of principal

1. 2. 2   PREFERRED STOCK

Preferred stock is an equity security because it represents a class of ownership in the issuing corporation. However, it does share some characteristics with a debt security. Just as with debt securities, the rate of return on a preferred stock is fixed rather than subject to variation as with common stock. As a result, its price tends to fluctuate with changes in interest rates rather than with the issuing company's business prospects unless, of course, dramatic changes occur in the company's ability to pay dividends. This concept, known as interest rate or money rate risk, will be covered in greater detail later in this unit during the discussion of fixed-income securities.

TAKE NOTE   Unlike common stock, most preferred stock is nonvoting.

TEST TOPIC ALERT   Like common stock, preferred stock represents ownership in a company, but its price reacts to the market more like a bond because with its fixed dividend payment, its price is sensitive to interest rate changes.

1. 2. 2. 1   Benefits of Preferred Stock

Although preferred stock does not typically have the same growth potential as common stock, preferred stockholders have four advantages over common stockholders. When the board of directors declares dividends, owners of preferred stock must be paid prior to any payment to common shareholders.

A preferred stock's fixed dividend is a key feature for income-oriented investors. Normally, a preferred stock is identified by its annual dividend payment stated as a percentage of its par value. A preferred stock with a par value of $100 that pays $6 in annual dividends would be known as a 6% preferred. The dividend of preferred stock with no par value is stated in a dollar amount (e.g., a $6 no-par preferred).

- If a corporation goes bankrupt, preferred stockholders have a priority claim over common stockholders on the assets remaining after creditors have been paid.
- Although it is generally regarded as a fixed-income investment, preferred stock, unlike debt securities, usually has no preset date at which it matures and no scheduled redemption date. Preferred stock is, thus, a perpetual security.

Because the primary objective met by investing in preferred stock is income, when analyzing a specific preferred stock, the most important determination should be the ability of the company to meet its dividend payments.

1. 2. 2. 2   Types of Preferred Stock

Separate categories of preferred may differ in several ways, including dividend rate and profit participation privileges. However, all maintain preference over common stock.

Remember, preferred stock is an equity security and, just as with common stock, dividends are paid at the discretion of the board of directors. What is special about preferred stock is that no dividend can ever be paid to the common stockholders unless the preferred is satisfied first.

Preferred stock may have one or more of the following characteristics.

1. 2. 2. 2. 1   Straight (Noncumulative)

Straight preferred has no special features beyond the stated dividend payment. Missed dividends are not paid to the holder.

1. 2. 2. 2. 2   Cumulative Preferred

Cumulative preferred stock accrues payments due its shareholders in the event dividends are reduced or suspended.

Dividends due cumulative preferred stock accumulate on the company's books until the corporation's board of directors decides to pay them. When the company resumes dividend payments, cumulative preferred stockholders receive current dividends plus the total accumulated dividends—dividends in arrears—before any dividends may be distributed to common stockholders.

EXAMPLE   In 2008, RST Corp. had both common stock and cumulative preferred stock outstanding. The common paid a dividend of $1, and the preferred paid a $2 dividend. Because of financial difficulties, the company stopped paying dividends during 2008. After resolving its problems in 2012, the company resumed dividend payments and paid the cumulative preferred holders an $8 dividend for the arrears in years 2008, 2009, 2010, and 2011 plus the current year's (2012) $2 dividend before paying any dividends to the common stockholders.

Because of this unique feature, found only with cumulative preferred stock, an investor seeking steady income would find this to be the most suitable of the different types of preferred stock.

1. 2. 2. 2. 3   Callable Preferred

Corporations often issue callable (or redeemable) preferred, which a company can buy back from investors at a stated price after a specified date. The right to call the stock allows the company to replace a relatively high fixed dividend obligation with a lower one when the cost of money has gone down. This is similar to refinancing a mortgage.

When a corporation calls a preferred stock, dividend payments cease on the call date. In return for the call privilege, the corporation may pay a premium exceeding the stock's par value at the call, such as $103 for a $100 par value stock. This can create a problem for your client who purchased callable preferred shares issued at a time when market conditions dictated relatively high dividend rates. If the cost of new money comes down, the company will call in the preferred, and the investor will now have to reinvest the proceeds at a lower rate.

1. 2. 2. 2. 4   Convertible Preferred

A preferred stock is convertible if the owner can exchange the shares for a fixed number of shares of the issuing corporation's common stock.

TAKE NOTE

Because the value of a convertible preferred stock is linked to the value of a common stock, the convertible preferred's price tends to fluctuate in line with the common.

Convertible preferred is generally issued with a lower stated dividend rate than nonconvertible preferred of the same quality because the investor may have the opportunity to convert to common shares and enjoy greater capital gain potential. The concept of a convertible security will be discussed in greater detail later in this unit when we cover convertible bonds.

1. 2. 2. 2. 5   Adjustable-Rate Preferred

Some preferred stocks are issued with adjustable (or variable) dividend rates. Such dividends are usually tied to the rates of other interest rate benchmarks, such as Treasury bills and money market rates, and can be adjusted as often as quarterly. Because the payment adjusts to current interest rates, the price of the stock remains relatively stable.

TEST TOPIC ALERT

For investors looking for income through preferred stocks, this would be their least appropriate choice.

QUICK QUIZ 1.A

1. Which of the following types of preferred stock typically has the highest stated rate of dividend (all other factors being equal)?

    A. Convertible
    B. Straight
    C. Cumulative
    D. Callable

2. Of straight and cumulative preferred, which would have the higher stated rate?
    A. Straight preferred
    B. Cumulative preferred

3. Which of the following types of preferred stock is most influenced by the price of an issuer's common stock?
    A. Cumulative
    B. Straight
    C. Convertible
    D. Callable

Quick Quiz answers can be found at the end of the unit.

1. 2. 2. 3   Risks of Owning Preferred Stock

Owners of preferred stock face several risks.

- As a fixed-income security, there is no inflation protection.
- As a fixed-income security, when interest rates rise, the value of preferred shares declines.
- As an equity security, there is the risk that dividends may be skipped.
- As an equity security, in the event of a corporate liquidation or bankruptcy, all creditors have a prior claim against the assets.

In summation, why would you include preferred stock in a client's portfolio?

- Fixed income from dividends
- Prior claim ahead of common stock
- Convertible preferred sacrifices income in exchange for potential appreciation

In doing so, the client would be incurring the following risks:

- Possible loss of purchasing power
- Interest rate (money rate) risk
- Business difficulties leading to possible reduction or elimination of the dividend and even bankruptcy leading to loss of principal

1. 2. 3   FOREIGN INVESTMENTS: AMERICAN DEPOSITARY RECEIPTS (ADRs)

American depositary receipts (ADRs), also known as American depositary shares (ADSs), facilitate the trading of foreign stocks in US markets because everything is done in English and in US dollars. An ADR is a negotiable security that represents a receipt for shares of stock in a non-US corporation, usually from 1 to 10 shares. ADRs are bought and sold in the US securities markets like any stock.

1. 2. 3. 1   Rights of ADR Owners

Most of the rights that common stockholders normally hold, such as the right to receive dividends, also apply to ADR owners.

1. 2. 3. 2   Currency Risk

In addition to the normal risks associated with stock ownership, ADR investors are also subject to currency risk. Currency risk is the possibility that an investment denominated in one currency (such as the Mexican peso) could decline if the value of that currency declines in its exchange rate with the US dollar. Because ADRs represent shares of stock in companies located in foreign countries, currency exchange rates are an important consideration.

1. 3 FIXED INCOME (DEBT SECURITIES)

Debt capital represents money loaned to a corporation by investors evidenced by that corporation's bonds. A bond is a certificate representing the corporation's indebtedness. It is a loan made to the corporation by an investor. These certificates state the corporation's obligation to pay back a specific amount of money on a specific date. They also state a corporation's obligation to pay the investor a specific rate of interest for the use of his funds. When an investor buys a bond, he is lending a corporation money for a set period of time at a fixed annual interest rate. For taxation purposes, all corporate bond interest is fully taxable as ordinary income on both federal and state tax returns.

It is important to understand that debt capital refers to long-term debt financing. Long-term debt, frequently called funded debt on the exam, is money borrowed for a minimum of five years, although more frequently the length of time is 20–30 years.

Even though only corporations have been mentioned to this point, it is important to know that there are two other major issuers of debt securities. The largest issuer of debt securities is the US government.

Substantial sums are also borrowed by state governments and those political entities that are subdivisions of a state, such as cities, counties, towns, and so forth.

These issues from state and local political entities are called municipal bonds. Whenever the word *government* is used in conjunction with a security on the exam, it means the federal government.

Whenever the term *municipal security* is used on the exam, it is referring to a security issued by a state or other municipality.

1. 3. 1   ROLE AS LENDER

The most important fact in discussing debt securities is the investor's position as lender: he is acquiring no ownership but is placing himself in the role of creditor.

Has anyone ever asked you to loan them money? If so, there were probably four questions that you needed to answer for yourself before you could agree to the loan.

■ How much am I lending?

■ How safe is my loan and how sure am I that I will get my money back?

■ How much interest will I be paid for the use of my money?

■ How and when will I get my money back?

Let's take a look at the first question because it's the simplest to answer. Although the overall size of the issue may be anywhere from several million dollars to billions of dollars in the case of government issues, the face amount, or par value, of each bond is always $1,000, unless otherwise specified. That is, loans in the form of bonds are always made in $1,000 units.

For common stock, par value is of no importance to the investor. With preferred stock, par value is the number on which the dividend is based. Par value is even more important with bonds because not only does it represent what the interest payment is based on, but it also represents the amount of principal to be repaid at maturity.

1. 3. 2　SAFETY OF PRINCIPAL—CORPORATE DEBT

Corporate debt securities, like any other loan, may be either secured or unsecured. Secured debt securities are backed by various kinds of assets of the issuing corporation, whereas unsecured debt securities are backed only by the reputation, credit record, and financial stability of the corporation.

1. 3. 2. 1　Mortgage Bonds

Just as the owner of a home pledges a real asset (the home and land) as collateral for the mortgage, a corporation will borrow money backed by real estate and physical assets of the corporation. Just as a home ordinarily would have a market value greater than the principal amount of its mortgage, the value of the real assets pledged by the corporation will be in excess of the amount borrowed under that bond issue. If the corporation develops financial problems and is unable to pay the interest on the bonds, those real assets pledged as collateral are generally sold to pay off the mortgage bondholders.

The principle is no different from having a mortgage on a home. Does the lender of a home mortgage feel his loan to a buyer is secure? If the buyer couldn't pay, could he sell the home for more than the mortgage? Probably so. A purchaser of a mortgage bond is in the same position of safety.

1. 3. 2. 2　Equipment Trust Certificate

When an automobile is purchased, a down payment is made, and the remaining balance is financed for an estimated three or four years. Because the asset would decrease in value, the buyer would have to make a down payment so that the value of the collateral (the automobile) would not be less than the amount financed. The buyer would pay off this note with monthly installments so that the value of the automobile was never worth less than the amount owed to the lender. If payment could not be made, the lender would repossess the automobile because he had first claim on the buyer's asset.

Corporations, particularly railroads and other transportation companies, do the same thing. They finance the acquisition of their rolling stock and locomotives by issuing an equipment trust certificate. When the railroad has finished paying off the loan, it receives clear title to its equipment from the trustee. If the railroad does not make the payments, the lender repossesses the collateral and sells it for his benefit.

1. 3. 2. 3　Collateral Trust Bonds

Sometimes a corporation wants to borrow money and has neither real estate (for a mortgage) nor equipment (for an equipment trust) to use as collateral. Instead, it deposits securities it owns into a trust to serve as collateral for the lenders. The securities it deposits can be securities in that corporation or of any other corporation as long as the securities are marketable, that is, readily liquidated. Obviously, the better the quality of the securities deposited as collateral, the better the quality and rating of the bond.

1. 3. 2. 4   Debenture (Unsecured Bond)

A debenture is a debt obligation of the corporation backed only by its word and general creditworthiness. Debentures are written promises of the corporation to pay the principal at its due date and interest on a regular basis. Although this promise is as binding as a promise for a mortgage bond, debentures are not secured by any pledge of property. They are sold on the general credit of the company; their security depends on the assets and earnings of the corporation.

Although debentures are unsecured, there are issuers whose credit standing is so good that their debentures are safer than mortgage bonds of less creditworthy companies.

1. 3. 2. 5   Guaranteed Bonds

A guaranteed bond is a bond that is guaranteed as to payment of interest, or both principal and interest, by a corporate entity other than the issuer. The value of the guarantee is only as good as the strength of the company making that guarantee. Guaranteed bonds were particularly popular in the railroad industry in which a major railroad seeking to lease trackage rights from a short line would guarantee that smaller company's debt. A more recent example is the ExxonMobil Corporation guaranteeing the debt issues of the Exxon Pipeline Company.

1. 3. 2. 6   Senior

The word *senior* is used to describe the relative priority of a security claim. Every preferred stock has a senior claim to common stock. Every debt security has senior claim to preferred stock. Secured bonds have a senior claim to unsecured bonds. The term *senior securities* means bonds and preferred stock because they have a claim senior to common stock. If an exam question described a corporation as having issued senior bonds, the answer would have to state that there were mortgage or equipment trust certificates issued by that corporation with prior claim ahead of unsecured creditors.

1. 3. 2. 7   Subordinated

The term *subordinated* means "belonging to a lower or inferior class or rank; secondary." It is usually describing a debenture. A subordinated debenture has a claim that is behind (junior to) that of any other creditor. However, no matter how subordinated the debenture, it is still senior to any stockholder.

TEST TOPIC ALERT

When examining the capital structure of a corporation, you must know the liquidation priority:

- ■ Secured creditors (e.g., mortgage bonds, equipment trust certificates, collateral trust bonds)

- ■ Unsecured creditors (e.g., general creditors including debenture holders)

- Subordinated debt holders

- Preferred stockholders

- Common stockholders

Features of Various Securities Issues

	Common Stock	Preferred Stock	Bonds
Ownership and control of the firm	Belongs to common stockholders through voting rights and residual claim to income	Limited rights, may include a participation feature	Limited rights under default in interest payments
Obligation to provide return	None	Must receive before common stockholder	Contractual obligation
Claim to assets in bankruptcy	Lowest claim of any security holder	Bondholders and creditors must be satisfied first	Highest claim
Risk-return trade-off	Higher risk, higher return	Moderate risk, moderate return (dollar amount of dividend is known before stock purchase)	Low risk, moderate return
Tax status of payment to recipient	Taxable as dividend in most cases	Taxable as dividend in most cases	Taxable as ordinary income in most cases

1. 3. 3   SAFETY OF PRINCIPAL—MUNICIPAL BONDS

The record of safety of principal of municipal bonds is second only to that of government issues. There are two basic types of municipal bonds.

1. 3. 3. 1   General Obligation Bonds (GOs)

General obligation bonds are backed by a pledge of the issuer's full faith and credit for prompt payment of principal and interest. Most city, county, and school district bonds have the further distinction of being secured by a pledge of unlimited ad valorem (property) taxes to be levied against all taxable property. In most cases, if taxes are not paid, the delinquent property is sold at a tax sale, giving the bondholder a superior claim above mortgages, mechanics' liens, and similar encumbrances. Because GOs are geared to tax resources, they are normally analyzed in terms of the size of the resources being taxed. They are generally very safe.

1. 3. 3. 2   Revenue Bond

Revenue bonds are payable from the earnings of a revenue-producing enterprise, such as a water, sewer, electric, or gas system; toll bridge; airport; college dormitory; or other income-producing facility.

Authorities and agencies are created by states or their subdivisions to perform specific functions, such as the operation of water, sewer, or electric systems; bridges; tunnels; or highways and in some states, to construct schools or public facilities. In some cases, the authority has the right to levy fees and charges for its services. In other cases, it receives lease rentals, which may be payable from specific revenues or may be general obligations of the lessee. They are usually analyzed in terms of their earnings, historical or potential, compared with bond requirements. The yield, generally, is higher for this type of bond than for a GO (taxes are more secure than revenues), although many have built up a good record over a long period of time and are sometimes rated higher than GOs.

1. 3. 4   TREASURY SECURITIES

Treasury bills are the bellwether of the money market. Because there is so much Treasury debt outstanding, the level of activity in Treasury bills and other short-term government issues is by far the highest and most carefully watched. Governments with short terms also refer to US Treasury notes or US Treasury bonds that are in their last year before maturity because, at that time, they would trade like any other security with one year or less to maturity. There are a number of advantages to Treasuries. First and foremost, at least for exam purposes, is the absence of credit risk. A second advantage is the extremely high liquidity in the secondary markets: the more active a security, the narrower the spread. The huge market activity in Treasuries keeps the spreads very low, making it easy for the investor to get in and out at a reasonable cost. A third benefit of investing in Treasuries is that the interest is exempt from state income tax. Because of these factors, the yields on these Treasuries are normally the lowest in the money market.

1. 3. 4. 1   Safety of Principal—Government Securities

US government bonds are the safest of all. There are two primary types of backing; direct government backing or guarantee, as in the case of Treasury issues, and the moral guarantee, as in the case of federal agencies.

Although most government issues trade in what is known as the capital market—that is, the market for long-term securities, stocks, and bonds—there are several issues that trade in the money market. The money market is where short-term instruments, those that mature in one year or less, are traded. The money market will be discussed later. No discussion of Treasury issues would be possible, however, without describing the widely held bellwether of the money market known as US Treasury bills.

1. 3. 4. 2   US Treasury Bills

Treasury bills are direct short-term debt obligations of the US government. They are issued every week by using a competitive bidding process. Each week, T-bills, as they are known, with maturities of 4 weeks, 13 weeks, 26 weeks, and 52 weeks are issued.

Treasury bills pay no interest in the way other bonds do; rather they are issued at a discount from par value and redeemed at par. An investor might purchase a $10,000, 26-week T-bill at a price of $9,800. He would receive no regular interest check, but, at maturity, the Treasury would send him a check for $10,000. The difference between the $9,800 he paid and the $10,000 he received would be considered his interest income even though he never received a separate interest check.

TAKE NOTE

Key points to remember regarding T-bills include:

■ Treasury bills are the only Treasury security issued at a discount;

■ Treasury bills are the only Treasury security issued without a stated interest rate;

■ Treasury bills are highly liquid; and

■ 13-week (also referred to as 90-day) Treasury bills are used in market analysis as the stereotypical "risk-free" investment.

1. 3. 4. 3   US Treasury Notes

US Treasury notes are direct debt obligations of the US Treasury with the following characteristics.

■ They pay semiannual interest as a percentage of the stated par value.

■ They have intermediate maturities (2–10 years).

■ They mature at par value.

1. 3. 4. 4   US Treasury Bonds

US Treasury bonds are direct debt obligations of the US Treasury with the following characteristics.

■ They pay semiannual interest as a percentage of the stated par value.

■ They have long-term maturities, generally 10–30 years.

■ Older 30-year bonds are usually callable at par beginning 25 years after issue. However, the last callable 30-year bond was issued in November 1984.

■ They mature at par value.

1. 3. 5   MONEY MARKET

The money market may be defined as the market for buying and selling short-term loan-able funds in the form of securities and loans. It is called the money market because that is what is traded there, money not cash. The buyer of a money market instrument is the lender of the money; the seller of a money market instrument is the entity borrowing the money.

Although there are many different kinds of money market instruments, there are several common factors. For example, they all have a maturity date of one year or less. In fact, the majority of money market instruments mature in less than six months. Another factor that many (but not all) money market instruments share is that they are issued at a discount. They do not pay interest because debt securities generally pay interest semiannually; as most money market instruments have a maturity of six months or less, the administrative costs of paying out interest would be very high. Therefore, the solution is to issue the security at a discount with the investor being paid back par at maturity, that difference being what he is paid for the use of his money. Money market instruments are safe. Although some are not quite as safe as others (e.g., commercial paper is not as safe as a Treasury bill), they are all considered to be low-risk securities.

1. 3. 5. 1   Negotiable Certificates of Deposit

Negotiable certificates of deposit (CDs) were created in the mid-1960s because the Federal Reserve Board had restrictions on the amount of money a bank could pay on savings and other time deposits (a time deposit has a fixed maturity) until 1986. Because the Fed's rules were somewhat restrictive, it was impossible for the banks to compete for money. If a corporation had $1 million that it would not need for several weeks, there was no way that a bank could pay it a rate competitive with other money market instruments until the introduction of negotiable CDs. These CDs are unsecured time deposits (no asset of the bank is pledged as collateral), and the money is being loaned to the bank for a specified period of time. A negotiable CD allows the initial investor, or any subsequent owner of the CD, to sell the CD in the open market prior to maturity date. The bank that issues the CD redeems the CD at face value plus interest on maturity date. CDs are the only money market instrument that pays periodic interest, usually semiannually. To be considered a negotiable CD, such CDs must have a face value of $100,000 or more, with $1 million and more being most common.

TAKE NOTE   In the industry (and sometimes on the exam), these are referred to as Jumbo CDs.

1. 3. 5. 2   Commercial Paper

Another money market instrument is commercial paper. This is short-term, unsecured paper issued by corporations, primarily to raise working capital (i.e., for current rather than long-term needs). Commercial paper is exempt from registration as long as the maximum maturity is 270 days.

Negotiable CDs are interest bearing and issued at face. Commercial paper is generally issued at a discount—instead of receiving interest, the investor receives the face amount at maturity.

In summation, why would you place money market securities in a client's portfolio?

■ Highly liquid
■ Very safe
■ The best place to store money that will be needed soon

In doing so, the client would be incurring the following risks.

■ Because of their many advantages, the rate of return is quite low, so these are not suitable for long-term investors.
■ Fluctuating income—due to short-term maturities, principal is potentially being reinvested at a different rate each time the instrument matures.

1. 4 PUBLIC SECURITIES OFFERING VERSUS PRIVATE SECURITIES OFFERING

1. 4. 1 SECURITIES ACT OF 1933

The primary purpose of the Securities Act of 1933 is to require full and fair disclosure in connection with the sale of securities to the public. Senate hearings in the 1920s and after the crash of 1929 uncovered widespread fraud in the issuance of securities. New issues were sold with little or no disclosure and could be purchased on margin with as little as 5% down.

The Act of 1933 requires that a new issue, unless exempt, must be registered with the SEC before public sale. All investors must receive a detailed prospectus prior to purchase. Also, if the US mail or other means of interstate commerce are used to sell a new issue, the requirements of the Act of 1933 apply.

Interstate commerce represents transactions between states. If the security involved in interstate commerce is a US-issued security, the definition is expanded. For instance, the wire transfer of US-issued securities between San Juan and Washington DC comes under the SEC, as this is considered interstate commerce, even though neither point in the transaction is a US state.

A basic rule: if the transaction is not intrastate, it is interstate.

1. 4. 1. 1   Definition of a Security

A **security** can be defined as any investment in a common enterprise for profit, with management performed by a third party. An element of risk must be present.

Excluded from the definition of a security are:

- CDs insured by the FDIC (no risk);
- fixed annuities (no risk);
- currencies (no third-party management); and
- futures contracts (no third-party management).

1. 4. 2   PRIVATE PLACEMENTS

A private placement occurs when the issuing company, usually with the assistance of its investment bank, sells securities to private investors as opposed to the general investing public. Although private placement buyers tend to be institutional investors, securities may be sold to small groups of wealthy individuals. When an issuer privately places securities with investors, there can be no solicitation of the general public. Private placements are generally exempt from the registration requirements of the Securities Act of 1933.

1. 4. 3   PUBLIC OFFERINGS

Public offerings can be publicly advertised, raise relatively large amounts of capital (stocks or bonds), and may attract investors with smaller budgets and less investment sophistication. Typically, they are more tightly regulated and subject to more stringent federal registration and prospectus requirements than private placements.

1. 4. 3. 1   Initial Public Offering (IPO) Versus Secondary Offering

An issuer transaction involving new securities is called a primary offering. If it is the first time an issuer distributes securities to the public, it is called an initial public offering (IPO).

Any subsequent issuance of new shares to the public is called a subsequent public offering (SPO) or additional public offering (APO). All primary offerings, IPOs and SPOs, are issuer transactions because the issuer (the company) receives the proceeds from the investor investing in the company.

EXAMPLE   The first time that ABC Shoe Co. issued shares to the public, ABC Shoe engaged in an IPO or a primary offering because it received the proceeds from distributing its shares to the public. After ABC Shoe went public, transactions between investors executed on exchanges through brokerage agents were secondary transactions in nonissuer securities.

1. 4. 3. 2   Types of Underwritings

The **new issue market** consists of companies going public—privately owned businesses raising capital by selling common stock to the public for the first time. New issue securities are also known as initial public offering (IPO) securities. The **additional issue market** is made up of new securities issues from companies that are already publicly owned. These companies are now increasing their equity capitalization by issuing more stock.

In addition to being classified by whether they represent initial or additional issues of new securities, offerings can be classified by the final distribution of their proceeds.

TAKE NOTE   Additional issue offerings are sometimes referred to as follow-on offerings.

1. 4. 3. 3   Primary Offerings (Primary Market)

A **primary offering** is one in which the proceeds of the underwriting go to the issuing corporation. The corporation increases its capitalization by selling stock (either a new issue or previously authorized but unissued stock). It may do this at any time and in any amount, provided the total stock outstanding never exceeds the amount authorized in the corporation's bylaws.

1. 4. 3. 4   Secondary Offerings

A **secondary offering** is one in which one or more major stockholders in the corporation are selling all or a major portion of their holdings. The underwriting proceeds are paid to the stockholders rather than to the corporation. Typically, secondary offerings occur in situations in which the founder of a business, and perhaps some of the original financial backers, determine that there is more to be gained by going public than by staying private.

Offerings and Markets

	New Issue (IPO) Market	Additional Issue Market
Primary Offering	Company is going public; underwriting proceeds go to the company	Company is already public; underwriting proceeds go to the company
Secondary Offering	Company is going public; underwriting proceeds go to the selling stockholders	Company is already public; underwriting proceeds go to the selling stockholders

1. 4. 3. 5   Exempt Securities

Certain new issues of securities are exempt from the registration requirements of the Act of 1933. An **exempt security** is any security exempt by law from having to register with the SEC prior to public sale.

1. 4. 3. 6 Nonexempt

A nonexempt security is a security subject to the registration provisions mandated by the 1933 Act and the SEC. By contrast, exempt means not subject to registration. If a security is not registered or exempt from registration, it cannot be sold in a state unless it is sold in an exempt transaction. As you will see, the sale of an unregistered nonexempt security, a prohibited practice, may subject an agent to criminal penalties.

T A K E N O T E

Think of what the legal terms actually mean in everyday usage. For example, a registered nonexempt security is most likely a common stock properly registered for sale in a state.

1. 5 MARKETS AND MARKET REGULATION

1. 5. 1 SECURITIES AND EXCHANGE ACT OF 1934

The Act of 1934 was passed primarily to curb abuse in the secondary (trading) markets. Among other things, the act accomplished the following:

- Created the SEC, which was delegated authority to enforce federal securities laws (the SEC subsequently delegated some of its authority to various SROs)
- Required the registration of broker/dealers
- Required the registration of all exchanges and all national securities associations
- Required the registration of registered representatives with the appropriate SRO
- Empowered the Federal Reserve to control the extension of credit on securities transactions
- Required publicly traded issuers to file financial reports with the SEC and the public
- Created rules dealing with insider trading
- Created rules dealing with secondary market trading activity of market makers and underwriters

1. 5. 1. 1   Markets

A **market** is the exchange or system where security trades occur. The trading market in the United States can be divided as follows.

The **first market**, a hybrid (open outcry and electronic) market, is where listed securities trade on an exchange floor. **Listed security** refers to any security listed (quoted) for trading on an exchange.

The **second market**, a negotiated market, is an over-the-counter market where unlisted securities trade. **Unlisted** means not listed for trading on any exchange. This market can be divided into Nasdaq and non-Nasdaq segments.

The **third market**, called the Intermarket, is the market where listed securities trade over the counter. Begun in the late 1970s, the third market represents competition for the exchanges.

The **fourth market**, also called the ECN market, is an over-the-counter market that allows transactions in both listed and unlisted securities between institutional investors without the use of a broker/dealer. Electronic communication networks (ECNs) are open 24 hours a day and match buy and sell orders as agents, not as principals.

Summary of the Trading Markets

Market	Securities	Type	Regulator
1st market	Listed securities	Hybrid	Exchanges FINRA
2nd market	Unlisted securities	Negotiated	FINRA
3rd market	Listed securities	Negotiated	FINRA
4th market	Listed and unlisted securities	Negotiated	FINRA

1. 5. 2   REGULATORY AND SELF-REGULATORY ORGANIZATIONS (SROs)

The Securities Exchange Act created the SEC. The act grants the SEC authority over all aspects of the securities industry, including the power to register, regulate, and oversee brokerage firms; transfer agents; clearing agencies; and the nation's securities self-regulatory organizations (SROs).

The various stock exchanges, such as the New York Stock Exchange (NYSE), American Stock Exchange (AMEX), Chicago Board Options Exchange (CBOE), and Nasdaq, are SROs. The largest SRO is FINRA, the organization to which most broker/dealers belong.

The act also identifies and prohibits certain types of conduct in the markets and confers to the SEC disciplinary powers over regulated entities and the persons associated with them.

The act also empowers the SEC to require periodic reporting of information by companies with publicly traded securities.

1. 5. 2. 1   FINRA

On July 26, 2007, the SEC approved the consolidation of NASD and NYSE regulation into a single self-regulatory organization (SRO) known as Financial Industry Regulatory Authority (FINRA). The purpose of the regulatory consolidation was to:

- eliminate duplicate regulation by NASD and NYSE; and
- strengthen the competitiveness of US markets.

Securities licensing exams are known as FINRA exams. Exam questions may refer to FINRA when speaking of the industry's SRO. However, you will continue to see exam questions refer to either NASD or NYSE, particularly when specific rules are referenced. It is expected that this will continue until all of the individual rules of NASD and NYSE have been consolidated.

1. 5. 3   THE SECURITIES AND EXCHANGE COMMISSION (SEC)

The SEC consists of five people, with one serving as chair, appointed by the US President with the advice and consent of the Senate. The SEC administrates all federal laws regulating the securities industry except those regulating the extension of credit and futures.

1. 5. 4   MARKETS AND MARKET PARTICIPANTS

After an initial offering of securities made by a company, many securities are bought and sold in the secondary market. The major exchanges include the New York Stock Exchange (NYSE), the American Stock Exchange (AMEX), and Nasdaq. Other trades take place in the nationwide network of broker/dealers known as the over-the-counter (OTC) market. We will now review the terminology and language of trading securities.

1. 5. 4. 1   Securities Markets

There are two terms used to describe the market for securities. The primary market is the market in which the proceeds of sales go to the issuer of the securities sold. The secondary market is where previously issued securities are bought and sold between individual investors.

1. 5. 4. 1. 1   Exchange Market

One method of trading in the secondary market is the exchange market such as the NYSE and other exchanges on which listed securities are traded. Listed security refers to any security listed for trading on an exchange. Each stock exchange requires corporations to meet certain criteria before it will allow its stock to be listed for trading on the exchange.

1. 5. 4. 1. 2   Price Dynamics

When a floor broker representing a buyer executes a trade by purchasing stock at a current offer price higher than the last sale, a plus tick occurs (market up); when a selling broker accepts a current bid price below the last sale price, a minus tick occurs (market down).

1. 5. 4. 1. 3   Designated Market Maker

The designated market maker (DMM) maintains an orderly market and provides price continuity. He fills limit and market orders for the public and trades for his own account to either stabilize or facilitate trading when imbalances in supply and demand occur.

The DMM's chief function is to maintain a fair and orderly market in the stocks for which he is responsible. An additional function is to minimize price disparities that may occur at the opening of the trading day. He does this by buying or selling, as a dealer, stock from his own inventory.

1. 5. 4. 1. 4   Over-the-Counter (OTC) Market (Negotiated)

The OTC market functions as an interdealer market in which both listed (such as Nasdaq) and unlisted securities—that is, securities not listed on any exchange—trade.

In the OTC market, securities dealers across the country are connected by computer and telephone. Thousands of securities are traded OTC, including stocks, corporate bonds, and all municipal and US government securities.

No central marketplace facilitates OTC trading. Trading takes place over the phone, over order management systems in trading rooms across the world.

The OTC market is an interdealer network. Registered market makers compete to post the best bid and ask prices. The OTC market is a negotiated market.

1. 5. 4. 1. 5   Market Makers

Market makers are broker/dealers who stand ready to buy and sell at least the minimum trading unit, usually 100 shares (or any larger amount they have indicated), in each stock in which they have published bid and ask quotes.

Market makers, that is, FINRA member firms acting in a dealer (principal) capacity, sell from their inventory (proprietary account) at their asking price and buy for their inventory at the bid price. When a market maker raises its bid price to attract sellers, the stock price rises; when a market maker lowers its ask price to attract buyers, the stock price declines.

1. 5. 5   DEPOSITORIES AND CLEARING FACILITIES

A **carrying firm** or clearing firm is a registered broker-dealer that carries customer accounts and accepts funds and securities from customers. Because they have greater financial responsibility than their correspondent firms (introducing firms), they are required to maintain a larger amount of minimum net capital. By far, most firms are introducing firms, also known as fully disclosed.

To function as a clearing firm, a broker/dealer must be a member of the Depository Trust & Clearing Corp. (DTCC), along with its subsidiary the National Securities Clearing Corp.

Listed option contracts are issued in standardized formats by the Options Clearing Corporation (OCC) and traded on the Chicago Board Options Exchange (CBOE) or another exchange. Because the CBOE and other exchanges provide forums to trade, and the OCC stands behind option contracts in the event of a firm's failure, options are easily tradable.

1. 5. 5. 1   DTCC

Interdealer trades are reported to ACT and submitted to National Securities Clearing Corp. (NSCC) for clearance and settlement. NSCC works on a **continuous net settlement**

(CNS) basis (interdealer buys and sells, per security, are netted each day for delivery and money settlement purposes). Delivery for many securities is accomplished through bookkeeping entries at a securities depository such as the depository trust company (DTC). DTC provides securities certificate safekeeping for member firms, and changes in ownership are made by computerized entries rather than physical delivery.

Depository Trust & Clearing Corp. (DTCC) was formed to clear transactions. Firms must be members of NSCC or clearing corporations associated with an exchange such as Midwest Clearing Corp. DTC itself is involved in custody and safekeeping, not in clearance. DTC also processes dividend and interest payments on securities it holds in safekeeping.

1. 6 DERIVATIVE SECURITIES—OPTIONS

Options are derivative securities, which means that they derive their value from that of an underlying instrument, such as a stock, stock index, interest rate, or foreign currency. Option contracts offer investors a means to hedge, or protect, an investment's value or speculate on the price movement of individual securities, markets, foreign currencies, and other instruments.

An option is a contract that establishes a price and time frame for the purchase or sale of a particular security. Two parties are involved in the contract: one party receives the right to exercise the contract to buy or sell the underlying security, and the other is obligated to fulfill the terms of the contract. In theory, options can be created on any item with a fluctuating market value. The most familiar options are those issued on common stocks; they are called equity options.

1. 6. 1 CALLS AND PUTS

There are two types of option contracts: calls and puts.

1. 6. 1. 1 Call Option

A call option gives its holder the right to buy a stock for a specific price within a specified time frame. A call buyer buys the right to buy a specific stock, and a call seller takes on the obligation to sell the stock.

1. 6. 1. 2 Put Option

A put option gives its holder the right to sell a stock for a specific price within a specified time frame. A put buyer buys the right to sell a specific stock, and a put seller takes on the obligation to buy the stock.

Each stock option contract covers 100 shares (a round lot) of stock. An option's cost is its premium. Premiums are quoted in dollars per share.

EXAMPLE   Because a contract covers 100 shares, a premium of $3 means $3 for each share multiplied by 100 shares, which equals $300.

1. 6. 2   OPTION TRANSACTIONS

Because two types of options (calls and puts) and two types of transactions (purchases and sales) exist, four basic transactions are available to an option investor:

- Buy calls
- Sell calls
- Buy puts
- Sell puts

Option buyers are long the positions; option sellers are short the positions.

1. 6. 3   EXPIRATION DATES

The test may ask you the difference between American- and European-style exercise. American style means the option can be exercised at any time the holder wishes, up to the expiration date. European-style options may only be exercised on their expiration date.

TAKE NOTE

A tool for remembering the difference between American and European exercise is to look at the first letter.

- A for American means Anytime.

- E for European means Expiration date.

TEST TOPIC ALERT

Now that you have become so focused on the difference in exercise dates between American and European styles, you need to be on the lookout for a question that goes something like this:

"A European option is a derivative because," and the first choice will probably say, "it can only be exercised on the expiration date." But, although this is true about exercise, it has nothing to do with why options are derivatives. The correct answer is, "because its value is based on some underlying asset."

1. 6. 4   OPTIONS STRATEGIES

Options strategies are either bullish or bearish positions on the underlying stock. The primary reason for buying or selling options is to profit from or hedge against price movement in the underlying security. A bullish investor may buy calls or write puts seeking profit if the price of the underlying assets rises. A bearish investor can write calls or buy puts seeking profit if the price of the underlying assets declines.

Bullish and Bearish Options Positions

	Long	Short
Calls	Right to buy Bullish	Obligation to sell Bearish
Puts	Right to sell Bearish	Obligation to buy Bullish

(Buyer, Holder, Owner)   (Seller, Writer, Grantor)

1. 6. 4. 1   Buying Calls

Investors expecting a stock to increase in value speculate on that price increase by buying calls on the stock. By buying a call, an investor can profit from the increase in the stock's price while investing a relatively small amount of money. The most a call buyer can lose is the money paid for the option. The most a call buyer can gain is unlimited because there is no limit to how high the stock price can go. Owners of options (puts or calls) do not receive dividends on the underlying stock.

1. 6. 4. 2   Writing Calls

A neutral or bearish investor can write a call and collect the premium. An investor who believes a stock's price will stay the same or decline can write a call to:

■ generate income from the option premium;

■ partially protect (hedge) a long stock position by offsetting any loss on the sale of the stock by the premium amount; or

■ speculate on the decline in the stock price.

If the stock price increases, the call may be exercised. The writer will be paid the strike price for the stock which, in total, is added to the premium he received for writing the call.

The call writer must then take that money and go out and buy the stock. The call writer's exposure is unlimited because there is no limit to how high the stock price can go. That is why naked call writing is the most risky option strategy.

TAKE NOTE

Covered call: If an investor holds a long stock position, buying puts provides nearly total downside protection. The upside potential of the stock is reduced only by the amount of premiums paid. Selling calls when holding a long stock position, also known as covered call writing, is partial protection that generates income and reduces the stock's upside potential.

1. 6. 4. 3   Buying Puts

A bearish investor—one who believes a stock will decline in price—can speculate on the price decline by buying puts. A put buyer acquires the right to sell 100 shares of the underlying stock at the strike price before the expiration date.

Puts can be used to speculate on or hedge (fully protect) against a decline in a stock's value in the following ways.

- An investor who expects a stock he does not own to decline can buy a put to profit from the decline.
- An investor who expects a stock he owns to decline can buy a put to lock in a minimum sale price.

If a put owner is correct and the stock falls in price, he could exercise the put option to sell the stock at the strike price or sell the put at a profit.

1. 6. 4. 4   Writing Puts

Generally, investors who write puts believe that the stock's price will rise. A put writer is obligated to buy stock at the exercise price if the put buyer puts it to the put writer. If a stock's price is above the put strike price at expiration, the put expires unexercised, allowing the put writer to keep the premium.

Some investors write puts with the intent of having the options exercised against them. Writing a put is a means to buy stock at a reduced price because the premium received, in effect, reduces the cost of the stock. If the put is not exercised, the writer keeps the premium.

TAKE NOTE

Covered put: An investor who is short stock is selling borrowed stock and expecting a price decline. The short seller must repay the stock loan and hopes to do so at a lower price. A short seller can buy calls to eliminate the risk of a rise in the stock's price. The investor may also sell puts for partial protection. This strategy, known as writing a covered put, limits the investor's potential profit and may subject the investor to unlimited loss.

QUICK QUIZ 1.B

Matching (each has two answers)

A. Long call
B. Short call
C. Long put
D. Short put

_____ 1. Which options positions are bearish?

_____ 2. Which options positions are bullish?

_____ 3. Which positions buy stock at exercise?

_____ 4. Which positions sell stock at exercise?

_____ 5. Which positions have rights?

_____ 6. Which positions have obligations?

1. 7 PACKAGED SECURITIES/ALTERNATIVE INVESTMENTS

1. 7. 1   REAL ESTATE INVESTMENT TRUSTS (REITs)

A real estate investment trust (REIT; pronounced reet) is a company that manages a portfolio of real estate investments to earn profits for shareholders. REITs are normally publicly traded and serve as a source of long-term financing for real estate projects. A REIT pools capital in a manner similar to an investment company. Shareholders receive dividends from investment income or capital gains distributions. REITs normally:

■ own commercial property (equity REITs);

■ own mortgages on commercial property (mortgage REITs); or

■ do both (hybrid REITs).

REITs are organized as trusts in which investors buy shares or certificates of beneficial interest either on stock exchanges or in the over-the-counter market.

Under the guidelines of Subchapter M of the Internal Revenue Code, a REIT can avoid being taxed as a corporation by receiving 75% or more of its income from real estate and distributing 90% or more of its taxable income to its shareholders.

TEST TOPIC ALERT

Four important points to remember about REITs follow.

■ An owner of REITs holds an undivided interest in a pool of real estate investments.

■ REITs trade on exchanges and over the counter.

■ REITs are not investment companies (mutual funds).

■ REITs offer dividends and gains to investors but do not pass through losses like limited partnerships and, therefore, are not considered to be direct participation programs.

In summation, why would a registered representative include REITs in a client's portfolio?

■ The opportunity to invest in real estate without the degree of liquidity risk found in direct ownership

■ Reasonable income and/or potential capital appreciation

In doing so, the client would be incurring the following risks.

■ Because the investor has no control, much of the risk in investing in REITs lies with the quality of the management.

■ Problem loans in the portfolio could cause income and/or capital to decrease.

■ Dividends are not considered qualified for purposes of the 15% maximum tax rate and are taxed at full ordinary income rates.

1. 7. 2   RIGHTS AND WARRANTS

Rights and warrants allow investors to buy additional shares of stock under defined circumstances.

1. 7. 2. 1   Rights

Preemptive rights entitle existing common stockholders to maintain their proportionate ownership shares in a company by buying newly issued shares before the company offers them to the general public.

A rights offering allows stockholders to purchase common stock below the current market price. The rights are valued separately from the stock and trade in the secondary market during the subscription period.

A stockholder who receives rights may:

- exercise the rights to buy stock by sending the rights certificates and a check for the required amount to the rights agent;

- sell the rights and profit from their market value (rights certificates are negotiable securities); or

- let the rights expire and lose their value.

1. 7. 2. 2   Warrants

A warrant is a certificate granting its owner the right to purchase securities from the issuer at a specified price, normally higher than the current market price. Unlike a right, a warrant is usually a long-term instrument that gives the investor the option of buying shares at a later date at the exercise price.

1. 7. 2. 2. 1   Origination of Warrants

Warrants are usually offered to the public as sweeteners in connection with other securities, such as debentures or preferred stock, to make those securities more attractive. Such offerings are often bundled as units.

1. 8 THE ROLE OF BROKER/DEALERS

Most securities firms act as both brokers and dealers but not in the same transaction.

1. 8. 1   BROKERS

Brokers are agents that arrange trades for clients and charge commissions. Brokers do not buy shares for inventory but facilitate trades between buyers and sellers.

1. 8. 2   DEALERS

Dealers, or principals, buy and sell securities for their own accounts. This practice is often called position trading. When selling from their inventories, dealers charge the buying customers a markup rather than a commission. A markup is the difference between the current interdealer offering price and the actual price charged the client. When a price to a client includes a dealer's markup, it is called the net price.

TAKE NOTE

The term *principal* has several meanings in the securities industry. A broker/dealer acts as a principal in a dealer transaction. A principal of a firm is a person who acts in a supervisory capacity. Principal can also mean the face value of a bond or asset in a trust.

A firm cannot act as both a broker and a dealer in the same transaction.

EXAMPLE

A firm cannot make a market in a stock, mark up that stock, and then add an agency commission. If the firm acts as a broker, it may charge a commission. If it acts as a dealer, it may charge a markup or markdown. Violation of this practice is called making a hidden profit.

Broker	Dealer
Acts as an agent, transacting orders on the client's behalf	Acts as a principal, dealing in securities for its own account and at its own risk
Charges a commission	Charges a markup or markdown
Is not a market maker	Makes markets and/or takes positions (long or short) in securities
Must disclose its role and the amount of its commission to the client	Must disclose its role to the client, but not necessarily the amount or source of the markup or markdown

1. 8. 3   INVESTMENT ADVISERS

An investment adviser is defined under the Investment Advisers Act of 1940 as "any person who, for compensation, engages in the business of advising others as to the value of securities or the advisability of investing in securities or, as part of a regular business, issues analyses or reports concerning securities."

The SEC interprets the definition of investment adviser under the Investment Advisers Act of 1940 to include financial planners, pension consultants, and others who offer investment advice as part of their financial practices.

TAKE NOTE

An investment adviser is anyone who:

■   provides investment advice, reports, or analyses with respect to securities;

■   is in the business of providing advice or analyses; and

■   receives compensation, directly or indirectly, for these services.

1. 8. 4   SUITABILITY OBLIGATION

Accounts may be opened by any legally competent person above the age of majority. Legally incompetent individuals may not open accounts.

TAKE NOTE

Rules also require the new account form to identify whether the customer is a director, officer, or shareholder of 10% or more of a publicly traded company. This helps monitor potentially unusual trading activity associated with insiders.

When opening an account, rules generally referred to as the "know your customer" rules require representatives to know all essential facts about a customer's current financial situation, present holdings, risk tolerance, needs, and objectives. Such information should be updated periodically, as situations change.

If a customer refuses to provide all information requested, the account may still be opened if the firm believes the customer has the financial resources necessary to support the account. The registered representative can make recommendations only if sufficient information has been given to determine suitability. Before recommending a security transaction for a noninstitutional customer (retail account), registered representatives must have reasonable grounds for believing that the recommendation is suitable in light of the customer's:

■   financial situation, including income and net worth;

■   tax status;

■   investment objectives;

■   risk tolerance; and

■   other holdings.

The key is suitability. Implicit in all dealings with customers is the responsibility for fair dealing. Sales efforts, including recommendations, must be judged on the basis of whether they represent fair and ethical treatment for the customer to whom the recommendation is being made.

Customers may place transactions that the registered representative considers unsuitable or has not recommended. In this case, the registered representative should mark the order ticket "Unsolicited." Unmarked order tickets are assumed to be solicited transactions.

ORDER TICKET   BUY

ACCOUNT NUMBER	RR#	QUANTITY	SECURITY DESCRIPTION	LIMIT PRICE	ORDER TYPE	A/C TYPE
					☐ DAY	
					☐ GTC	
CUSTOMER NAME	TTO				☐ GTX	
				EXECUTED PRICE	☐ MKT	S/N
		☐ SHARES ☐ CALLS	SYMBOL/CUSIP		☐ SPREAD DR/CR	
		☐ UNITS ☐ PUTS ☐ OTHER				

OPTIONS	SELLER	EXCHANGE	CAPACITY	COMMISSION		TIME STAMP
☐ OPEN	U-LONG SEG	☐ NYSE ☐ BOS	☐ OTC		% ¢	
☐ CLOSE	V-LONG C/N	☐ AMEX ☐ PCSE	ACT		F Z	
☐ COVERED	W-WILL DEL	☐ MWSE ☐ CBOE	SOES	GROSS CREDIT	R/I	
☐ UNCOVERED	SS-SHORT	☐ PHLX ☐ OTHER	SNET			
			☐ AGENCY ☐ AGENCY CROSS ☐ PRINCIPAL			

ORDER QUALIFIERS									
STOP	STOP LIMIT	DNR	AON	ND	CASH	WOW	OB	NH	

CONTRA ACCOUNT #	CONTRA NAME/SYMBOL	FACTOR	REPORTED PRICE	DISCRETION
				Y-YES
				N-NO

PRE-FIGURE	PRINCIPAL	INTEREST	COMMISSION/GROSS	SEC FEE	SVC CHG	NET	SPEC-TYPE
CUSTOMER							
CONTRA							

TRADE DATE	SETTLEMENT DATE	MARK UP/DOWN	MESSAGE/FLOOR

CONFIRM NOTE	SPECIAL INSTRUCTIONS

1. 8. 5   COMMISSIONS, MARKUPS, AND FEE-BASED ACCOUNTS

1. 8. 5. 1   Commissions

Brokers are agents that arrange trades for clients and charge commissions. Brokers do not buy shares for inventory but facilitate trades between buyers and sellers.

1. 8. 5. 2   Markups

Dealers, or principals, buy and sell securities for their own accounts. This practice is often called position trading. When selling from their inventories, dealers charge the buying customers a markup rather than a commission. A markup is the difference between the current interdealer offering price and the actual price charged the client. When a price to a client includes a dealer's markup, it is called the net price.

1. 8. 5. 3   Fee-Based Accounts

Fee-based accounts are those that are charged a fixed fee monthly or annually as an alternative to traditional commission-based charges for brokerage services. Unlike wrap accounts, these accounts do not provide advisory services. They are generally appropriate for customers with a moderate to high level of trading activity. They are not appropriate for customers with a buy-and-hold strategy. FINRA rules require firms to periodically review all fee-based accounts to determine if they remain appropriate.

1. 8. 5. 4   Customer Statement Versus Performance Report

A performance report is a form of sales literature that must be approved by a principal of the firm and kept on file for three years. A customer statement is a document showing a customer's trading activity, positions, and account balance. The SEC requires that customer statements be sent quarterly, but customers generally receive them monthly.

1. 8. 6   REGULATORY REQUIREMENTS OF BROKER-DEALERS

1. 8. 6. 1   Net Capital

All member firms are subject to minimum net capital requirements rules. These minimum requirements are designed to ensure that members have enough capital to meet their obligations to other members and the investing public. In general, the greater the risk assumed by a member, the higher the firm's minimum net capital requirement.

Net capital represents the liquid net worth of a firm. It differs from net worth in that net worth includes the value of all of a member's assets, whereas net capital subtracts those assets that are illiquid. An example of an illiquid asset would be common stock that has no interest in the secondary market or is restricted from resale.

$$\text{Net worth} = \text{total assets} - \text{total liabilities}$$

Net capital excludes the value of a member's illiquid assets.

$$\text{Net capital} = \text{liquid assets} - \text{total liabilities}$$

In theory, if a member goes into liquidation, the amount realized after all assets are sold and all liabilities paid off is net capital.

1. 8. 6. 2   Reserve Formula Calculation

We will address this in greater detail later in the text, but as an overview, each week, as of the close of business on Friday, carrying firms must perform a computation as to how much money (or equivalent) the firm owes to its customers and how much money the customers owe to the member firm.

If the firm has more customer money than its own, in theory, the firm is using customer monies in the conduct of its business. Any excess of customer funds must be on deposit in a special reserve account. The only acceptable deposits into this account are cash and securities guaranteed by the US government.

1. 8. 6. 3   Financial and Operational Combined Uniform Single (FOCUS) Report

Member firms must file electronic FOCUS reports with the regulatory authorities. These reports show the financial condition of the member, include a net capital computation, include a reserve computation, and provide operational information. For example, carrying firms must file the FOCUS II reports both monthly and quarterly. Noncarrying firms must file FOCUS IIA quarterly, unless FINRA notifies the firm in writing that it must file monthly.

Sample Cover Sheet

UNITED STATES
SECURITIES AND EXCHANGE COMMISSION
Washington, D.C. 20549

OMB APPROVAL	
OMB Number:	3235-0123
Expires:	April 30, 2013
Estimated average burden hours per response......12.00	

Form X-17A-5

FOCUS REPORT

(Financial and Operational Combined Uniform Single Report)

PART II ☐11

(Please read instructions before preparing Form.)

This report is being filed pursuant to (Check Applicable Block(s)):

1) Rule 17a-5(a) ☐ 16   2) Rule 17a-5(b) ☐ 17   3) Rule 17a-11 ☐ 18

4) Special request by designated examining authority ☐ 19   5) Other ☐ 26

NAME OF BROKER-DEALER

SEC FILE NO. ☐ 14

☐ 13

FIRM I.D. NO. ☐ 15

ADDRESS OF PRINCIPAL PLACE OF BUSINESS (Do Not Use P.O. Box No.)

FOR PERIOD BEGINNING (MM/DD/YY) ☐ 24

☐ 20

(No. and Street)

AND ENDING (MM/DD/YY) ☐ 25

☐ 21 (City)   ☐ 22 (State)   ☐ 23 (Zip Code)

NAME AND TELEPHONE NUMBER OF PERSON TO CONTACT IN REGARD TO THIS REPORT

(Area Code) — Telephone No.

☐ 30   ☐ 31

NAMES OF SUBSIDIARIES OR AFFILIATES CONSOLIDATED IN THIS REPORT:

OFFICIAL USE

☐ 32   ☐ 33

☐ 34   ☐ 35

☐ 36   ☐ 37

☐ 38   ☐ 39

DOES RESPONDENT CARRY ITS OWN CUSTOMER ACCOUNTS?   YES ☐ 40   NO ☐ 41

CHECK HERE IF RESPONDENT IS FILING AN AUDITIED REPORT   ☐ 42

EXECUTION:
The registrant/broker or dealer submitting this Form and its attachments and the person(s) by whom it is executed represent hereby that all information contained therein is true, correct and complete. It is understood that all required items, statements, and schedules are considered integral parts of this Form and that the submission of any amendment represents that all unamended items, statements, and schedukes remain true, correct and complete as previously submitted.

Dated the _____ day of _____ , _____
Manual signatures of:

1) _____
Principal Executive Officer or Managing Partner

2) _____
Principal Financial Officer or Partner

3) _____
Principal Operations Officer or Partner

ATTENTION — Intentional misstatement or omissions of facts constitute Federal Criminal Violations. (See 18 U.S.C. 1001 and 15 U.S.C. 78:f(a))

Persons who respond to the collection of information contained in this form are not required to respond unless the form displays a currently valid OMB control number.

SEC 1695 (07-02) 1 of 28

1. 8. 6. 4   Financial and Operations Principal (FINOP)

The preparation and submission of FOCUS reports must be supervised by someone holding a financial and operations limited principal license, the Series 27. The Series 27 license entitles the FINOP to supervise the financial administration of a brokerage firm.

1. 8. 6. 5   General Ledger

The **general ledger** contains accounting records of the firm's assets, liabilities, and net worth accounts. From the general ledger, a firm prepares its financial statements. The general ledger must be prepared as frequently as necessary to determine compliance with the net capital rule, but in no event less frequently than monthly.

1. 8. 6. 6   Carrying Firms

A **carrying firm**, also known as a clearing firm, is one that carries customer accounts and accepts funds and securities from its customers and those of its correspondent firms that have signed clearing and settlement arrangements in place. The minimum net capital requirement for carrying firms is $250,000. These firms nearly always clear for other broker/dealers, which they refer to as correspondent firms. A clearing firm is not to be confused with a clearing facility such as the Depository Trust Clearing Corp.

1. 8. 6. 7   Introducing Firms (Fully Disclosed Firms)

A **fully disclosed firm** is one that introduces its customers to a clearing firm. The clearing firm holds funds and securities of its correspondent, the introducing firm's customers, and performs related functions, such as sending confirmations and statements. Essentially, the clearing firm acts as the introducing firm's back office. The minimum net capital requirement for introducing firms can be as little as $5,000, depending on their lines of business.

1. 8. 6. 8   Commission Sharing Arrangements (Soft Dollars)

Both carrying firms and introducing firms with membership agreements permitting commission sharing arrangements known as "soft dollars" may set aside a portion of the commission for a trade and pay for legitimate trading expenses of their institutional customers, such as order management systems, research, and subscriptions to information processors like Bloomberg Professional Service. The SEC does not permit the use of soft dollars for computer hardware, telecommunications lines, office equipment, reimbursement of travel expenses to attend seminars, and other operational overhead such as rent.

The difference between soft dollars and hard dollars is that instead of paying a broker/dealer with cash (hard dollars), the investor will pay in-kind with brokerage business (soft dollars), that is, sending business to the broker/dealer in such large amounts that the money manager's bills can be paid and enough left over for the broker/dealer to be happy.

QUICK QUIZ 1.C

1. FOCUS IIA reports must be filed by a clearing firm

    A. weekly
    B. monthly
    C. quarterly
    D. annually

2. Which of the following is permitted to submit a FOCUS report under his signature?

    A. Registered representative
    B. Registered operations professional
    C. Chief operations officer
    D. Financial and operations principal

3. A general ledger must be prepared no less frequently than

    A. weekly
    B. monthly
    C. bimonthly
    D. quarterly

4. Broker/dealers required to make a reserve computation must do so no less frequently than

    A. weekly
    B. every 10 business days
    C. monthly
    D. quarterly

5. Which of the following most closely defines net capital?

    A. Net worth
    B. Liquid net worth
    C. General ledger
    D. Net income

6. Which of the following statements is most CORRECT?

    A. Soft dollars is a form of money laundering.
    B. Commission sharing arrangements are illegal.
    C. Soft dollars is the same thing as a commission.
    D. It is acceptable to pay the bills of a money manager with part of the trading commissions.

1. 8. 7   SECURITIES INVESTOR PROTECTION CORPORATION (SIPC)

The **Securities Investor Protection Corporation (SIPC)**, created under the Securities Investor Protection Act of 1970, is a nonprofit membership organization. SIPC members pay assessments into a general insurance fund that is used to meet customer claims in the event of a broker/dealer bankruptcy.

All broker/dealers registered with the SEC must be SIPC members except:

■ banks that deal exclusively in municipal securities;

■ firms that deal exclusively in US government securities; and

■ firms that deal exclusively in redeemable investment company securities.

If the SEC or any SRO finds indications that a broker/dealer is in financial difficulty (usually this will entail net capital violations), SIPC will be notified immediately. If SIPC determines that the member has failed or is in imminent danger of failing, it may petition a federal court to take action by appointing a trustee to liquidate the firm and protect its customers. A **customer** can be broadly defined as anyone who has cash or securities in the possession of a broker/dealer.

The court, upon receipt of SIPC's petition, will issue a protective decree if the broker/dealer is, in fact, insolvent and will then promptly appoint a trustee for the liquidation of the broker/dealer's business.

Once a trustee has been appointed, the member firm is prohibited from engaging in business as a broker/dealer. It also is prohibited from attempting to conceal assets, file false statements, or alter securities records to defraud the trustee or SIPC.

1. 8. 7. 1   Customer Account Coverage

The basic coverage under SIPC is no more than $500,000 per separate customer, not per separate account. Of that total, SIPC covers no more than $250,000 in cash claims.

1. 8. 7. 2   Corporate and Partnership Accounts

Each corporate and partnership account is entitled to separate customer status—separate from the accounts of its directors, partners, and owners.

1. 8. 7. 3   Cash and Margin Accounts

If a customer has both a cash and a margin account, these accounts would be combined for SIPC coverage purposes.

The following claims are not permitted under SIPC:

■ Claims of officers or partners from the failed firm

■ Claims of other member firms for proprietary accounts

■ Claims of subordinated lenders (their funds are at risk)

■ Claims of persons who own 5% or more of the failed firm's equity

In addition, SIPC does not cover losses relating to currencies or futures contracts, as these are not securities. For amounts not covered in a SIPC liquidation, the customer becomes a general (unsecured) creditor of the failed firm.

There are customer accounts in which one person is related to each account, but each account is considered a separate customer for SIPC coverage purposes.

TAKE NOTE

SIPC should not be confused with the FDIC. The FDIC only insures deposits up to $250,000 at insured banks. These deposits may include CDs, checking, savings, and money market deposit accounts.

UNIT TEST

1. An executing broker-dealer who offers over-the-counter securities must be associated with all the following EXCEPT

   A. the Securities and Exchange Commission (SEC)
   B. Financial Industry Regulatory Authority (FINRA)
   C. the Securities Industry and Financial Markets Association (SIFMA)
   D. the Securities Investor Protection Corporation (SIPC)

2. List the following in order of precedence of claims to a bankrupt company's assets.

   I. Common shareholders
   II. Secured bondholders
   III. Preferred shareholders
   IV. Debenture holders
   A. I, II, III, IV
   B. II, I, IV, III
   C. III, II, IV, I
   D. II, IV, III, I

3. Extra commissions charged by a broker/dealer to pay a customer's research expenses is called

   A. markups
   B. commission recapture
   C. soft dollars
   D. additional paid-in capital

4. Stock trades settling "regular way" settle on

   A. trade date
   B. T+1
   C. T+2
   D. T+3

5. In order to trade without restriction, all the following securities must be registered EXCEPT

   A. municipal securities
   B. corporate bonds
   C. Treasury bonds
   D. rights

6. The principal responsible for filing a FOCUS report must be registered as

   A. a Financial and Operations Principal
   B. a General Securities Principal
   C. a Branch Manager
   D. an Operations Manager

7. If an investor believes a stock's price will go down, the investor

   I. is bullish
   II. is bearish
   III. will buy put options
   IV. will buy call options
   A. I and III
   B. I and IV
   C. II and III
   D. II and IV

8. Customer holdings in the following are covered by SIPC EXCEPT

   A. cash
   B. limited partnerships
   C. preferred stocks
   D. BB-rated corporate bonds

9. A broker/dealer must register as an investment advisor if it offers which of the following services?

   A. Research reports
   B. Trade execution
   C. Investment advice
   D. Securities custody

10. Carrying broker/dealers must maintain a minimum net capital of

    A. $5,000
    B. $50,000
    C. $100,000
    D. $250,000

ANSWERS AND RATIONALES

1. **C.** All broker/dealers offering OTC securities must be registered with the SEC and be members of SIPC and FINRA. There is no obligation for any broker/dealer to associate with SIFMA.

2. **D.** During a liquidation of a company's assets, the order of security owner's claims to residual assets is secured bondholders, debenture (unsecured bond) holders, preferred shareholders, and common shareholders.

3. **C.** If a broker/dealer pays for an expense through commission dollars for a customer, the additional commission is called soft dollars. Commission recapture is where the excess commission dollars are paid directly back to the customer. Markups are used in place of commission on principal trades.

4. **D.** The standard settlement date for stocks is T+3, or 3 business days after the trade date. This is referred to as "regular way" settlement.

5. **C.** Treasury securities are exempt from the registration requirements of the Securities Act of 1933. All the other listed securities are nonexempt securities.

6. **A.** Only a financial and operations principal who has qualified by examination (Series 27 or 28, depending on firm's net capital requirement) may file a broker/dealer's FOCUS report.

7. **C.** If an investor is bearish, he believes prices will go down. Purchasing a put option will allow the investor to sell at the higher strike price if the markets go down. Call options are used to purchase shares at a lower strike price if the stock increases in price.

8. **B.** While SIPC covers cash and most securities, it does not cover futures, limited partnerships, or unregistered fixed annuities.

9. **C.** Broker/dealers that offer to advise clients on investment decisions or on the valuation of securities must register as an investment advisor. Research reports do not constitute advising the client as to an investment decision and may be provided by a broker/dealer.

10. **D.** Broker/dealers who hold customer securities or funds must maintain a minimum net capital of $250,000.

QUICK QUIZ ANSWERS

Quick Quiz 1.A

1. **D.** Callable preferred. When the stock is called, dividend payments are no longer made. To compensate for that possibility, the issuer must pay a higher dividend.

2. **A.** Straight preferred. Cumulative preferred is safer, and there is always a risk reward tradeoff. Because straight preferred has no special features, it will pay a higher stated rate of dividend.

3. **C.** Because convertible can be exchanged for common shares, its price is closely linked to the price of the issuer's common.

Quick Quiz 1.B

1. **B and C.**

2. **A and D.**

3. **A and D.**

4. **B and C.**

5. **A and C.**

6. **B and D.**

Quick Quiz 1.C

1. **B.** A FOCUS report must be filed by a clearing firm monthly.

2. **D.** A FINOP is required to sign and submit a FOCUS report on behalf of his broker/dealer.

3. **B.** A general ledger must be prepared at least monthly.

4. **A.** A reserve computation must be made at least weekly.

5. **B.** Net capital is very liquid net worth.

6. **D.** It is permissible for soft dollars to pay for the legitimate bills of an institutional "buy-side" trading firm such as a mutual fund.

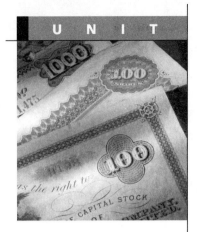

2

Broker-Dealer Operations

Much of the work done in the securities industry is done in the back office. For every front office transaction, a series of processes must be conducted to ensure a smooth transaction for the customer. These processes include account openings, asset transfers, trade reporting and corrections, stock loan, and generating customer statements and confirmations. These items are at the core of the Series 99 examination and must be understood by operations professionals to ensure a secure and efficient back office.

This unit will cover information that will account for 48 questions on the Series 99 exam.

When you have completed this unit, you should be able to:

■ **describe** the process of opening new accounts;

■ **explain** the AML review process;

■ **describe** Suspicious Activity Reports and Currency Transaction Reports;

■ **list** the types of customer accounts;

■ **describe** the process of maintaining customer records;

■ **list** the types of disclosures required for different accounts and products;

■ **list** and **describe** the processes of transferring funds and securities;

■ **describe** the use of stock legends;

■ **describe** the process of transferring securities;

■ **explain** how trades are executed and reported;

■ **describe** the effects of corporate actions;

■ **define** margin, hypothecation, and rehypothecation;

■ **identify** margin requirements for various securities and trading patterns;

■ **describe** the documents and disclosures required to open a margin account;

■ **describe** the settlement process;

■ **list** the information on account statements and trade confirmations; and

■ **identify** the retention requirements for books and records.

2. 1 ACCOUNT OPENING AND MAINTENANCE

2. 1. 1   TYPES OF ACCOUNTS

2. 1. 1. 1   Retail Account

Retail customers are an ever-growing portion of the securities marketplace. There are two options for individual investors to gain access to the markets: through individual trading accounts or through managed, pooled accounts such as a mutual fund or a hedge fund.

Many of the securities rules and regulations have been created in order to protect retail customers. Because they can be easily taken advantage of by investment professionals, retail accounts need to be closely monitored, and investments should be carefully selected to fits the individual's suitability.

2. 1. 1. 2   Institutional Accounts

Institutional investors are companies that either trade for their own account or manage the funds of other investors. Institutional investors are covered by fewer protective regulations than retail customers because it is assumed that they are more knowledgeable and better able to protect themselves. Examples of institutional investors include:

- insurance companies;
- pension funds;
- endowments;
- venture capital firms;
- private equity firms; and
- employee stock option plans (ESOPs).

2. 1. 1. 3   Prime Brokerage Accounts

A **prime brokerage account** is one in which a customer, generally an institution, selects one member firm (the **prime broker**) to provide custody and financing of securities while other firms, called **executing brokers**, handle all trades placed by the customer. Under SEC rules, prime brokerage customers must maintain a minimum of $500,000 in equity in the account.

To open a prime brokerage account for a customer, a member (the prime broker) must sign an agreement with the customer spelling out the terms of the agreement as well as names of all executing brokers the customer has contracted with. The prime broker will then enter into written agreements with each executing broker named by the customer.

The customer receives trade confirmations and account statements from the prime broker, while responsibility for compliance with the short sale rule rests with the executing brokers.

Route of Trade

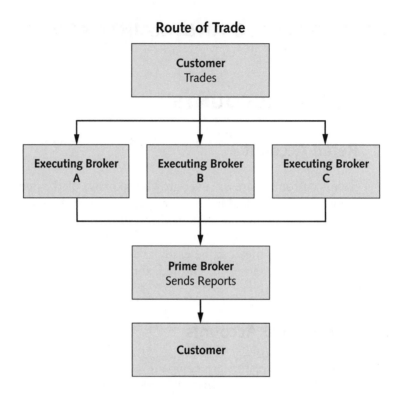

2. 1. 2   ACCOUNT DESIGNATIONS

When an account is opened, it is registered in the name(s) of one or more persons. These persons are the account owners and the only individuals allowed access to and control of the investments in the account.

2. 1. 2. 1   Single Accounts

A single account has one beneficial owner. The account holder is the only person who can control the investments within the account and request distributions of cash or securities from the account.

2. 1. 2. 1. 1   Transfer on Death (TOD)

Transfer on death is a relatively new type of individual account that allows the registered owner of the account to pass all or a portion of it, upon death, to a named beneficiary. This account avoids probate (i.e., having the decedent's will declared genuine by a court of law) because the estate is bypassed. However, the assets in the account do not avoid estate tax, if applicable.

2. 1. 2. 2   Joint Accounts

In a joint account, two or more adults are named on the account as co-owners, with each allowed some form of control over the account.

In addition to the appropriate new account form, a joint account agreement must be signed, and the account must be designated as either tenants in common (TIC) or joint tenants with right of survivorship (JTWROS).

The account forms for joint accounts require the signatures of all owners.

Both types of joint account agreements provide that any or all tenants may transact business in the account. Checks must be made payable to the names in which the account is registered and endorsed for deposit by all tenants, although mail need be sent to only a single address. To be in good delivery form, securities sold from a joint account must be signed by all tenants.

2. 1. 2. 2. 1 Tenants in Common

TIC ownership provides that a deceased tenant's fractional interest in the account is retained by that tenant's estate and is not passed to the surviving tenant(s).

2. 1. 2. 2. 2 Joint Tenants with Right of Survivorship

JTWROS ownership stipulates that a deceased tenant's interest in the account passes to the surviving tenant(s).

TEST TOPIC ALERT

- JTWROS—all parties have an undivided interest in the account

- TIC—each party must specify a percentage interest in the account

Checks or distributions must be made payable to all parties and endorsed by all parties.

2. 1. 2. 3 Partnership Accounts

A partnership is an unincorporated association of two or more individuals.

Partnerships frequently open cash, margin, retirement, and other types of accounts necessary for business purposes.

The partnership must complete a partnership agreement stating which of the partners can make transactions for the account. If the partnership opens a margin account, the partnership must disclose any investment limitations.

An amended partnership agreement must be obtained each year if changes have been made. A partnership agreement is similar to a corporate resolution.

2. 1. 2. 4 Fiduciary and Custodial Accounts

When securities are placed in a fiduciary, or custodial, account, a person other than the owner initiates trades. The most familiar example of a fiduciary account is a trust account. Money or securities are placed in trust for one person, often a minor, but someone else manages the account. The manager or trustee is a fiduciary.

In a fiduciary account, the investments exist for the owner's beneficial interest, yet the owner has little or no legal control over them. The fiduciary makes all of the investment, management, and distribution decisions and must manage the account in the owner's best interests. The fiduciary may not use the account for his own benefit, although he may be reimbursed for reasonable expenses incurred in managing the account.

Securities bought in a custodial account must be registered in such a way that the custodial relationship is evident.

EXAMPLE   Marilyn Johnson, the donor, has appointed her daughter's aunt, Barbara Wood, as custodian for the account of her minor daughter, Alexis. The account and the certificates would read "Barbara Wood as custodian for Alexis Johnson."

The beneficial owner's Social Security number is used on the account.

A fiduciary is any person legally appointed and authorized to represent another person, act on his behalf, and make whatever decisions are necessary to the prudent management of his account. Fiduciaries include a(n):

- trustee designated to administer a trust;
- executor designated in a decedent's will to manage the affairs of the estate;
- administrator appointed by the courts to liquidate the estate of a person who died intestate (without a will);
- guardian designated by the courts to handle a minor's affairs until the minor reaches the age of majority or to handle an incompetent person's affairs;
- custodian of a Uniform Gift to Minors Act (UGMA) or Uniform Transfer to Minors Act (UTMA) account;
- receiver in a bankruptcy; and
- conservator for an incompetent person.

Any trades the fiduciary enters must be compatible with the investment objectives of the underlying entity.

2. 1. 2. 4. 1   Opening a Fiduciary Account

Opening a fiduciary account may require a court certification of the individual's appointment and authority. An account for a trustee must include a trust agreement detailing the limitations placed on the fiduciary. No documentation of custodial rights or court certification is required for an individual acting as the custodian for an UGMA or UTMA account.

The registered representative for a fiduciary account must be aware of the following rules.

- Proper authorization must be given—the necessary court documents must be filed with and verified by the broker/dealer.
- Speculative transactions are generally not permitted.
- Margin accounts are only permitted if authorized by the legal documents establishing the fiduciary accounts.
- The prudent investor rule requires fiduciaries to make wise and safe investments.
- Many states publish a legal list of securities approved for fiduciary accounts.
- A fiduciary may not share in an account's profits but may charge a reasonable fee for services.
- No margin accounts.

2. 1. 2. 5   Power of Attorney

If a person not named on an account will have trading authority, the customer must file written authorization with the broker/dealer giving that person access to the account. This trading authorization usually takes the form of a power of attorney. Two basic types of trading authorizations are full and limited powers of attorney. Both would be cancelled upon the death of either party.

2. 1. 2. 5. 1   Full Power of Attorney

A full power of attorney allows someone who is not the owner of an account to:

■ deposit or withdraw cash or securities; and

■ make investment decisions for the account owner.

Custodians, trustees, guardians, and other people filling similar legal duties are often given full powers of attorney.

2. 1. 2. 5. 2   Limited Power of Attorney

A limited power of attorney allows an individual to have some, but not total, control over an account. The document specifies the level of access the person may exercise. Limited power of attorney, also called limited trading authorization, allows the entering of buy and sell orders but no withdrawal of assets. Entry of orders and withdrawal of assets is allowed if full power of attorney is granted.

TEST TOPIC ALERT   A durable power of attorney (POA) will survive a declaration of mental incompetence.

2. 1. 2. 6   Discretionary Accounts

An account set up with preapproved authority for a registered representative to make transactions without having to ask for specific approval is a discretionary account. Discretion is defined as the authority to decide:

■ what security;

■ the number of shares or units; or

■ whether to buy or sell.

Discretion does not apply to decisions regarding the timing of an investment or the price at which it is acquired.

EXAMPLE   An order from a customer worded, "Buy 100 shares of ABC for my account whenever you think the price is right," is not a discretionary order.

2. 1. 2. 6. 1   Discretionary Authority

A customer can grant discretionary power over his account(s) only by filing a trading authorization or a limited power of attorney with the broker/dealer. No transactions of a discretionary nature can take place without this document on file. Once authorization is given, the customer is legally bound to accept the decision made by the person holding discretionary authority, although the customer may continue to enter orders on his own.

2. 1. 2. 6. 2   Regulation of Discretionary Accounts

In addition to requiring the proper documentation, discretionary accounts are subject to the following rules.

- Each discretionary order must be identified as such at the time it is entered for execution.
- An officer or a partner of the brokerage house must approve each order promptly and in writing, but not necessarily before order entry.
- A record must be kept of all transactions.
- No excessive trading, or churning, may occur in the account relative to the size of the account and the customer's investment objectives.
- To safeguard against the possibility of churning, a designated supervisor or manager must review all trading activity frequently and systematically.

2. 1. 2. 6. 3   Discretionary Accounts and Nonconventional Investments

Nonconventional investments (NCIs) are alternative investments that do not fit a common category. Examples would include the following.

- Hedge funds: Aggressively managed and unregulated portfolio of investments that uses advanced investment strategies
- Distressed debt: Debt instruments of companies that have declared bankruptcy or are considering declaring bankruptcy
- Equity-linked notes (ELNs): A debt instrument where the final payment at maturity is based on the return of a single stock, a basket of stocks, or an equity index

FINRA is concerned that retail investors, especially senior citizens, do not fully understand the risks associated with these NCIs. Accordingly, FINRA requires members that sell these products to conduct the appropriate due diligence. Regarding discretionary accounts and these products, appropriate due diligence may require members to receive prior written consent before purchasing them.

TEST TOPIC ALERT

If you are having difficulty identifying a discretionary order, try this method: an order is discretionary if any one of the three As is missing. The three As are:

- activity (buy or sell);
- amount (number of shares); and
- asset (the security).

EXAMPLE

If a customer asks a representative to sell 1,000 shares of XYZ stock, the order is not discretionary, even though the customer did not specifically say when or at what price.

Activity = sell

Amount = 1,000 shares

Asset = XYZ stock

All three As were defined.

However, if a customer asks a representative to buy 1,000 shares of the best computer company stock available, the order is discretionary. The asset is missing because the company was not defined.

EXAMPLE

A customer wishes to buy 1,000 shares of XYZ whenever the floor broker thinks he can get the lowest price. The order is nondiscretionary. The three As were all defined. Omitting the time or price does not make an order discretionary.

Any order for which the customer gives you authority over price or time, as in the previous example, is not discretionary. Rather, it is termed a market not held order or NH for short. In other words, you are not held to secure a specific price for the order. Market not held orders must be executed on the day received (day orders) unless the customer has given written instructions to the contrary.

QUICK QUIZ 2.A

Match each type of account with the appropriate description.

A. Partnership account
B. TOD
C. TIC
D. JTWROS
E. Numbered account

—— 1. Each party specifies a percentage interest in the account. If one party dies, his interest in the account passes to his estate.

—— 2. An account identified by a number or symbol.

—— 3. Parties share an undivided interest in the account. If one party dies, his interest passes to the other owner(s) of the account.

—— 4. A person with a power of attorney can manage this individual account and be the beneficiary of the account. The assets in the account become the property of the beneficiary on the death of the account owner.

—— 5. An unincorporated interest of 2 or more individuals. An annual agreement specifies which individuals can trade the account.

Quick Quiz answers can be found at the end of the unit.

2. 1. 2. 7   Uniform Gift and Uniform Transfers to Minors Act

Uniform Gift to Minors Act (UGMA) and Uniform Transfers to Minors Act (UTMA) accounts require an adult to act as custodian for a minor (the beneficial owner). Any kind of security or cash may be given to the account without limitation.

Under UGMA, when the minor reaches the age of majority, the property in the account is transferred into the name of the new adult. Under UTMA, the custodian can withhold transfer of property in the account until the new adult reaches age 25 (21 in some states).

2. 1. 2. 7. 1   Donating Securities

When a person makes a gift of securities to a minor under the UGMA or UTMA laws, that person is the donor of the securities. A gift under these acts conveys an indefeasible title; that is, the donor may not take back the gift, nor may the minor return the gift. Once the gift is donated, the donor gives up all rights to the property.

2. 1. 2. 7. 2   Custodian

Any securities given to a minor through an UGMA or UTMA account are managed by a custodian until the minor reaches the age of majority. The custodian has full control over the minor's account and can:

- buy or sell securities;
- exercise rights or warrants; or
- liquidate, trade, or hold securities.

The custodian may also use the property in the account in any way deemed proper for the minor's support, education, maintenance, general use, or benefit. However, the account is not normally used to pay expenses associated with raising a child because the parents can incur negative tax consequences.

Registered representatives must know the following rules of custodial accounts.

- An account may have only one custodian and one minor or beneficial owner.
- Only an individual can be a custodian for a minor's account.
- A minor can be the beneficiary of more than one account, and a person may serve as custodian for more than one account as long as each account benefits only one minor.
- The donor of securities can act as custodian or can appoint someone else to do so.
- Unless they are acting as custodians, parents have no legal control over a custodial account or the securities in it.

2. 1. 2. 7. 3   Opening a Custodial Account

When opening a custodial account, a representative must ensure that the account application contains the custodian's name, the minor's name and Social Security number, and the state in which the account is registered.

2. 1. 2. 7. 4   Registration of Custodial Securities

Any securities in a custodial account are registered in the custodian's name for the benefit of the minor; they cannot be registered in street name.

Typically, the securities are registered to "Joan Smith as custodian for Brenda Smith," for example, or a variation of this form.

2. 1. 2. 7. 5 Fiduciary Responsibility

A custodian is charged with fiduciary responsibilities in managing the minor's account. Certain restrictions have been placed on what is deemed to be proper handling of the investments in these accounts. The most important limitations follow.

- Custodial accounts may be opened and managed as cash accounts only.

- A custodian may not purchase securities in an account on margin or pledge them as collateral for a loan.

- A custodian must reinvest all cash proceeds, dividends, and interest within a reasonable time. Cash proceeds from sales or dividends may be held in a non-interest-bearing custodial account for a reasonable period but should not remain idle for long.

- Investment decisions must take into account a minor's age and the custodial relationship. Commodities futures, naked options, and other high-risk securities are examples of inappropriate investments. Options may not be bought in a custodial account because no evidence of ownership is issued to an options buyer. Covered call writing is normally allowed.

- Stock subscription rights or warrants must be either exercised or sold.

- A custodian cannot delegate away fiduciary responsibility but can grant trading authority and investment decisions to a qualified third party.

- A custodian may loan money to an account but cannot borrow from it.

A custodian may be reimbursed for any reasonable expenses incurred in managing the account unless the custodian is also the donor.

2. 1. 2. 7. 6 Taxation

The minor's Social Security number appears on a custodial account, and the minor must file an annual income tax return and pay taxes on any investment income produced by the account at the parent's tax rate until the minor reaches the age of 18, and in the case of full-time students, until the age of 24.

Exclusions are available, and they are indexed for inflation.

TAKE NOTE

When the minor reaches age 18, the account will be taxed at his tax rate rather than his parents' rate.

Although the minor is the account's beneficiary and is responsible for any and all taxes on the account, in most states, it is the parent's or legal guardian's responsibility to see that the taxes are paid.

2. 1. 2. 7. 7 Death of the Minor

If the beneficiary of a custodial account dies, the securities in the account pass to the minor's estate, not to the parents' or custodian's estate.

2. 1. 2. 7. 8 Death of the Custodian

In the event of the custodian's death or resignation, either a court of law or the donor must appoint a new custodian.

QUICK QUIZ 2.B

1. Which of the following persons are considered fiduciaries?

   I.   Executor of an estate
   II. Administrator of a trust
   III. Custodian of an UGMA/UTMA account
   IV. Conservator for a legally incompetent person

   A. I and II
   B. I, II and III
   C. III and IV
   D. I, II, III and IV

2. If a customer would like to open a custodial UGMA or UTMA account for his nephew, a minor, the uncle

   A. can open the account, provided the proper trust arrangements are filed first
   B. can open the account and name himself custodian
   C. needs a legal document evidencing the nephew's parents' approval of the account
   D. can be custodian for the account only if he is also the minor's legal guardian

3. All of the following statements regarding customer accounts are true EXCEPT

   A. stock held in a custodial account may not be held in street name
   B. the customer who opens a numbered account must sign a statement attesting to ownership
   C. stock held under JTWROS goes to the survivor(s) in the event of a tenant's death
   D. margin trading in a fiduciary account does not require any special consideration

4. Which of the following individuals may NOT open a joint account?

   A. Two spouses
   B. Three sisters
   C. Two strangers
   D. Parent and a minor

5. Securities owned by a donor and given to a minor under the Uniform Gift to Minors Act become the property of the minor

   A. when the securities are paid for by the minor
   B. on the settlement date
   C. when the securities are registered in the custodian's name for the benefit of the minor
   D. when the donor decides to give the securities to the minor

2. 1. 3   RETIREMENT ACCOUNTS

2. 1. 3. 1   Qualified Versus Nonqualified Plans

Retirement plans are generally tax deferred. Plans can be established by individuals or employers. If a plan meets the requirements of ERISA and is approved by the IRS, the plan is said to be tax qualified. If a plan does not meet these requirements, the plan is non-tax qualified. Both plans are tax deferred, which means that earnings in the plan are not taxed until withdrawal.

Qualified plans allow the person (individual or corporate) making a contribution to take a tax deduction for the amount of the contribution. Contributions to nonqualified plans are made with after-tax dollars (i.e., the person making the contribution cannot deduct the contribution amount for tax purposes).

TAKE NOTE

When withdrawals are made from qualified plans, 100% of the withdrawal is taxable as ordinary income at the recipient's tax rate. Withdrawals from nonqualified plans are taxable only to the extent of earnings.

2. 1. 3. 1. 1   Employee Retirement Income Security Act (ERISA)

The Employee Retirement Income Security Act (ERISA) was passed in 1974 to protect the retirement assets of persons in the private sector of the economy. Specifically, ERISA protects participants in corporate pension plans against employer mismanagement. ERISA guidelines include the following.

- Participation. If a company has a retirement plan, employees must be covered within a reasonable time (defined by ERISA as no more than three years).

- Funding. Funds contributed to the plan must be segregated from other corporate assets. The plan's trustees have a fiduciary responsibility to invest prudently and manage funds in a way that represents the best interest of all participants.

- Vesting. Employees must be entitled to their entire retirement benefit amount within a certain time period, even if they are no longer with the employer.

- Communication. The retirement plan must be in writing, and employees must be kept informed of plan benefits, availability, account status, and vesting procedure.

- Nondiscrimination. A uniformly applied formula determines benefits and contributions of all employees. Such a method ensures equitable and impartial treatment.

- Party-in-interest. A party-in-interest is anyone who participates in the plan, provides services to the plan, or manages the plan. These persons are prohibited from selling assets to the plan or receiving any benefit from the operations of the plan. An exception is granted to member firms that offer advice to the plan, as well as to registered representatives of member firms. These persons may be compensated (e.g., commissions) on transactions effected for the plan.

2. 1. 3. 2   Corporate Retirement Plans

All corporate pension and profit-sharing plans must be established under a trust agreement. A trustee is then appointed to act as a fiduciary for the plan and the beneficial owners (the planholders).

All qualified retirement plans fall into one of two categories. Those that shelter contributions of otherwise taxable income without promise of specific future benefits are called defined contribution plans. Those that promise a specific retirement benefit but do not specify the level of current contributions are called defined benefit plans.

2. 1. 3. 2. 1   Defined Contribution Plans

Many types of plans are considered defined contribution plans. These include profit-sharing plans, money-purchase pension plans, thrift plans, 401(k) plans, and 403(b) plans.

All of these plans share a basic feature: the provisions cover amounts going into the plan currently or the plan's current allocation. These plans identify the participant's interest and vested balance. Funds then accumulate to some future event, generally retirement, when the values may be withdrawn. The future final accumulation or account balance depends on the total amount contributed, interest and dividends earned, and increase in value (asset appreciation).

A 401(k) plan may be established by any for-profit corporation. A 403(b) plan, on the other hand, is available to employees of nonprofit organizations such as schools and universities, hospitals, and charitable foundations.

Through payroll deductions, the amount withheld from an employee's payroll check is excluded from reported income. Therefore, the employee in both 401(k) and 403(b) plans gets a tax deduction for amounts contributed to the plan. On withdrawal, 100% is taxable.

2. 1. 3. 2. 2   Defined Benefit Plans

In contrast, the phrase *collecting a pension* usually describes a defined benefit pension plan. Defined benefit plans are designed to provide a specified benefit for their participants.

 E X A M P L E   Such a plan may provide a fixed dollar amount of monthly income at retirement.

Although these plans may also provide benefits in the event of early retirement, death, or disability, the key concept remains: definitely determinable benefits are provided at some future date.

No matter what is actually earned on the underlying assets, the promised benefit is paid under the terms of the contract. Similarly, these plans use actuarial assumptions including mortality, turnover, and interest to derive the appropriate current outlay necessary to fund the future benefits.

2. 1. 3. 3   Nonqualified Corporate Retirement Plans

A nonqualified plan is an employee benefit provided by an employer that does not meet the standards required for qualified plan status. The plan does not require advanced approval from the IRS or the Department of Labor. As a result, the plan does not receive advantageous tax treatment.

A nonqualified plan is not required to comply with the nondiscrimination rules. The employer may make a nonqualified benefit available to certain classes of employees and exclude others. This is drastically different from the manner in which a qualified plan must operate.

Nonqualified plans are not subject to the same stringent reporting and disclosure requirements as qualified plans. This means the employer that sponsors the nonqualified plan need not adhere to strict guidelines regarding the specific information that must be communicated to employees about the benefit plan.

2. 1. 3. 3. 1 Taxation

Contributions to nonqualified plans are not exempt from current income tax. With nonqualified plans, the tax is paid on the amount of contribution in the year the contribution is made (whether the contribution is made by the employer or directly by the employee).

2. 1. 3. 3. 2 Plans

In a payroll deduction program, the employee authorizes a deduction from his check on a weekly, monthly, or quarterly basis. The money is deducted after taxes are paid and may be invested in any number of investment vehicles at the employee's option.

2. 1. 3. 3. 3 Deferred Compensation Plans

Deferred compensation plans represent a contractual agreement between a firm and an employee by which the employee agrees to defer receipt of current compensation in favor of a payout at retirement (or at the employee's disability or death)—when it is assumed that the employee will be in a lower tax bracket. The agreement underlying a deferred compensation plan will usually include:

- a list of the conditions and circumstances under which some or all of the benefits may be forfeited (a contract may specify that an employee gives up all benefits if the employee moves to a competing firm—sometimes known as a golden handcuffs clause);

- a statement to the effect that the employee is not entitled to any claim against the assets of the employer until retirement, death, or disability; and

- a disclaimer that the agreement may be void if the firm suffers a business failure or bankruptcy.

TAKE NOTE

Outside directors of the company are not considered employees for purposes of establishing eligibility for a deferred compensation plan, and as a result, may not participate in the plan.

Also note that any monies set aside to pay benefits are not segregated by the company and may be attached in a lawsuit.

2. 1. 3. 4   Individual Retirement Accounts (IRAs)

IRAs were created as a way of encouraging people to save for retirement. All employed individuals, regardless of whether they are covered by a qualified corporate retirement plan, may open and contribute to an IRA. IRAs are considered qualified plans by the IRS.

2. 1. 3. 4. 1   Tax Benefits

The Economic Recovery Tax Act of 1981 (ERTA) allowed all IRA participants to fully deduct the amount contributed to their IRAs from their taxable income. In 1986, Congress changed the deductibility rules. If an individual is not actively participating in other qualified plans, the full amount of the contribution to the IRA is still deductible. For an individual covered by another qualified plan, the portion deductible is determined by that person's income level. The tax deduction gradually fades away as the taxpayer's adjusted gross income climbs. The exact income levels above which tax deductible contributions are prohibited is not critical because these levels are, by law, raised each year. However, contributions may still be made because the earnings on these amounts are still tax deferred.

2. 1. 3. 4. 2   Participation in an IRA

Any taxpayer reporting income for a given tax year may participate in an IRA. However, the person's income must be earned income—that is, from the performance of personal services (as in a job) and not passive income from rental real estate or portfolio income such as interest, dividends, or capital gains. The taxpayer may not participate if he has reached age 70½ during the tax year.

2. 1. 3. 4. 3   IRA Contributions

The maximum annual IRA contribution that an employed individual can make is subject to the following limitations:

- For 2012, 100% of earned income or $5,000, whichever is less
- For a spousal account, 100% of earned income or $10,000 (divided between two accounts), whichever is less

The IRS allows an individual who has an unemployed spouse to contribute to a separate retirement account established for the nonworking spouse (known as the spousal account). The contribution may be divided between the two accounts in any way, as long as the total contribution is no more than $10,000 with no more than $5,000 in any one account.

2. 1. 3. 4. 4   IRA Investments

The only permissible contribution to an IRA is cash. Once cash is in the account, investments can be made in stocks, bonds, investment company securities, US-minted gold and silver coins, and many other securities. Margin accounts are unsuitable for IRAs.

There are certain investments that are considered ineligible for use in an IRA. Collectibles (e.g., antiques, gems, rare coins, works of art, stamps) are not acceptable IRA investments. Life insurance contracts (cash value, term, and decreasing term insurance with no cash surrender value) may not be purchased in an IRA.

2. 1. 3. 4. 5   IRA Rollovers

Individuals may take possession of the funds and investments in a qualified plan to move them to another qualified plan but may do so no more than once a year. Such a rollover into another account must be completed within 60 calendar days of withdrawal.

EXAMPLE   If an individual changes employers, the amount in his pension plan may be distributed to him in a lump-sum payment. He may then deposit the distribution in an IRA rollover account, where the amount deposited retains its tax-deferred status.

Transfers of funds between qualified retirement accounts differ from rollovers in that the account owner never actually takes physical possession of the funds: the money or investments are sent directly from one IRA custodian to another. There is no limit to the number of times per year a person can transfer investments between custodians, provided the assets in the accounts do not pass through the hands of the taxpayer.

2. 1. 3. 4. 6   IRA Withdrawals

IRA earnings are tax deferred until the money is received, usually at retirement. Withdrawals may not begin without penalty before age 59½ and must begin by April 1 of the year after the year in which the account owner reaches age 70½.

EXAMPLE   If the IRA owner reaches age 70½ on January 1, 20X1, he would have to begin withdrawals by April 1, 20X2. If an individual fails to begin withdrawing by age 70½, a 50% penalty tax will be imposed on amounts that, according to IRS tables, should have been withdrawn.

Withdrawals may be made in a lump sum, in varying amounts, or in regular installments. Withdrawals, except those that result from contributions made with after-tax (nonqualified) contributions, are taxable as ordinary income.

IRA withdrawals before age 59½ incur a 10% penalty (in addition to ordinary income taxation) unless they occur because of:

- the death or permanent disability of the individual;
- the payment of medical expenses exceeding 7.5% of the individual's adjusted gross income (the expenses must be allowed under the Internal Revenue Code);
- the payment of health insurance premiums by an unemployed or self-employed individual who has received state or federal unemployment compensation for 12 consecutive weeks during the year in which the withdrawal is made or the year after;
- first-time home purchase ($10,000 lifetime limit); or
- qualified higher education expenses.

2. 1. 3. 5   Roth IRAs

Unlike a traditional IRA, contributions to a Roth IRA are not tax deductible. In addition, taxpayers are subject to phaseout rules if their adjusted gross income is above certain levels. For taxpayers with income above these levels, contributions to a Roth IRA are prohibited. Contributions could, however, be made to a traditional IRA.

The contribution limits are the same: 100% of earned income not to exceed $5,000. If a taxpayer has both a traditional IRA and a Roth IRA, the aggregate amount that may be contributed to both is $5,000.

Unlike traditional IRAs, contributions to a Roth IRA may be made after age 70½, as there is no requirement to take minimum distributions at that age.

If a withdrawal from a Roth IRA is a qualified distribution, the withdrawal is tax free. A qualified distribution is one made after a five-year holding period and after the taxpayer has reached age 59½.

TEST TOPIC ALERT   Individuals age 50 or older may make an additional catch-up contribution into either Roth or traditional IRAs. For 2012, the amount is $1,000.

2. 1. 3. 5. 1   Roth 401(k) Plans

Roth 401(k) plans became a plan option on January 1, 2006. A Roth 401(k), like a Roth IRA, requires after-tax contributions and allows tax-free withdrawals, provided the plan participant is at least age 59½.

Like a 401(k), it allows the employer to make matching contributions, but the employer's contribution must be made into a traditional 401(k) account. The employee, who would then have two accounts, could make contributions into either but could not transfer money from one to the other.

Unlike a Roth IRA, there are no income limitations on who may have such a plan, there is no five-year holding period for tax-free withdrawals, and the account owner must begin withdrawals by age 70½.

To summarize, a traditional 401(k) allows tax-deductible contributions, but withdrawals are taxable. A Roth 401(k) allows nondeductible contributions but permits tax-free withdrawals.

2. 1. 3. 5. 2   Education IRAs (Coverdell ESAs)

Education IRAs allow after-tax contributions of up to $2,000 per student, per year, for children younger than age 18. Contributions may be made by any adult, as long as the total contribution per child does not exceed $2,000 in one year. Distributions are tax free, as long as the funds are used for education (elementary, secondary, or college).

Taxpayers are subject to phaseout rules if their adjusted gross income is above certain levels. For taxpayers with income above these levels, contributions to a Coverdell ESA are prohibited.

TAKE NOTE

A review of the important features of Roth and Education IRAs follows.

Roth IRA

■ Maximum contribution of $5,000 per year per individual

■ Contributions are not tax deductible

■ Distributions are tax free if taken after age 59½ and money has been in the account for at least five years

■ Distributions not required to begin at age 70½

■ No 10% early distribution penalty for death, disability, and first-time home purchase

■ Contribution levels phased out for high-income individuals

Education IRA (Coverdell)

■ Contribution limit is $2,000 per year per child under age 18

■ Contributions can be made by adults other than parents; total for one child is still $2,000

■ Contributions are not tax deductible

■ Distributions are tax free if taken before age 30 and used for education expenses

■ Contribution levels phased out for high-income individuals

QUICK QUIZ 2.C

1. An individual who is younger than age 70½ may contribute to a traditional IRA

   A. if he has earned income
   B. provided he is not covered by a pension plan through an employer
   C. provided he does not have a Keogh plan
   D. provided his income is between $40,000 and $50,000 if married and $25,000 and $35,000 if single

2. An individual who is 50 years old wants to withdraw funds from her IRA. The withdrawal will be taxed as

   A. ordinary income
   B. ordinary income plus a 10% penalty
   C. capital gains
   D. capital gains plus a 10% penalty

3. Premature distribution from an IRA is subject to

   A. a 5% penalty plus tax
   B. a 6% penalty plus tax
   C. a 10% penalty plus tax
   D. a 50% penalty plus tax

4. Which of the following will NOT incur a penalty on an IRA withdrawal?
    A. Man who has just become totally disabled
    B. Woman who turned age 59 a month before the withdrawal
    C. Person, age 50, who decides on early retirement
    D. Man in his early 40s who uses the money to buy a second home

5. Which of the following statements regarding IRAs is NOT true?
    A. IRA rollovers must be completed within 60 days of receipt of the distribution.
    B. Cash value life insurance is a permissible IRA investment, but term insurance is not.
    C. The investor must be younger than 70½ years old to open and contribute to an IRA.
    D. Distributions may begin at age 59½ and must begin by the year after the year in which the investor turns age 70½.

6. Which of the following is TRUE of both traditional IRAs and Roth IRAs?
    A. Contributions are deductible.
    B. Withdrawals at retirement are tax free.
    C. Earnings on investments are not taxed immediately.
    D. To avoid penalty, distributions must begin the year after the year the owner reaches age 70½.

2. 1. 3. 6   Keogh (HR-10) Plans

For anyone who is self-employed or owns a small business or professional practice, a Keogh plan offers virtually the same tax advantages and retirement coverage found with corporate retirement programs.

Keogh plans are ERISA-qualified plans intended for self-employed individuals and owner-employees of nonincorporated business concerns or professional practices. Included in the self-employed category are independent contractors, consultants, freelancers, and anyone else who files and pays self-employment Social Security taxes. Owner-employee refers to sole proprietors who rely on their business for their livelihood.

Income Must Be Earned. As required for IRAs, full-time or part-time income must be earned income from personal services, not passive income from investments or other unearned sources.

Business Must Show a Profit. Owner-employees of businesses or professional practices must show a gross profit to qualify for a tax-deductible contribution to a Keogh plan. If there is no business profit, no contribution is allowed.

Plan Must Be Nondiscriminatory. Owner-employees who have full-time employees on their payrolls must provide for these people's retirement security under a Keogh plan in the same manner and to the same extent that the owner-employee's retirement security is provided.

2. 1. 3. 6. 1 *Employee Eligibility*

Employee Coverage. If the owner of a sole proprietorship or the partners in a partnership have common law employees (payroll employees), these people must be covered under the employer's Keogh plan. However, employee participation in an employer's Keogh plan is subject to the following employee eligibility rules.

- **Full-time employees**. All employees who receive compensation for at least 1,000 hours of work per year must be covered.
- **Tenured employees**. All employees who have completed one or more years of continuous employment must be covered.
- **Adult employees**. By law, employees under age 21 can be excluded from Keogh plan coverage.

2. 1. 3. 6. 2 *Comparison of Qualified Retirement Plans*

HR-10 (Keogh) plans and IRAs are tax-deferred retirement plans designed to encourage individuals to set aside funds for retirement income. Both IRAs and Keoghs are considered qualified plans, but an IRA does not involve employer contributions and cannot be termed an ERISA-qualified plan. The principal similarities between Keoghs and traditional IRAs are as follows.

- **Age limits**. Anyone younger than age 70½ who is otherwise eligible may contribute to a Keogh or to an IRA plan.
- **Tax deferral of income contributed to plans**. Taxes are deferred on the amount of contributions until the individual receives distributions.
- **Tax-sheltered**. Investment income from dividends, interest, and capital gains is deferred until distribution.
- **Cash-only contributions**. An investor may contribute cash to a plan, but not stocks, bonds, or other securities.
- **Distributions**. Retirement income distributions can begin as early as age 59½ or as late as the year after the year in which the taxpayer reaches age 70½. The tax penalties for early withdrawals or failure to start withdrawals are the same for both.
- **Rollovers and transfers**. Retirement benefits from IRAs and Keoghs may be rolled over once every 12 months. The rollover must be completed within 60 days.
- **Available payout options**. Lump-sum distributions and regular, periodic payments are both permissible.
- **Beneficiary(ies)**. Upon the planholder's death, payments are made to a beneficiary—rights to the cash and securities accumulated in the account do not end with the death of the owner.

2. 1. 4 ACCOUNT OPENING

2. 1. 4. 1 Entities Authorized to Open and Transact Business in the Account

When opening an account for a corporation, a member must obtain a copy of the corporate charter as well as a corporate resolution replete with corporate seal. The charter is proof that the corporation does exist, and the resolution authorizes both the opening of the account and the officers designated to enter orders.

2. 1. 4. 2   New Account Paperwork and Approvals

An account opened by a broker/dealer requires a completed new account form or new account card.

A registered representative must fill out the following information on all new account forms:

- Full name of each customer who will have access to the account
- Date of birth
- Address and telephone number (business and residence)
- Social Security number if the customer is an individual or tax identification number if the customer is another legal entity
- Occupation, employer, and type of business
- Citizenship
- Whether the customer is of legal age
- Annual income and net worth (excluding value of primary residence)
- Investment objectives
- Bank and brokerage references
- Whether the customer is an employee of another broker/dealer
- How the account was acquired
- Name and occupation of the person(s) with authority to make transactions in the account
- Signatures of the representative opening the account and a principal or branch manager accepting the account

---

TAKE NOTE   The customer's signature is not required on the new account form.

All of the items listed are required by FINRA rules. The Municipal Securities Rulemaking Board (MSRB) also requires the customer's tax status.

2. 1. 4. 3   Standing Settlement Instructions (SSIs)

As part of the account opening process, the customer and the registered representative establish registration and delivery instructions. These instructions may be changed for individual transactions. For purchase orders, the customer must stipulate whose name is to be on the security and who will keep the security certificate.

Customers may select any of the following delivery instructions.

- **Transfer and ship.** Securities are transferred into the name of the customer and shipped.
- **Transfer and hold in safekeeping.** Securities are transferred into the customer's name but are held by the broker/dealer.
- **Hold in street name.** Securities are transferred into the broker/dealer's name and held by the broker/dealer. Although the broker/dealer is the nominal owner of the securities, the customer is the beneficial owner.

■ **Delivery versus payment**. The customer instructs the representative to deliver any securities purchased to an agent bank, which will pay the member upon delivery. The customer provides the member firm with the name, address, and account number on file with the agent bank.

2. 1. 5 ANTI-MONEY LAUNDERING (AML) REVIEWS

The Bank Secrecy Act establishes the US Treasury Department as the lead agency for developing regulations in connection with anti-money laundering programs. It also requires broker/dealers to establish internal compliance procedures to detect abuses. Before September 11, 2001, money laundering rules were concerned with the origin of the cash.

Under the act, regulators are more concerned with where the funds are going. The idea is to prevent "clean" money from being used for "dirty" purposes (such as funding terrorist activities).

The three basic stages of money laundering are as follows.

2. 1. 5. 1 Placement

This first stage of laundering is when funds or assets are moved into the laundering system. This stage is recognized as the time when illegal funds are the most susceptible to detection.

2. 1. 5. 2 Layering

The goal of money launderers during this stage is to conceal the source of the funds or assets. This is done through a series of layers of transactions that are generally numerous and can vary in form and complexity.

2. 1. 5. 3 Integration

In the final stage, illegal funds are commingled with legitimate funds in what appear to be viable legitimate business concerns. This can be accomplished using front companies operating on a cash basis, import/export companies, and many other types of businesses.

2. 1. 5. 4 Required Customer Information and Documentation

Under provisions of the USA PATRIOT Act, broker/dealers are required to:
■ verify the identity of any new customer;
■ maintain records of the information used to verify identity; and
■ determine whether the person appears on any list of known or suspected terrorists or terrorist organizations.

These rules are designed to prevent, detect, and prosecute money laundering and the financing of terrorism. Under the act, financial institutions are encouraged to share information regarding terrorism and money laundering activity.

As part of its customer identification program, a broker/dealer must, before opening an account, obtain at least:

■ customer name;

■ date of birth;

■ physical address (no PO box); and

■ Social Security number.

An exception is granted to persons who do not currently have but who have applied for a Social Security number. The firm, in this instance, must obtain the number within a reasonable period of time.

The firm must also verify the identity of each new customer. This can be done by obtaining a copy of the person's valid driver's license or a copy of a valid passport. Furthermore, the firm must determine whether the customer's name appears on any list of known or suspected terrorists. This is done by contacting the US Treasury.

Finally, new customers must be advised, before the account is opened, that the firm is requesting information to verify their identities. This notification may be placed on the firm's Website, delivered verbally, or placed on the new account form.

TAKE NOTE
The Office of Foreign Asset Control (OFAC) maintains a list of individuals viewed as a threat to the United States. An officer of the firm must be designated to monitor the list and the rules and regulations as set forth by OFAC.

2. 1. 5. 5   Suspicious Activity Reports (SARs)

The USA PATRIOT Act requires firms to report to Financial Crimes Enforcement Network (FinCEN) when there is an event, transaction, or series of events or transactions that appear to be questionable. The act requires firms to report to FinCEN any transaction that alone or in the aggregate involves at least $5,000 in funds or other assets if the firm suspects that it falls within one of the following four classes.

■ The transaction involves funds derived from illegal activity.

■ The transaction is designed to evade the requirements of the Bank Secrecy Act.

■ The transaction appears to serve no business or lawful purpose.

■ The transaction involves the use of the firm to facilitate criminal activity.

EXAMPLE
A pattern of cash deposits over time, none of which individually would require a Form 104 filing, could trigger a suspicious activity report (SAR) filing.

TAKE NOTE
Structuring refers to handling currency transactions in a way designed to avoid reporting requirements.

Firms must file a SAR within 30 days of becoming aware of the suspicious transaction(s). Copies of each SAR filing and the related documentation must be retained for five years from the date of the filing.

The act also requires that the filing of a SAR must remain confidential. The person involved in the transaction that is the subject of the report must not be notified. If subpoenaed, the firm must refuse to provide the information and must notify FinCEN of the request unless the disclosure is required by FinCEN, the SEC, an SRO, or other law enforcement authority.

In addition, the USA PATRIOT Act requires firms to make and retain records relating to wire transfers of $3,000 or more. Information to be collected includes the name and address of both sender and recipient, the amount of the transfer, the name of the recipient's financial institution, and the account number of the recipient.

Sample Cover Sheet

<table>
<tr>
<td colspan="2">

FinCEN
Form 101

March 2011

</td>
<td colspan="2">

Suspicious Activity Report by the
Securities and Futures Industries

▶ **Please type or print. Always complete entire report. Items marked with an asterisk * are considered critical. (See instructions.)**

</td>
<td>

OMB No. 1506 - 0019

</td>
</tr>
</table>

1 Check the box if this report corrects a prior report (See instructions) ☐

Part I   Subject Information   2 Check box a ☐ if multiple subjects   box b ☐ subject information unavailable

*3 Individual's last name or entity's full name	*4 First name	5 Middle initial

6 Also known as (AKA - individual), doing business as (DBA - entity)	7 Occupation or type of business

*8 Address	*9 City

*10 State	*11 ZIP code	*12 Country code (If not U.S.) (See instructions)	13 E-mail address (If available)

*14 SSN/ITIN (individual), or EIN (entity) | *15 Account number(s) affected, if any. Indicate if closed.

Acc't #_____ yes ☐   Acc't #_____ yes ☐
Acc't #_____ yes ☐   Acc't #_____ yes ☐

16 Date of birth   __/__/__   MM   DD   YYYY

*17 Government issued identification (If available)

a ☐ Driver's license/state ID   b ☐ Passport   c ☐ Alien registration   d ☐ Corporate/Partnership Resolution

e ☐ Other _____

f ID number |_____| g Issuing state or country (2 digit code) _____

18 Phone number - work   (   )   —   19 Phone number - home   (   )   —

20 Is individual/business associated/affiliated with the reporting institution? (See instructions)
a ☐ Yes   b ☐ No

Part II   Suspicious Activity Information

*21 Date or date range of suspicious activity

From ___/___/___   To ___/___/___
   MM DD YYYY   MM DD YYYY

*22 Total dollar amount involved in suspicious activity

$ |___,___,___,___|.00

23 Instrument type (Check all that apply)

a ☐	Bonds/Notes	i ☐	Commodity options	q ☐	Commodity type _____ (Please identify)	
b ☐	Cash or equiv.	j ☐	Security futures products			
c ☐	Commercial paper	k ☐	Stocks	r ☐	Instrument description _____	
d ☐	Commodity futures contract	l ☐	Warrants			
e ☐	Money Market Mutual Fund	m ☐	Other securities	s ☐	Market where traded |___|___|___|	
f ☐	Mutual Fund	n ☐	Other non-securities		(Enter appropriate three or four-letter code.)	
g ☐	OTC Derivatives	o ☐	Foreign currency futures/options	t ☐	Other (Explain in Part VI)	
h ☐	Other derivatives	p ☐	Foreign currencies			

24 CUSIP® number	25 CUSIP® number	26 CUSIP® number

27 CUSIP® number	28 CUSIP® number	29 CUSIP® number

*30 Type of suspicious activity:

a ☐	Bribery/gratuity	h ☐	Identity theft	o ☐	Significant wire or other transactions without economic purpose	
b ☐	Check fraud	i ☐	Insider trading			
c ☐	Computer intrusion	j ☐	Mail fraud	p ☐	Suspicious documents or ID presented	
d ☐	Credit/debit card fraud	k ☐	Market manipulation	q ☐	Terrorist financing	
e ☐	Embezzlement/theft	l ☐	Money laundering/Structuring	r ☐	Wash or other fictitious trading	
f ☐	Commodity futures/options fraud	m ☐	Prearranged or other non-competitive trading	s ☐	Wire fraud	
g ☐	Forgery	n ☐	Securities fraud	t ☐	Other (Describe in Part VI)	

2. 1. 6   ACCOUNT MAINTENANCE

2. 1. 6. 1   Escheatment Process

With regard to individual accounts, once a firm becomes aware of the death of the account owner, the firm must cancel all open orders, mark the account *Deceased*, and freeze the assets in the account until receiving instructions and the necessary documentation from the executor of the decedent's estate. If the account has a third-party power of attorney, the authorization is revoked.

TAKE NOTE   Discretionary authority ends at the death of the account owner.

Depending on the account type, the documents necessary to release the assets of a decedent are:

- a certified copy of the death certificate;
- inheritance tax waivers; and
- letters testamentary.

If one party in a JTWROS account dies, the account cannot be transferred to the name of the new owner (the other party) until a certified copy of the death certificate is presented to the member firm. The other documents noted previously are not needed to transfer ownership at death in a JTWROS account.

If one party in a TIC account dies, the decedent's interest in the account goes to his estate. The executor for the decedent must present the proper documents before the assets belonging to the decedent can be released. In some states, the death of a tenant in a TIC account requires that the executor present an affidavit of domicile to the member that shows the decedent's estate will be handled under the laws of that state.

Also note that in TIC accounts, the death of a tenant requires that the member firm freeze the account and acceptance of orders until the required documents are presented. Compare this with a JTWROS account, for which the death of one tenant does not preclude the remaining tenant from entering orders.

With regard to partnership accounts, if one partner dies, the member needs written authority from the remaining partners before executing any further orders. This written authorization generally takes the form of an amended partnership agreement.

TEST TOPIC ALERT   Three basic steps apply at the death of a customer:

- Cancel open orders
- Freeze the account (mark it deceased)
- Await instructions from the executor of the estate

2. 1. 6. 2   Updating Customer Account Records

If the customer should notify the firm of any changes to the account record such as change in name, address, or investment objectives, the firm must send a copy of the updated account record within 30 days of receiving notice of the change. Account information is required to be sent to all customers at least every 36 months to ensure the information is accurate.

2. 1. 6. 3   Accounts for Associated Persons of Member Firms

If an account is held by an associated person of a separate member firm, duplicate statements and confirms must be provided upon request of the customer's employer. This may either be established at the account's opening or during any time throughout the life of the account. Only member firms that the customer is currently associated with, however, may make this request.

2. 1. 7   DISCLOSURES

2. 1. 7. 1   Product-Specific Disclosures

2. 1. 7. 1. 1   Penny Stocks

A penny stock is a non-Nasdaq, unlisted stock trading at less than $5 per share. A penny stock is a low-priced Bulletin Board or Pink Sheet stock. The SEC rules on designated securities are the 15(g) rules.

Rule 15(g)2 requires that customers, before their initial transaction in a penny stock, be given a copy of a Risk Disclosure Document. The member must receive a signed and dated acknowledgment from the customer that the document has been received. Not surprisingly, a disclosure document fully describes the risks associated with penny stock investments.

2. 1. 7. 2   Account-Specific Disclosures

Accounts that provide investors with additional amounts of risk over a cash account require that the investor be notified prior to the account opening of the additional risk. Prime examples of these accounts are option and margin accounts.

2. 1. 7. 2. 1   Options

Options are unique insomuch that the risk disclosure that must be provided is standardized throughout the industry. The Options Clearing Corporation (OCC) publishes the Options Disclosure Document (ODD), which must be provided to every options investor prior to their option account being opened. Additional, firm-specific disclosures may also be provided.

2. 1. 7. 2. 2   Margin

Prior to opening a margin account, and at least annually thereafter, a risk disclosure must be provided to the account holders identifying and discussing the risks associated with a margin account. This is explained in greater detail in Section 2.6.3.4.

2. 2 CASHIERING AND ACCOUNT TRANSFERS

2. 2. 1 MOVEMENT OF FUNDS AND SECURITIES

2. 2. 1. 1 Methods of Fund Transfer

There are several methods in which customers can transfer their funds in and out of their accounts. Funds can be sent by the following methods.

- **Wire transfer.** Wire transfer is an electronic funds transfer from one person to another. A wire transfer can be made from one bank account to another bank account. Wire transfer systems offer more individualized transactions than bulk payment systems such as ACH and check.

- **Automated Clearing House transfer.** Automated Clearing House (ACH) is an electronic network for financial transactions in the United States. ACH processes large volumes of credit and debit transactions in batch that includes direct deposit payroll payments. Businesses increasingly use ACH online to have customers pay, rather than via credit or debit cards.

- **Check.** A check is a document ordering a payment of money from a bank account. Checks are a convenient type of bill of exchange developed as a way to make payments without the need to carry large sums. In a way, paper currency is not too dissimilar to a check in that that currency too was originally a written order to pay the given amount to the "bearer."

A check is a negotiable instrument instructing a bank or thrift to pay a specific amount of currency from the drawer's account. The payee may endorse the check, allowing a third party to cash it. Check usage has fallen in recent years in favor of electronic payment systems. Some countries have phased out checks completely.

2. 2. 1. 2 Methods of Giving Instructions

Funds cannot be moved out of a customer account without the customer's permission (or anyone with a power of attorney to move funds). To authorize a fund transfer, the customer will generally require a letter of authorization. The letter of authorization should include the customer's name, account number, quantity of funds to move, method of transfer, and any transfer instructions (e.g., wire instructions or address to mail check).

TEST TOPIC ALERT   Due to the increased risk with foreign and third-party fund transfers, additional precautions should be taken to authenticate the transfer instructions, such as having the letter of authorization notarized.

2. 2. 1. 3 Medallion Signature Guarantee Program

To avoid rejection by the transfer agent, all signatures on certificates must be guaranteed by a party acceptable to the transfer agent, such as a member clearing firm or a bank that participates in the **NYSE medallion program**. The NYSE developed the Medallion Signature Guarantee Program, which provides for the use of medallions by participants in place of signatures in effecting assignments.

In addition to an annual fee, the administrative expenses are borne by the program's participants. The program covers all signatures placed on securities, stock and bond powers, CDs, deeds, and so forth and provides for indemnification insurance for participants in the case of fraud. The program does not guarantee the certificate but rather the signature only.

For nonparticipants, signature requirements are as follows.

- For stock registered to an individual, the signature must exactly match the name registered on the face of the certificate.

- For stock registered in joint names, the exact signature of all owners is required.

- For stock registered in corporate name, interchangeable endorsements are acceptable (e.g., Acme Inc., Acme & Co., Acme and Co., Acme Company).

- For stock registered in the name of a deceased person, the only acceptable endorsement is that of the decedent's estate executor.

- For stock registered in the name of a minor child, the only acceptable endorsement is that of the custodian.

- For stock registered in the name of a trust, the only acceptable endorsement is that of the trustee.

2. 2. 1. 4 Currency Transaction Reports (CTRs)

The Bank Secrecy Act requires broker/dealers to report, on Form 104, any currency received in the amount of more than $10,000 on a single day. Though paying for purchased securities with currency is not prohibited, many firms do not permit this. Failure to report can result in fines of up to $500,000, 10 years in prison, or both. Records relating to Form 104 must be retained for five years.

Form 104 must be filed within 15 days of receipt of the currency. This rule is part of the regulatory effort to deal with money laundering. The two federal agencies empowered to deal with this abuse are the Federal Reserve and the Department of the Treasury.

Sample Cover Sheet

FINCEN Form **104**	**Currency Transaction Report**	
(March 2011) Department of the Treasury FinCEN	▶ **Previous editions will not be accepted after September, 2011.** ▶ **Please type or print.** *(Complete all parts that apply--See Instructions)*	OMB No. 1506-0004

1   Check all box(es) that apply: **a** ☐ Amends prior report   **b** ☐ Multiple persons   **c** ☐ Multiple transactions

---

Part I   Person(s) Involved in Transaction(s)

Section A--Person(s) on Whose Behalf Transaction(s) Is Conducted

2 Individual's last name or entity's name	**3** First name	**4** Middle initial

5 Doing business as (DBA)	**6** SSN or EIN

7 Address (number, street, and apt. or suite no.)	**8** Date of birth ___/___/___ MM DD YYYY

9 City	**10** State	**11** ZIP code	**12** Country code (if not U.S.)	**13** Occupation, profession, or business

14 If an individual, describe method used to verify identity: **a** ☐ Driver's license/State I.D.   **b** ☐ Passport   **c** ☐ Alien registration

d ☐ Other _____   **e** Issued by: _____   **f** Number: _____

Section B--Individual(s) Conducting Transaction(s) (if other than above).
If Section B is left blank or incomplete, check the box(es) below to indicate the reason(s)

a ☐ Armored Car Service   **b** ☐ Mail Deposit or Shipment   **c** ☐ Night Deposit or Automated Teller Machine   **d** ☐ Multiple Transactions   **e** ☐ Conducted On Own Behalf

15 Individual's last name	**16** First name	**17** Middle initial

18 Address (number, street, and apt. or suite no.)	**19** SSN

20 City	**21** State	**22** ZIP code	**23** Country code (If not U.S.)	**24** Date of birth ___/___/___ MM DD YYYY

25 If an individual, describe method used to verify identity: **a** ☐ Driver's license/State I.D.   **b** ☐ Passport   **c** ☐ Alien registration

d ☐ Other _____   **e** Issued by: _____   **f** Number: _____

Part II   Amount and Type of Transaction(s).   Check all boxes that apply.

26   Total cash in $_____ 0.00   **27**   Total cash out $_____ 0.00   **28** Date of transaction ___/___/___ MM DD YYYY

26a   Foreign cash in_____ 0.00 *(see instructions, page 4)*   **27a**   Foreign cash out _____ 0.00 *(see instructions, page 4)*

29 ☐   Foreign Country_____   **30** ☐   Wire Transfer(s)   **31** ☐   Negotiable Instrument(s) Purchased

32 ☐   Negotiable Instrument(s) Cashed   **33** ☐   Currency Exchange(s)   **34** ☐   Deposit(s)/Withdrawal(s)

35 ☐   Account Number(s) Affected (if any):   **36** ☐   Other (specify)

Part III   Financial Institution Where Transaction(s) Takes Place

37 Name of financial institution	Enter Regulator or BSA Examiner code number (see instructions) ▶

38 Address (number, street, and apt. or suite no.)	**39** EIN or SSN

40 City	**41** State	**42** ZIP code	**43** Routing (MICR) number

	44 Title of approving official	**45** Signature of approving official	**46** Date of signature ___/___/___ MM DD YYYY
Sign Here ▶	**47** Type or print preparer's name	**48** Type or print name of person to contact	**49** Telephone number (___) ___ - ___

▶ **For Paperwork Reduction Act Notice, see page 4.**   Cat. No. 37683N   FinCEN Form **104** (Rev. 03-2011)

2. 2. 1. 5   Reinvestments and Sweeps

In a sweep account, extra cash above the average balance that may be required by the broker/dealer will be invested in a money market, CD, or some highly liquid investment enabling the investor to have some return on his money when it is not invested in stocks or longer-term debt.

2. 2. 2   TRANSFERS OR PARTIAL TRANSFERS OF ACCOUNTS BETWEEN BROKER-DEALERS

2. 2. 2. 1   Automated Customer Account Transfer Service (ACATS)

When a customer whose securities account is carried by a member (the carrying member) wants to transfer the account to another member (the receiving member), the customer must sign an account transfer form (ACAT form), which is sent to the carrying member by the receiving member. For purposes of this rule, customer authorization could be the customer's actual signature or an electronic signature.

TAKE NOTE   When your firm receives an ACAT form from a prospective customer, it must forward the form to the carrying member immediately.

The carrying member, within one business day following receipt, must validate and return the transfer instruction to the receiving member with an attachment showing all securities positions.

The carrying firm may take exception to the transfer instruction if:

- the account is flat and reflects no transferable assets;
- the Social Security number on the instruction does not match the number on the carrying firm's records;
- the account title does not match the title on the carrying firm's record; or
- the customer signature on the instruction is improper.

TAKE NOTE   A carrying member may not take exception to a transfer instruction and thereby deny validation because of a dispute over securities positions or the money balance in the account.

Both firms must promptly (within five business days) resolve any exceptions taken.

Upon validation, the carrying member must freeze the account and refuse any new orders. In addition, all open orders such as stops or limits must be canceled. The only exception to the acceptance of new orders is option positions, which expire within seven business days.

Within three business days following validation, the carrying firm must complete the transfer of the account. If any positions are not transferred to the receiving firm due to a failure to receive at the carrying firm, fail to receive and fail to deliver contracts must be established by the members. Fail contracts, dealer to dealer, are discussed later.

Certain assets are nontransferable. These include proprietary products such as unit trusts managed by the carrying firm. In these situations, the customer can retain these assets at the carrying firm or liquidate and have the resulting cash balance transferred. The securities underlying when-issued contracts are subject to delayed delivery. Rather than transfer the contract, the carrying firm retains the contract until the underlying securities are issued. At this point, the securities are transferred. Also note that partial transfers are acceptable. For example, a customer could elect to transfer only his equity securities, leaving the remainder at the carrying firm.

TAKE NOTE

The bulk transfer of customer accounts is permitted in certain circumstances. Assume, for example, that a registered representative at Firm A has 200 variable annuity customers where the contracts are held by the insurance company issuer. This person now joins Firm B and wishes to have the broker/dealer of record changed for these accounts with the insurance company carrier. This can be done in bulk but only after the customers have provided their consent via an affirmative consent letter. Under FINRA rules, the use of a negative consent letter is not permitted.

2. 2. 2. 2   Non-ACATS Transfers

Not all securities are eligible to be transferred via ACATS. These securities include:

- securities sold exclusively by the sending firm;
- mutual funds or money market funds not available at the receiving firm (sometimes referred to as a mutual fund clean-up);
- limited partnerships that are private placements;
- annuities;
- bankrupt securities; and
- restricted securities.

Occasionally, customers may choose to have some specific part of their assets (partial) transferred outside of ACATS. This is sometimes referred to as a non-standard transfer. When a customer gives alternate instructions for the transfer of specifically designated assets from one broker/dealer to another, it creates an exemption from the member's obligation to transfer through ACATS. This is available *only* for partial transfers.

TAKE NOTE

Customers may use an electronic signature in a format that is valid under federal law.

2. 2. 2. 3   Residual and Residual Credit Processing

A residual credit position may be both cash and securities that have come into the account *after* the account has been transferred. In that case, if securities account assets were transferred, in whole, the clearing agency is required to transfer residual credit positions from the carrying member to the receiving member.

2. 2. 2. 4   Safeguard

In order to safeguard all customer assets and to meet their supervisory obligations, bro-ker/dealers must enforce procedures governing the withdrawal or transmittal of money or other assets from their customers' accounts. A broker/dealer's procedures should be reasonably designed to review and monitor all instructions to transmit or withdraw assets from customer accounts, including instructions from an investment adviser or other third party acting on behalf of the customer. FINRA firms are required to test and verify their procedures and update them as often as necessary.

2. 2. 3   HANDLING CHECKS

2. 2. 3. 1   Characteristics of Negotiable Checks

A negotiable check is a money instrument that allows the recipient of the check to endorse it to a third party. To indorse the check, the payee must sign her name and write on the check to whom it is to be paid. Not all checks, however, are negotiable. Non-negotiable checks may not be changed in any way and are only valid for the original payee.

TAKE NOTE   Amount of payment cannot be changed in either a negotiable or non-negotiable check.

2. 2. 3. 2   Check Issuance

Although many clearing firms do not accept or disperse cash, checks that come in and go out are recorded on a check blotter, also called the "cash" blotter, though most brokerage firms will no longer accept cash, money orders, traveler's checks, and of course stale dated checks (six months or older). A firm is also under no obligation to distribute cash.

Checks drawn on customer accounts must be made out in the full account name. For example, if the account name is William & Carol Rudolph, the check must state that fully, without any alteration. It would be unacceptable to make the check payable to Carol Rudolph alone.

2. 2. 3. 3   Maintenance of a Check Blotter

Broker/dealers are required to keep a blotter for all checks receive. This blotter, updated at least daily, should include the date checks were received, from whom checks were received, and amount of checks. If the checks were forwarded (such as to a clearing firm), the blotter should also include the date checks were forwarded and to whom checks were forwarded.

Daily Check Blotter
Direct Business

Date: ___Feb 29, 2012___

Office: ___Wayne PA___

Date Received from Client	Date Sent to Headquarters	Customer Name	Customer Account Number	Check #	Dollar Amount	Payable to	Method Used to Send Check
2/29/12	2/29/12	Adam Andrews	20584/RRT	215	$26,000.00	Alex Br.	UPS 10AM
3/1/12	3/1/12	Victoria Jones	30001/RRT	3074	107,400.00	Alex Br.	UPS 10AM

2. 2. 4   PROHIBITED CASHIERING AND ACCOUNT TRANSFER ACTIVITIES

2. 2. 4. 1   Anti-Money Laundering

As discussed previously, member firms have a requirement to ensure they are in compliance with anti-money laundering regulations. While tests are performed on new accounts for customer identification and funding of the account, continual surveillance is required throughout the life of the account to detect any placement, layering, or integration as part of a money laundering scheme.

2. 2. 4. 2   Check Fraud

Any form of check fraud is a serious offense, classified as a felony in many jurisdictions, and is a basis for a statutory disqualification from registration with FINRA. Check fraud may include altering checks and kiting, the process of writing a check for more than the account balance to use the funds in the depositing account prior to the check bouncing. To reiterate, once a check is drawn, it may not be altered.

TAKE NOTE

Kiting is the illegal practice of writing a check for an amount greater than the available account balance from an account in one bank and then writing another check from another bank with non-sufficient funds to cover the non-existent funds from the first account in an effort to avoid bouncing.

2. 2. 4. 3   Holding Checks for Extended Periods

Checks must be processed in a timely manner—usually meaning same day—for clearing, but in the event of a disaster, the members must determine as soon as possible the dollar amount of any customer checks held at an affected business that cannot be located or accounted for. That information must be provided in writing to FINRA.

2. 2. 4. 4   Holding Account Transfers for an Extended Period

The uniform practice code requires that all broker/dealers expedite and coordinate transfer activities. A broker/dealer may not, therefore, hold (or fail to transfer) securities for an extended period.

TAKE NOTE

While the UPC requires transfer requests to be expedited, care still needs to be taken during the transfer process to ensure the appropriate securities and funds are transferred to the receiving firm. Delays may also occur due to either the customer or the broker/dealer improperly filing required documents or transfer instructions.

---

2. 3 CUSTODY AND CONTROL OF SECURITIES

Carrying firms have the daily requirement to bring under possession (in-house) or control (in an account controlled by the firm) all fully paid-for customer securities and all excess margin securities. Each day, from the prior day's settlement records, a carrying firm must take steps to ensure that it has obtained physical possession or control over such securities. Stocks of a customer that are held in the name of a broker/dealer for safekeeping and easy transferring are referred to as being held in "street name."

A customer's securities must always be held in a safe location, but those held in the name of the customer must be segregated from those of the firm so as to avoid comingling.

TAKE NOTE

Margin securities are not subject to this requirement. The securities are at a bank collateralizing customer debit balances. Excess margin securities, however, must be under the possession or control of the firm and may not be used as collateral.

Good control locations include securities depositories such as depository trust company (DTC), commercial banks, and other broker/dealers. DTC is the world's largest securities depository. It provides custody services for virtually all securities except those subject to transfer or ownership restrictions. Securities eligible for DTC services are said to be on the approved list. Foreign depositories, foreign clearing agencies, and foreign custodian banks are acceptable control locations if approved by the SEC.

Credit unions and savings and loans are not good control locations.

2. 3. 1 CUSTOMER PROTECTION RULE

SEC Rule 15c3-3, the Customer Protection Rule, was enacted in conjunction with SIPC legislation in response to a wave of broker/dealer liquidations in the late 1960s and early 1970s. The rule has two basic components: possession or control requirements and the reserve requirement.

2. 3. 1. 1 Possession or Control

Carrying firms have the daily requirement to bring under possession (in-house) or control (in an account controlled by the firm) all fully paid-for customer securities and all excess margin securities. Each day, from the prior day's settlement records, a carrying firm must take steps to ensure that it has obtained physical possession or control over such securities.

Margin securities are not subject to this requirement. The securities are at a bank collateralizing customer debit balances. Excess margin securities, however, must be under the possession or control of the firm and may not be used as collateral.

2. 3. 1. 2 Reserve Requirement

Each week, as of the close of business on Friday, carrying firms make the following determinations:

- Monies owed to the member by customers (debits)
- Monies owed by the member to customers (credits)

If credits exceed debits, the firm, in theory, is using customer monies in the conduct of business. The rule requires that any excess of credits over debits must be on deposit in a special reserve account within one hour after the banks open on the second business day following computation (this generally means by 10:00 am, Tuesday). The only acceptable deposits into this account are cash and qualified securities, which are securities guaranteed by the US government. Qualified securities are Treasury bills, Treasury notes, Treasury bonds, and Ginnie Maes.

Reserve Requirement

Debits (Assets)	Credits (Liabilities)
Money owed to the brokerage firm by customers	Money owed to customers by the brokerage firm
$1,000,000	$1,200,000

BANK
SUBJECT TO FEDERAL REGULATION

$200,000 excess deposited in Special Reserve Account

Failure to make a required deposit into a special reserve account requires immediate electronic notice to the SEC and FINRA. The member must promptly confirm the contents of the electronic notice in writing.

2. 3. 1. 2. 1   Special Reserve Account

In opening a special reserve account, a member must inform the bank that the monies on deposit are for the exclusive benefit of the member's customers and that there can be no cross liens on this account (the bank cannot go after funds in this account if the member is delinquent in meeting other obligations it may have with the bank).

A member is permitted to withdraw monies from the special reserve account as long as the withdrawal is supported by a computation indicating there is an excess on deposit.

QUICK QUIZ 2.D

1. Match the following terms with the appropriate descriptions.
   A. Weekly
   B. 105%
   C. 6 years
   D. 3 years
   E. Lifetime
   F. Monthly
   G. Settlement date
   H. 45 days
   I. Quarterly

   —— 1. Term for which Focus reports must be retained

   —— 2. Typical frequency of a firm's customer reserve calculation

   —— 3. Term for which customer account records must be retained

   —— 4. Term for which minute books must be retained

—— 5. Amount of excess of credits over debits that must be deposited by monthly reserve account calculators

—— 6. Number of days after which unresolved short securities differences must be bought in

—— 7. Frequency with which trial balances must be prepared

—— 8. Date by which customer ledgers must be posted

—— 9. Frequency of securities counts

2. 3. 1. 3   Periodic Physical Count of Securities

SEC Rule 17a-13 requires carrying firms to count all securities being held by the firm at least quarterly. The count cannot be performed by persons whose responsibilities include the care and custody of securities or the creation or preservation of records relating to the count. The quarterly count is sometimes referred to as a box count.

In performing the count, the firm must count all securities, including those underlying repurchase agreements. The firm must also count all securities at a transfer agent, in transit, and securities that are not in the firm's possession such as fails to deliver and fails to receive.

2. 3. 1. 4   Maintenance of a Stock Record and Verifying Securities

The quarterly count must verify all securities maintained on the stock record book. Occasionally, the count will show too many shares, called a long securities difference, or too few, a short securities difference. In this case, the expression *short* does not mean to "sell short," but rather the firm simply does not have the securities in either its possession or in a good control location.

2. 3. 1. 4. 1   Long Securities Difference

For instance, as a result of a quarterly count, a member is confronted with the following: its records show it should have under its possession or control 1 million shares of XYZ stock owned by its customers. A count shows it has 1.1 million shares. The firm has a long securities difference of 100,000 shares, which it must resolve as promptly as possible.

It might be tempting to sell the 100,000 shares, thereby balancing the count with the records. The SEC does not prohibit the sale of a long securities difference.

If a firm chooses this route, it must charge its net worth (and, thus, its capital) by the sales proceeds. Sooner or later, according to the SEC, the member will determine the owner of those shares and will be forced to buy back the position (so there is no benefit to selling the long difference).

TAKE NOTE   The sale of a long difference is charged to net worth. A long securities difference (unsold) has no effect on net worth.

2. 3. 1. 4. 2   Short Securities Difference

A greater problem arises if the count shows fewer shares than indicated on the stock record. Using the prior example, assume the count shows the firm has only 900,000 shares of XYZ under its possession or control. The firm now has a short securities difference of 100,000 shares.

If the short difference remains unresolved for more than seven business days from discovery, the firm must begin changing its net capital by 25% of the market value of the short securities difference.

Over time, additional charges to net capital are made if the difference has not been resolved. After 28 business days from discovery, the entire market value of the difference will have been charged to net capital. If unresolved for 45 days from discovery, the difference of 100,000 shares must be bought in.

2. 3. 1. 5   Securities Information Center (SIC)

SEC rules call for the Securities Information Center (SIC) to maintain records of lost, counterfeit, missing, or stolen securities. This rule was created in an effort to reduce trafficking in lost, stolen, missing, and counterfeit securities. The database of securities maintained by the SIC can only be accessed by registered BDs and other financial institutions to ascertain if securities that have come into their possession have been reported as lost, stolen, missing, or counterfeit.

2. 3. 1. 5. 1   Reporting Requirements

Upon discovery of a security loss, if no criminal action is suspected, a member has two business days to locate the security. If it is still missing on the third day, the loss must be reported to the SIC and the transfer agent.

If securities are missing and criminal action is suspected, a member has one business day to report the loss to the SIC and the transfer agent. In addition, the FBI must be notified promptly. If the securities are later recovered, those parties that were originally notified must be advised of the recovery within one business day.

2. 3. 1. 5. 2   Securities Inquiries

Every member is required to inquire the SIC regarding certain securities coming into its possession as to whether the security has been reported as missing, lost, counterfeit, or stolen. Exceptions are made to this inquiry rule if the security is:

- received directly from the issuer;
- received from another reporting institution (e.g., member firm);
- received from an existing customer of the firm and registered in the customer's name; or
- was previously sold to that customer as verified by the member's records and part of a transaction valued at $10,000 or less.

2. 3. 2   SECURITIES TRANSFERS

2. 3. 2. 1   Registered Versus Bearer Certificates

Bonds are registered, in varying degrees, to record ownership should a certificate be lost or stolen. Tracking a bond's ownership through its registration has been common in the United States since the early 1970s.

2. 3. 2. 1. 1   Coupon (Bearer) Certificates

Though no longer issued, in past years, most bonds were issued in coupon, or bearer, form. Issuers kept no records of purchasers, and securities were issued without an investor's name printed on the certificate. Coupon bonds are not registered, so whoever possesses them can collect interest on, sell, or redeem the bonds.

Interest coupons are physically attached to bearer bonds, and holders collect interest by clipping the coupons with scissors and delivering them to an issuer's paying agent which is typically a bank.

Individual coupons are payable to the bearer. When a bond matures, the bearer delivers it to the paying agent and receives the principal.

No proof of ownership is needed to sell a bearer bond. Even though bearer bonds are not issued today, the term *coupon* is still used to describe interest payments received by bondholders. Bearer bonds are expected to be extinct by 2013.

2. 3. 2. 1. 2   Registered Certificates

A common form of bond issued today is the registered bond. When a registered security is issued, the issuer's transfer agent records the holder's name. The buyer's name appears on the certificate's face.

2. 3. 2. 2   Delivery

Before a security that has been sold can be delivered to the buyer, it must be in good deliverable form. Good delivery describes the physical condition, signatures, attachments, and denominations of the certificates involved in a securities transaction. Although good delivery is mostly a matter of street-side settlements between buying and selling dealers, it also applies to deliveries from customers on sell orders.

In any dealer-to-dealer transaction, the delivered securities must be accompanied by a properly executed uniform delivery ticket. The transfer agent is the final arbiter of whether a security meets good delivery.

The transfer and registration of stock certificates are two distinct functions that, by law, cannot be performed by a single person or department operating within the same institution. Issuers typically use commercial banks and trust companies to handle these functions.

2. 3. 2. 2. 1   Assignment

All stock and bond certificates must be assigned (endorsed by signature) by the owner, whose name is known to the registrar and printed on the face of the certificate. Upon the sale or transfer of the security, the owner must affix his signature on the place indicated on the back of the certificate. Alternatively, an endorsement may be made by signing a detached (separate) assignment, also known as a stock power or power of substitution.

Any separate assignment must contain all of the same information as the assignment on the back of the certificate, including an irrevocable appointment of attorney (with power of substitution) and a full description of the security (e.g., name of issuer, issue, certificate number, amount). One stock or bond power can be used with any number of certificates for one security, but a separate power is required for each different security.

TEST TOPIC ALERT

The assignment must be guaranteed by a member of the NYSE medallion program discussed earlier.

2. 3. 2. 2. 2   Transfer Agent

The transfer agent for a corporation is responsible for:

- ensuring that its securities are issued in the correct owner's name;
- canceling old and issuing new certificates;
- maintaining records of ownership;
- handling problems relating to lost, stolen, or destroyed certificates; and
- validating a certificate in question.

The transfer agent distributes additional shares in the event of a stock split or new certificates in the event of a reverse split. If a stock dividend or stock split results in fractional shares, under most circumstances, the transfer agent sends the beneficial owner a check for a fractional share's value.

TAKE NOTE

In a stock split, par value changes, as does the market price of a stock. In the event of a stock split, the customer will receive the additional shares directly from the transfer agent. In addition, the investor will receive a sticker to put on his existing certificate to change its par value.

EXAMPLE

In a 2:1 split, the price of the shares and the par value of the stock are halved, whereas the number of shares outstanding doubles. It's like having two nickels instead of one dime. Unlike stock splits, with a stock dividend, par value does not change.

2. 3. 2. 2. 3   Registrar

Any stock or bond transaction requiring the registration and issuance of new certificates is routed through a registrar as well as the transfer agent. The registrar does not, however, keep a list of the names of the owners of the company's securities.

The registrar ensures that a corporation does not have more shares outstanding than have been authorized. The registrar is also responsible for certifying that a bond represents a legal debt of the issuer. Unlike the transfer agent, the registrar must be independent of the issuing corporation and is usually a bank or trust company.

2. 3. 2. 3   Electronic Movement of Securities to Transfer Agent

There are two ways securities can move to or from a transfer agent electronically, the DRS and DWAC. The **Direct Registration System** (DRS) is supported by DTCC to allow electronic (or certificateless) securities to be registered in the investor's name, rather than street name, and transferred between the transfer agent and the carrying firm electronically.

A **Deposit/Withdrawal At Custodian** (DWAC) is similar to a DRS except that while a DRS is entirely electronic, a DWAC requires the stockholder to submit a medallioned stock power along with the request. The option may be limited by the how the issue is carried with DTCC and the transfer agent.

2. 3. 2. 4   Types of Securities That Are Depository Eligible

Most types of securities may be made depository eligible, including but not limited to

- equities;
- warrants;
- rights;
- corporate debt and notes;
- municipal bonds;
- government securities;
- money market instruments;
- American/global depositary receipts; and
- shares of closed-end funds.

General eligibility requirements for a security to be handled through an SEC-registered depository include but are not limited to:

- registration under the 1933 Securities Act;
- a security issued in a transaction exempt from registration under a 1933 Act and at the time of the request for DTC eligibility no longer has transfer or ownership restrictions; or
- a security eligible for resale pursuant to Rule 144A or Regulation S under the 1933 Act. Remember that these criteria for eligibility are not exhaustive but are the basic requirements.

2. 3. 3   RULE 144

Rule 144 regulates the sale of control and restricted securities. Control securities are those owned by directors, officers, affiliated persons (e.g., a spouse of an officer), or persons who own more than 10% of a company's outstanding securities. Such persons are subject to volume limitations on the sale of these securities for as long as they are affiliated with the company.

Unless it is unregistered, such as privately placed stock, control stock is not subject to the holding period requirements imposed on restricted stock but is subject to volume limits throughout the time the owner holds the control position.

TAKE NOTE

If an unaffiliated individual owns 7% of the voting stock of XYZ, that person is not a control person. However, if that person's spouse owns 5% of the voting stock, then both would be considered control persons. In other words, if there is a 10% or more interest held by immediate family members, then all those family members owning voting stock are control persons.

Restricted securities are those acquired through a private placement or any means other than a registered public offering. Restricted securities may not be sold until they have been held fully paid for six months. According to Rule 144, after holding restricted stock fully paid for six months, an affiliate may begin selling shares but is subject to the volume restriction rules as enumerated in the following. Furthermore, restricted stock is not subject to the 30-second reporting requirement. In any 90-day period, an investor may sell the greater of:

■ 1% of the total outstanding shares of the same class at the time of sale; or

■ the average weekly trading volume in the stock over the past four weeks on all exchanges or as reported through Nasdaq.

After the six-month holding period, affiliated persons are subject to the volume restrictions for as long as they are affiliates. For unaffiliated investors, the stock may be sold completely unrestricted after the six-month holding period has been satisfied.

Selling shares under Rule 144 effectively registers the shares. In other words, buyers of stock being sold subject to Rule 144 are not subject to any restrictions if they choose to resell.

Summary of the Provisions of Rule 144

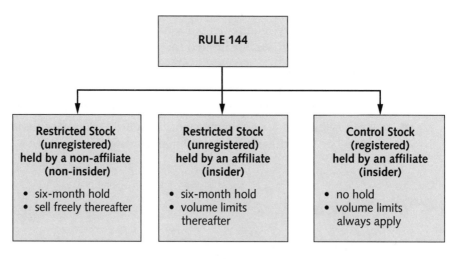

TEST TOPIC ALERT

When you encounter a Rule 144 question, ask yourself the following.

■ What kind of stock is being sold? (restricted or control)

■ Who is selling it? (an insider or noninsider)

Only restricted stock has a holding period. Unless unregistered, control stock can be sold immediately, but volume limits always apply.

2. 3. 3. 1   Restrictions

The SEC restricts broker/dealers from actively soliciting buyers for control shares or arranging private negotiations between buyers and sellers of control stock. Additionally, all sales under Rule 144 are to be executed as agency transactions, meaning that the firm matches a buyer and seller.

Buyers of 144 stock must come to firms on an unsolicited basis. Initiating contact with customers or other broker/dealers for the purpose of selling the stock is prohibited, but callbacks are allowed under the following circumstances.

■ Customer callbacks may be made to customers who expressed interest in the stock within the past 10 business days.

■ Broker/dealer callbacks may be made to those firms that expressed interest within the past 60 calendar days.

Broker/dealers may not register as market makers in anticipation of Rule 144 transactions. If a firm is currently registered as a market maker in the stock, the firm can purchase the stock for its inventory. This is an exception from the rule that firms may act in an agent capacity only in Rule 144 transactions.

A firm may purchase as dealer under one additional exception. Block positioners are firms defined under SEC Rule 3b-8 as firms that purchase long or sell short blocks of stock worth $200,000 or more. These firms may be treated as market makers for Rule 144 transactions.

TEST TOPIC ALERT

Review the following points regarding Rule 144.

■ Restricted stock has a six-month holding period unless the holder is the estate of a deceased person.

■ Restricted stock held by an estate is exempt from both the holding period requirements and the volume limitations of Rule 144.

■ There is no holding period on registered control stock, but volume limits always apply.

■ Rule 144 transactions should be agency-only, unless the firm is a registered market maker or block positioner in the stock.

■ Callbacks are allowed to customers who indicated interest within the past 10 business days and to firms that indicated interest within the past 60 calendar days.

TAKE NOTE

Insiders cannot short. They are prohibited from taking short-swing profits and cannot engage in short naked options positions or short sales.

Insiders are permitted, however, to write calls against a long stock position. On the other hand, a corporation cannot write calls against its own stock (e.g., stock held in its treasury). If exercised, the company must deliver shares, thereby increasing the number of shares outstanding. This would require shareholder approval.

2. 3. 4   RULE 144A

Rule 144A allows nonregistered foreign and domestic securities to be sold to certain institutional investors in the United States without holding period requirements.

To qualify for this exemption, the buyer must be a qualified institutional buyer (QIB).

TAKE NOTE   A QIB must have a minimum of $100 million in securities unaffiliated with the institution.

2. 3. 5   REGULATION S

Offers and sales made outside the United States are excluded from the registration provisions of the Act of 1933. Securities distributed offshore by US issuers need not be registered with the SEC. To avoid registration under Regulation S:

■ the offer and sale must be made in an offshore transaction; and

■ there can be no directed selling efforts in the United States in connection with the offering.

To be an offshore transaction, offers and sales cannot be made to any person or entity in the United States. However, US citizens residing outside the United States could purchase these securities. All sales made under Regulation S must be reported to the SEC on Form 8-K.

TAKE NOTE   Regulation S deals with the sale of unregistered securities by US-based issuers to non-US residents. Sales made to non-US citizens cannot be resold in the United States for 12 months.

However, sales may be made immediately to any SEC-designated offshore securities market.

TAKE NOTE   Regulation S applies to US issuers. Foreign issuers are not subject to this regulation as long as certain requirements are met: to be a foreign issuer, no more than 50% of its voting securities and no more than 20% of its debt securities can be owned by persons with a US address. If a foreign issuer does not meet these requirements, it will be subject to the provisions of Regulation S (no sales to entities in the United States).

1. Match the following amounts to the appropriate following description. Some choices may be used more than once

   A. 500
   B. 147
   C. 35
   D. 20
   E. 10
   F. 9
   G. $1 million
   H. $100 million
   I. 60

   ——— 1. Number of nonaccredited investors that can buy a private placement under Regulation D

   ——— 2. Form 144 does not need filing if a shareholder sells less than this amount of shares

   ——— 3. Number of months a state resident must hold securities before sale to a nonstate resident under an intrastate offering

   ——— 4. Intrastate offering is also known by this rule number

   ——— 5. Minimum number of days in the SEC cooling-off period

   ——— 6. Under Rule 144, customers may be called back if they expressed interest within this number of business days

   ——— 7. Minimum amount of net worth for an accredited individual investor under Regulation D

   ——— 8. Minimum amount of assets for QIBs under Rule 144A

   ——— 9. Ownership of at least this percentage of a firm's outstanding stock qualifies an unaffiliated investor as a control person

2. 4 TRADE REPORTING AND TRADE CORRECTIONS

2. 4. 1 TRADE REPORTING SYSTEMS

2. 4. 1. 1 Automated Confirmation Transaction (ACT) Service

The **Automated Confirmation Transaction (ACT) Service** is an automated TRF operated by FINRA/Nasdaq using a Web-based system that compares trade information submitted by ACT participants and submits locked-in trades to the National Securities Clearing Corporation (NSCC) for clearing and settlement. All trades reported by ACT that have been locked in and sent to NSCC are considered firm obligations and must be honored on the scheduled settlement date.

Members have the capability to upload as many as 500 trades to the TRF in a single file if they choose. Firms may also take action on their trades by accepting, declining, canceling, or breaking specific trades.

Clearing firms can use Nasdaq Weblink ACT to manage their risk by placing limitations on correspondent buying and selling as well as blockbuster limits.

Sample ACT Trade Entry

Role:	Side:	Share Quantity:	Security:	Price:	Contra:	Trade Time:
● Market Maker ○ Order Entry	Sell	100	zvzzt	● 84.00	nqmo	

Short Sale:	TOOL Info: Capacity:	Contra Info: Capacity:	Clearing & Reporting	○ Contract	Special Instruction	Settlement (Level 1)
None	Principal	None	● Neither ☑ Clear ○ AGU ☐ Report ○ QSR	☑ Price Override ☐ Fee	☐ Special ☐ Step Out ☐ NDQ Step Out ☐ NDQ Sales Fee	● Standard 3-Day ○ Same Day - Cash ○ Next Day ○ Other

☐ As-Of ☐ Reversal ☑ Trade Thru Exempt

Give up: ____ Give up: ____

Branch Seq#: ____ Branch Seq#: ____

Trade Date: 07312011

Clearing #: ____ Clearing #: ____

Clearing Price $ 0.00

Memo: ____

Trade Modifiers: Level 2 [F-Intmkt Swp] Level 3 ____ Level 4 ____

[Send] [Unlock]

TEST TOPIC ALERT   ACT is not an order system. Its purpose is two-fold: to compare and submit transactions to the NSCC for clearing and settlement and to disseminate last sale information.

As noted earlier, Nasdaq became a registered stock exchange in late 2006. One of the requirements to be considered an exchange was to separate its trade execution services from its trade reporting facility. Because the ACT System both compares trades and reports completed trades, it had to be broken apart. To do this, Nasdaq created the trade reporting facility (FINRA/Nasdaq TRF), which operates as part of the ACT platform. Technically, the TRF reports trades for Nasdaq stocks and exchange-listed stocks traded in the third market, whereas ACT continues to report trades in OTCBB and OTC Pink stocks.

Firms that use Weblink ACT for their trade reporting of OTC trades must comply with the 30-second rule. As a cautionary note, it is unwise to delay a trade report to the last second. A pattern of late reporting may trigger a violation of FINRA Rule 2010 (i.e., behavior inconsistent with high standards of commercial honor and just and equitable principles of trade).

2. 4. 1. 2   TRACE "Trade Reporting and Compliance Engine"

TRACE is FINRA's automated trade reporting system for OTC primary and secondary market transactions in TRACE-eligible debt. This mandatory reporting by market participants is facilitated through the Trade Reporting and Compliance Engine (TRACE). Trades are generally reported immediately to the investing public for improved market transparency. Member firms are identified by an MPID. MPID is an abbreviation for Market Participant

Identification and must use that identifier for trade reporting and for an audit trail. An MPID is obtained from FINRA. A firm may have more than one if, for example, there are multiple clearing firm arrangements.

Most corporate debt securities, including church bonds, agency debentures, and mortgage and asset-backed securities, fall within the definition of a TRACE-eligible security. Specifically excluded from TRACE reporting are:

■ debt of foreign countries and provinces;

■ US Treasury debt;

■ money market instruments;

■ debt securities that are not DTC eligible or are in physical form;

■ convertible corporate bonds (these are reported to ACT); and

■ agency debentures and primary market transactions.

TEST TOPIC ALERT   Municipal securities are not TRACE-eligible securities. Municipal securities transactions are reported by MSRB's EMMA system.

TRACE is not an execution system. It is a trade reporting system only. It does not accept quotations, nor does it provide settlement and clearance functions. The reporting rules follow.

■ Both sides to an interdealer trade must report (dual side reporting).

■ Trades must be reported within 15 minutes of execution. Otherwise, the transaction report will be late.

TRACE displays:

■ execution date and time;

■ quantity;

■ price;

■ yield;

■ whether price reflects that a commission was charged;

■ whether there was any special settlement or condition that may have affected the price; and

■ whether the trade was reported late.

Once FINRA receives trade information on TRACE-eligible debt securities, it will disseminate this information immediately to the public.

2. 4. 1. 3   Trade Reporting and Comparison Service (TRACS)

Because they are not part of Nasdaq and cannot use ACT, TRACS was developed for alternative display facility (ADF) members to report trades within 30 seconds, executed through the ADF. Securities eligible for TRACS reporting include global market, capital market, Consolidated Quotation System (CQS), and Nasdaq-listed convertible bonds. Trades not reported within 30 seconds must be marked as late, and each ADF-eligible trade ticket must be time-stamped.

TRACS reporting rules are similar to those of ACT, with one exception: TRACS will allow market participants the option to enter a three-party trade. This option makes it easier to report riskless principal trades and for an electronic communication network (ECN) to report trades between itself and its subscribers.

TRACS also provides a trade comparison service, which compares trade data from participants, submits locked-in trades to DTCC, and transmits last sale information for public dissemination.

Note that FINRA members with dual status as market makers in Nasdaq and the ADF have the option to report trades to TRACS or ACT.

2. 4. 2   TRADING PRACTICES

2. 4. 2. 1   Best Execution

In customer transactions, firms must determine the best market for a security and buy or sell so that the resulting price to the customer is as favorable as possible under prevailing market conditions.

In reviewing customer transactions, FINRA will consider the following to determine whether members are executing in the best available market:

- Character of the market for the security (e.g., price, volatility, and liquidity)
- Size and type of transaction
- Number of markets checked
- Accessibility of quotations

Best execution means more than best price; **execution quality** (which includes speed of execution, fill rates, price improvement, and so forth) is also important. Member firms are required to have procedures in place to monitor their trade executions and to take action where appropriate.

2. 4. 2. 2   Trading Capacity

All customer trades executed on an exchange floor are done on an agency basis—the firm executing the trade on behalf of the customer acts as a broker, charging the customer a commission. Acting as a broker means finding a buyer for a seller and vice versa.

In the over-the-counter market, however, a member firm may act as either a broker (agency) or a dealer (principal). When acting as a dealer, the member is on the other side of a trade with a customer; when a customer buys, it is the member who is selling to that customer from its inventory, and when a customer sells, it is the member who is buying from that customer for its inventory. To act as a dealer, the member must maintain an inventory of that particular security.

In addition, when acting as a dealer, a member will mark up when a customer buys and mark down when a customer sells. When a price to a customer includes a markup or markdown, it is termed a net price. A firm may never charge a commission in addition to a markup or markdown. This is called a hidden profit and is a rules violation.

2. 4. 2. 3   Quotations

A quote is a dealer's current bid and offer on a security. The current bid is the highest price at which the dealer will buy, and the current offer is the lowest price at which the dealer will sell. The difference between the bid and ask is known as the spread.

A typical quote might be expressed as bid 63–offered 63.07. The highest price the dealer will pay is 63, and the lowest price the dealer will accept is 63.07. The spread is .07 of a point between the bid and ask. The broker could also say 63 bid–63.07 ask or 63 to .07.

The Customer's and the Market Maker's Relationship to the Quote

	Bid-63	Ask/Offer-63.07
Quoting dealer	Buys	Sells
Customer	Sells	Buys

When a customer buys a stock from a firm acting as principal, the broker marks up the ask price to reach the net price to the customer. Likewise, when a customer sells stock to a firm acting as principal, the dealer marks down from the bid price to reach the net proceeds to the customer.

EXAMPLE

If WXYZ is quoted as 43.25 to .50, for instance, and the dealer wants a half-point for the trade, a customer buying would pay 44 net, and a customer selling would receive 42.75 net.

2. 4. 2. 3. 1   Firm Quote

A firm quotation is the price at which a market maker stands ready to buy or sell at least one trading unit—100 shares of stock or five bonds—at the quoted price with other member firms. When an OTC firm makes a market in a security, the broker/dealer must be willing to buy or sell at least one trading unit of the security at its firm quote. All quotes are firm quotes unless otherwise indicated.

As is true of market order executions on an exchange floor, an OTC trader may attempt to negotiate a better price with a market maker by making a counter offer or a counter bid, especially if the spread between the market maker's bid and ask is fairly wide. However, the only way to guarantee an immediate execution is to buy stock at the market maker's ask price or sell at the bid price.

In a typical bond transaction, a trader at one broker/dealer calls a trader at another broker/dealer (a market maker) to buy a specific bond. A market maker might give another broker/dealer a quote that is firm for an hour with five-minute recall. This is a firm quote that remains good for an hour.

If, within that hour, the market maker receives another order for the same security, the trader calls the broker/dealer back and gives it five minutes to confirm its order or lose its right to buy that security at the price quoted.

A market maker can revise a firm quote in response to market conditions and trading activity, but a market maker that refuses to do business at the price(s) quoted is backing away from the quote. Backing away is a violation of trading rules.

2. 4. 2. 3. 2 Spread

The difference between a security's bid and ask prices is known as the spread. Many factors influence a spread's size, including the:

- issue's size;
- issuer's financial condition;
- amount of market activity in the issue; and
- market conditions.

2. 4. 2. 3. 3 Size

Unless otherwise specified, a firm quote is always good for one round lot (100 shares).

EXAMPLE

A firm quote of 8.25–.50 means the market maker stands ready to buy 100 shares of stock from another broker/dealer at the 8.25 bid price or sell 100 shares at the 8.50 ask price.

2. 4. 2. 3. 4 Non-Nasdaq

For securities quoted on either OTC Pink or the Over-the-Counter Bulletin Board (OTCBB), the three-quote rule often applies. Unless there are at least two market makers displaying firm quotes, broker/dealers receiving orders to buy or sell non-Nasdaq securities must contact a minimum of three dealers to determine the prevailing price.

2. 4. 2. 3. 5 Manipulative and Deceptive Practices

The Conduct Rules mandate that any quote given must represent a real bid or offer. No fictitious quotes are allowed.

Following is a list of important test points about OTC quotes.

- Markups and markdowns are charged when a market maker is acting as a principal (dealing from inventory with financial risk).

- Firm quotes are good for a round lot only, unless otherwise stated. A quote of 11–11.5 3 × 5 is firm between dealers for 300 shares at the bid of 11 and 500 shares at the asked of 11.5.

- Nominal quotes can be given for informational purposes and can be printed only if clearly labeled as such.

- A relatively wide spread indicates a thin trading market for the security.

2. 4. 3   MARKET HOURS

The NYSE trades between 9:30 am and 4:00 pm ET each business day. Normal hours for retail OTC trading are the same as those of the NYSE, although many market makers remain open until 6:30 pm in extended hours trading. The after-hours market is much less liquid because order flow is limited. As a result, the spreads between bid and ask prices are wider, and there is greater price volatility.

2. 4. 4   TRADER CORRECTIONS

When a trade has been reported incorrectly, a bona fide correction may be made. These corrections, made after the trade date, are entered "as/of." Back office systems will show the trade entered on the processing date; however, the trade will be marked as of the trade date reported. The settlement date will be calculated from the as/of trade date (i.e., calculated from the trade date, not the processing date). Corrections made beyond the settlement date are processed in a similar manner; however, the settlement date will change to the process date, rather than the original settlement date, because an unsettled trade cannot settle in the past.

2. 4. 5   ERROR ACCOUNTS

Occasionally, a trader will make an error such as trading through a customer's limit or over-buying or selling a customer's order. In these cases, the firm will need to allocate the erroneous trades and cover them in the open market. These trades will be booked into the firm's **error account**. The error account is only used to hold and cover erroneous trades on a short-term basis. It is not permitted for use as an account for regular proprietary trading.

2. 4. 6   UNETHICAL TRADING PRACTICES

2. 4. 6. 1   Front Running

If a firm or any associated person has nonpublic knowledge of an impending block order to buy or sell, that firm or person may not place an order in front of the block order. For purposes of this rule, a block order is an order for 10,000 shares or more.

 EXAMPLE

Assume that a representative has nonpublic knowledge of an impending order to buy 100,000 shares of a Nasdaq stock. If the representative places an order to buy stock for her personal account in front of the order, the representative would likely benefit from a free ride because the stock would rise on the execution of a large block.

2. 4. 6. 2   Excessive Trading

Excessive trading in a customer's account to generate commissions rather than to help achieve the customer's stated investment objectives is an abuse of fiduciary responsibility known as **churning**. Churning occurs because of excessive frequency or excessive size of transactions.

To prevent such abuses, self-regulatory organizations require that a principal of the member firm review all accounts, especially those for which a registered representative or an investment adviser has discretionary authority.

2. 4. 6. 3   Market Manipulation

Any attempt to manipulate options' markets is considered unlawful. There is no regard for market impact or the economic result, profit, or loss caused by the activity once evidence presented support that the offense has occurred.

Although manipulation can be attempted by any investor, these violations most often occur where large positions are at stake, more likely among traders and institutional trading entities. Following are the most common types of market manipulation involving options.

- **Capping**: This is the act of entering sell orders in a stock for the purpose of keeping the stock from rising above the strike price of calls one is short. If successful, the stock will stay below the strike price, and the short call options will be out-of-the-money and will not be exercised.

- **Supporting**: This is the act of entering purchase orders in a stock for the purpose of keeping the price from falling below the strike price of puts one is short. The intent is to keep the puts out-of-the-money and unexercised.

- **Pegging**: This is a generic term that applies to any activity intended to keep the price of a stock from moving. This can involve entering either buy or sell orders or both. For example, a short straddle writer will profit most if the stock price and strike prices of the position are the same at expiration—that is, the short options are right at-the-money.

- **Front running**: This is the act of taking an option position when a firm has received a block order but before the block has been entered for execution. The intent is to establish an option position likely to profit or protect against loss once the block is executed.

- **Spinning:** Spinning is the prohibited practice of allocating highly sought-after IPO shares (also known as hot stock) to persons who are in a position to direct securities business to the firm. Portfolio managers are categorized as restricted persons. These people are able to direct business to a firm and may be willing to do so based on the size of their allocation.

2. 4. 6. 4   Excessive Markups

The 5% markup policy was adopted to ensure that the investing public receives fair treatment and pays reasonable rates for brokerage services in both exchange and OTC markets. It is considered a guideline only and is not a firm rule for markups and markdowns. A firm charging a customer more or less than a 5% markup may or may not be in violation of fair and equitable trade practices. The markup may be considered excessive once all of the relevant factors are taken into account.

A broker/dealer can fill a customer order in the following three ways.

- If the broker/dealer is a market maker in the security, it will (as principal) buy from or sell to the customer, charging a markup or markdown.

■ If the firm is not a market maker in the security, it can fill the order as agent, without taking a position in the security, and charge a commission for its execution services.

■ An order can be filled as a riskless and simultaneous transaction.

2. 4. 6. 4. 1 Markup Based on Representative Market Prices

The 5% markup is based on the price representative of prevailing (inside) market prices at the time of a customer transaction. The 5% markup policy applies to all transactions in nonexempt listed or unlisted securities traded on an exchange or OTC, regardless of whether the transactions are executed as agency or principal trades.

TAKE NOTE

The 5% policy applies to markups, markdowns, and commissions.

2. 4. 6. 4. 2 Fixed Public Offering Price Securities

The 5% markup policy does not apply to mutual funds, variable annuity contracts, or securities sold in public offerings, all of which are sold by a prospectus, nor does it apply to municipal securities.

2. 4. 6. 4. 3 Dealer's Inventory Costs

If a customer's buy order is filled from a broker/dealer's inventory, the net price to the customer is based on the prevailing market price, regardless of whether the broker/dealer selling to the customer is also making a market in the stock and what the firm's quote might be.

The price at which the broker/dealer acquired the stock being sold to the customer has no bearing on the net price to the customer; the price to the customer must be reasonably related to the current market.

2. 4. 6. 4. 4 Riskless and Simultaneous Transactions

A riskless and simultaneous transaction is an order to buy or sell stock in which the firm receiving the order is not a market maker. The dealer has the following two options for filling the order.

■ As agent for the customer, it could buy or sell on the customer's behalf and charge a commission, subject to the 5% policy.

■ It could buy or sell for its riskless principal account, then buy or sell to the customer as principal, charging a markup or markdown subject to the 5% policy.

When the order is filled as a principal transaction, the broker/dealer must disclose the markup to the customer.

2. 4. 6. 4. 5 Proceeds Transactions

When a customer sells securities and uses the proceeds to purchase other securities in a proceeds transaction, the broker/dealer's combined commissions and markups must be consistent with the 5% markup policy. In other words, member firms must treat proceeds transactions as one transaction for markup and markdown purposes.

2. 4. 6. 4. 6   *Markup Policy Considerations*

In assessing the fairness of a broker/dealer's commission and markup practices, the following factors are considered.

- **Type of Security**. In general, more market risk is associated with making markets and trading common stocks than is associated with dealing in bonds. The policy gives guidance to markups specific to both stock and bond transactions, including government securities. The more risk a broker/dealer assumes, the greater the justification for higher markups.

- **Inactively Traded Stocks**. The thinner the market for a security, the more volatile the stock and the greater the market risk to anyone dealing in the stock. Thus, a broker/dealer is justified in charging higher markups on inactively traded stocks.

- **Selling Price of Security**. Commission and markup rates should decrease as a stock's price increases.

- **Dollar Amount of Transaction**. Transactions of relatively small dollar amounts generally warrant higher percentage markups than large-dollar transactions.

- **Nature of the Broker/Dealer's Business**. This standard pertains to full service brokers versus discount brokers. In most cases, a general securities firm has higher operating costs than does a discount broker and, thus, may justify higher commissions and markups.

- **Pattern of Markups**. Although the regulators are concerned primarily with detecting cases where broker/dealers have established patterns of excessive markups, a single incident could still be considered an unfair markup.

- **Markups on Inactive Stocks (Contemporaneous Cost)**. For inactive stocks and situations where no prevailing market quotes are available, a broker/dealer may base a markup on its cost in the stock.

TEST TOPIC ALERT

The 5% markup policy is peculiarly named for two reasons.

- It applies to markups, markdowns, and commissions, meaning it is applicable to principal and agency transactions.

- Five percent is not the limit. A transaction charge of more than 5% might be fine if it is reasonably based on the circumstances of the trade.

Examples of subject transactions are REITs; closed-end company shares; ADRs; third market trades; and listed and unlisted stocks, bonds, and government securities.

New issues sold by prospectus and municipal securities are not subject to this policy.

Remember that all computations must be based on the inside quote (the best available from all the market makers), not the firm's quote.

2. 4. 6. 5   Breakpoint Sales

Breakpoints are quantity discounts: the greater the dollar amount of a purchase, the lower the sales charge.

Breakpoint sales, on the other hand, is jargon in the securities industry that means sales just below the breakpoint in an effort by representatives to share in the higher sales charges applicable on sales below the breakpoint. This is inconsistent with just and equitable principles of trade.

The member must advise the customer that, for a few dollars more, the customer could qualify for a lower sales charge.

FINRA does not define *near a breakpoint*. Therefore, members must make certain that customers are advised of a fund's breakpoint schedule. The rule is in place because members, and indirectly, registered representatives, could earn more concession dollars on a smaller customer investment (with a higher sales charge) than on a larger customer investment (with a smaller sales charge).

A single mutual fund generally offers more than one class of shares to investors. Each class represents the same interest in the fund's portfolio but has different fees and expenses. A typical class structure follows.

2. 4. 6. 6   Improper Sharing in Customer Accounts

As a basic rule, associated persons are not permitted to share in the profit and loss in customer accounts unless:

■ profit or loss is shared in proportion to the capital contributed by each party (note that an associated person's knowledge or expertise cannot be considered that person's contribution); and

■ the arrangement is approved by a principal.

It is unlikely that a principal would approve such a sharing agreement, as it would be virtually impossible to monitor the proportionate test. However, if there is an immediate family relationship between the customer and the associated person, the proportionate test does not apply.

TAKE NOTE   Firms cannot have joint accounts with customers. Representatives may have joint accounts with customers only if the arrangement has been approved by the principal and account proceeds are shared in proportion to each party's contribution.

2. 5 CORPORATE ACTIONS

When a company initiates a corporate action, it will bring some change to its stock. The effect the action has on shares of stock is important to investors who try to have a clear understanding of a company's financial picture. How a particular corporate action influences the share price would likely have an effect on the decision by investors as to whether to buy, hold, or sell a particular stock.

A company's board of directors and voting shareholders control corporate actions. Examples of corporate actions include:

■ dividends (board of directors only);

■ rights issues (board of directors only);

■ stock split/reverse stock split;

- spin offs (a distribution of the stock of subsidiary to the shareholders of the parent company without cost to the shareholder of the parent issue);
- mergers and acquisitions;
- bankruptcy;
- delisting;
- name change; and
- Dutch auction.

2. 5. 1   STOCK SPLITS

As the name implies, a stock split (also referred to as a bonus share) divides each of the outstanding shares of a company, thereby lowering the price per share—the market will adjust the price on the day the action is implemented. A stock split, however, is a non-event, meaning that it does not affect a company's equity or its market capitalization. Only the number of shares outstanding change, so a stock split does not directly change the value or net assets of a company.

2. 5. 1. 1   Adjustments

A company announcing a 2-for-1 (2:1) stock split, for example, will distribute an additional share for every one outstanding share, so the total shares outstanding will double. If the company had 50 shares outstanding, it will have 100 after the stock split. At the same time, because the value of the company and its shares did not change, the price per share will drop by half. So if the pre-split price was $100 per share, the new price will be $50 per share.

So why would a firm issue such an action? More often than not, the board of directors will approve (and the shareholders will authorize) a stock split in order to increase the liquidity of the share on the market.

The result of the 2-for-1 stock split in our previous example is two-fold: (1) the drop in share price will make the stock more attractive to a wider pool of investors, and (2) the increase in available shares outstanding on the stock exchange will make the stock more available to interested buyers. So, do keep in mind that the value of the company, or its market capitalization (shares outstanding multiplied by market price/share), does not change, but the greater liquidity and higher demand on the share will typically drive the share price up, thereby increasing the company's market capitalization and value.

A split can also be referred to in percentage terms. Thus, a 2-for-1 (2:1) split can also be termed a stock split of 100%. A 3-for-2 split (3:2) would be a 50% split, and so on.

A reverse split might be implemented by a company that would like to increase the price of its shares. If a $1 stock had a reverse split of 1-for-10 (1:10), holders would have to trade in 10 of their old shares for one new one, but the stock would increase from $1 to $10 per share (retaining the same market capitalization). A company may decide to use a reverse split to shed its status as a "penny stock." Other times, companies may use a reverse split to drive out small investors.

2. 5. 1. 1. 1   Change in Number of Shares Outstanding

A Nasdaq-listed company should notify the exchange no later than 10 days after the occurrence of any aggregate increase or decrease of any class of securities listed on Nasdaq that exceeds 5% of the amount of securities of the class outstanding.

2. 5. 2   DIVIDENDS

Many corporations pay regular quarterly cash dividends to stockholders. A company's dividends may increase over time as profitability increases. Dividends, which can be a significant source of income for investors, are a major reason many people invest in stocks. Issuers may also pay stock dividends (additional shares in the issuing company) or property dividends (shares in a subsidiary company or a product sample). In the case of any cash or stock dividend action, the company must no later than 10 calendar days prior to the record date of the action notify the exchange by filing the appropriate form and provide public notice using a Regulation Fair Disclosure compliant method.

TEST TOPIC ALERT   Stock dividends are frequently paid by companies that wish to reinvest earnings for research and development. Technology companies, aggressive growth companies, and new companies are examples of companies likely to pay stock dividends. Property dividends are the least common form of dividend payment.

2. 5. 2. 1   Dividend Department

The dividend department collects and distributes cash dividends for stocks held in street name. In addition to processing cash dividends, the department handles registered bond interest payments, stock dividends, stock splits, rights offerings, warrants, and any special distributions to a corporation's stockholders or bondholders.

2. 5. 2. 2   Transfer Agent

Dividends are actually disbursed, on the payable date, by a party known as the transfer agent. The corporation itself may have the transfer agent on its payroll, or the transfer agent may be a bank or trust company that keeps track of the stockholders and disburses dividends when declared.

2. 5. 2. 3   Dividend Disbursing Process

The process of disbursing a dividend begins on the **declaration date**. The declaration date is when a company's board of directors approves a dividend payment; it also designates the payment date and the dividend record date. The SEC requires any corporation that intends to pay cash dividends or make other distributions to notify FINRA or the appropriate exchange at least 10 business days before the record date. This enables FINRA, or another SRO if appropriate, to establish the ex-date.

2. 5. 2. 4   Ex-Dividend Date

The SRO posts an ex-date on the basis of the dividend record date, or the date on which an investor must be the stockholder on record to receive the dividend. The ex-date is two business days before the record date. Because most trades settle regular way—three business days after the trade date—a customer must purchase the stock three business days before the record date to qualify for the dividend.

TAKE NOTE

For dividend purposes, an investor does not own the stock until settlement date, three business days after the trade date.

On the ex-date, the stock's opening price drops to compensate for the fact that customers who buy the stock that day or later do not qualify for the dividend. Trades executed regular way on or after the ex-date do not settle until after the record date.

A customer who buys the stock before the ex-date receives the dividend but pays a higher price for the stock. The customer who buys the stock on or after the ex-date does not receive the dividend but pays a lower price for the stock.

The **payable date** is two or three weeks after the record date and is the date the dividend-disbursing agent sends dividend checks to all stockholders whose names appeared on the books as of the record date.

TAKE NOTE

The acronym DERP will help you remember the order in which the dates involving dividend distributions occur. The Declaration takes place first; the Payment of the dividend is actually the last step in the process. The dividend is paid to owners on the date of Record. The corporation's board of directors determines the declaration, record, and payable dates. The ex-date is determined by the SRO.

EXAMPLE

			June			
Sun	Mon	Tue	Wed	Thu	Fri	Sat
				1	2	3
4	5	6	7	8	9	10
11	12	13	14	15	16	17
18	19	20	21	22	23	24
25	26	27	28	29	30	

Record Date → 21

Will an investor who purchases stock on Friday, June 16, receive the dividend?

The investor would receive the dividend because regular way settlement takes place three business days after the trade. Monday, Tuesday, and Wednesday are the three business days that must be counted. The investor settles on Wednesday, June 21, which means he owns the stock on the record date and is entitled to the dividend, which is paid on the payable date.

What if the transaction had taken place on Monday, June 19?

Counting the three business days required, regular way settlement would take place on Thursday, June 22. The investor would own the stock on the business day after the record date—too late to receive the dividend.

This example illustrates that June 19 is the first day the investor buys the stock without the dividend (the ex-date) when the record date is June 21. An investor must buy the stock before the ex-date to get the dividend. The seller receives the dividend if the transaction takes place on or after the ex-date.

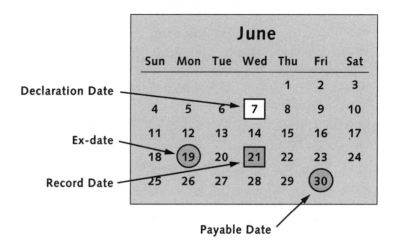

The ex-date is two business days before the record date in transactions executed with regular way settlement. Consider an investor who purchases the stock on Wednesday, June 21, in a cash settlement transaction. Because the settlement takes place the same day, the investor receives the dividend and owns the stock on the record date of June 21. As you will learn in the next unit, mutual fund ex-dates are typically the business day after the record date.

We have prepared this chart to help you remember the sequence. Just as a refresher, we've started with trade date and settlement date, and then we list DERP.

Event	Definition	Duration/Expiration
Trade date	Date on which the transaction occurs	Initiation date for all types of payment contracts; due date for cash settlements
Settlement date	Date on which payment must be received under the rules of its SRO	The investor must have settled the transaction to be considered the stockholder of record on the record date
Declaration date	Date on which the board of directors announces a dividend	Initiates the dividend payment process
Ex-date (ex-dividend date)	Set by the Uniform Practice Committee after being informed of the distribution declaration by the issuer; stock is sold without (ex) the right to receive the dividend	One-day period dictated by the record date for distributions; normally two business days before the record date; stock trades without (ex) rights or dividends
Record date	Determines who is eligible to receive dividends or rights distributions; fixed by the issuing corporation	The investor must have settled the transaction to be considered the stockholder of record on the record date
Payable date	Date on which dividend is paid	Date appears on dividend checks

---

QUICK QUIZ 2.F   Match the following items to the appropriate following description.

- A. Trade date
- B. Settlement date
- C. Ex-date
- D. Declaration date

———   1. When the board announces a dividend

———   2. The day that obligates the parties to the terms of the trade

———   3. First date on which a security trades without entitling the buyer to receive a previously declared distribution

———   4. Date on which ownership changes between buyer and seller

True or False?

———   5. To receive a dividend, a shareholder must own the stock on the ex-date.

———   6. The ex-date is 2 business days following the record date.

———   7. A frozen account means no more trading.

———   8. The payable date is usually before the record date.

2. 5. 3   RIGHTS ISSUANCE

Existing stockholders have preemptive rights that entitle them to maintain their proportionate ownership in a company by buying newly issued shares before the company offers them to the general public. A rights offering allows stockholders to purchase common stock below the current market price. The rights are valued separately from the stock and trade in the secondary market during the subscription period.

A stockholder who receives rights may:

- exercise the rights to buy stock by sending the rights certificates and a check for the required amount to the rights agent;
- sell the rights and profit from their market value (rights certificates are negotiable securities); or
- let the rights expire and lose their value.

2. 5. 3. 1   Subscription Right Certificate

A subscription right is a certificate representing a short-term (typically less than 60 days) privilege to buy additional shares of a corporation. One right is issued for each common stock share outstanding.

2. 5. 3. 2   Terms of the Rights Offering

The terms of a rights offering are stipulated on the subscription right certificates mailed to stockholders. The terms describe how many new shares a stockholder may buy, the price, the date the new stock will be issued, and the final date for exercising the rights.

EXAMPLE   ABC Co. plans to raise capital by issuing additional stock and, on April 1, declares a rights offering. Common stockholders as of May 1, the record date, can subscribe to one new share, at a price of $30, for each 10 shares of stock they own. ABC stock trades in the open market for $41 per share. The rights will expire on June 18. The corporation will issue rights to stockholders of record May 1. Stock is traded cum rights until the ex-date. An investor who buys stock cum rights receives the right. An investor who buys stock ex-rights does not.

The number of rights required to buy one new share is based on the number of shares outstanding and the number of new shares offered.

2. 5. 3. 3   Tender Offer

When a person publicly announces intentions to acquire, in a tender offer, shares of a target company, the following rules apply.

Once the tender is announced, the person making the offer can no longer buy the target company's share in the open market. The only shares the person can purchase are those tendered by shareholders.

The person making the offer is also prohibited from buying convertible securities or call options (equivalent securities) of the target company in the open market. The person could, however, make open market purchases of other nonconvertible securities of the issuer.

The tender offer, under SEC rules, must remain open for at least 20 business days from the date the offer is first announced.

If the terms of the offer are changed, the revised offer must remain open for at least 10 business days from the date the terms are changed (but in no event less than 20 business days from the original announcement).

The target company, within 10 business days of the announcement, must provide its shareholders with a statement:

- accepting or rejecting the offer;
- expressing no opinion on the offer; or
- that it is unable to take a position on the offer.

2. 5. 4   PROXIES AND PROXY VOTING

2. 5. 4. 1   The Proxy

Every publicly traded company must have an annual general shareholder meeting where management presents several decisions that need shareholder approval. The approval (or disapproval) is given by means of voting for each decision. Shareholders may attend the meeting in person or vote by proxy—electronically or by mail via their brokers and custodian (i.e., proxy voting).

A corporation's stockholders usually vote by means of a proxy, like an absentee ballot. A proxy is a limited power of attorney that a stockholder gives to another person, transferring the right to vote on the stockholder's behalf.

A proxy is automatically revoked if the stockholder attends the shareholder meeting or, if the proxy is replaced by another proxy, the stockholder executes at a later date.

2. 5. 4. 2   Proxy Solicitation

Stockholders can receive multiple proxy solicitations for controversial company proposals. If proxies are solicited, the SEC requires a company to give stockholders information about the items to be voted on and allow the SEC to review this information before it sends the proxies to stockholders. In a proxy contest, everyone who participates must register with the SEC. Also, anyone who is not a direct participant but who provides stockholders with unsolicited advice must register as a participant.

2. 5. 4. 3   Forwarding Proxies and Other Materials

Member firms must cooperate with issuers by ensuring that customers whose stock is held in street name are alerted to all financial matters concerning issuers (e.g., quarterly reports and proxy statements). To do so, members act as forwarding agents for all proxies and other corporate materials received from an issuer for street name stock.

Member firms that are nominal owners of record must vote street name stock in accordance with the wishes of the beneficial owners. If a customer signs and returns a proxy statement and fails to indicate how the shares are to be voted, the member must vote the shares as recommended by management.

If a customer does not return the proxy by the 10th day before the annual shareholders' meeting, the member may vote the shares as it sees fit as long as the matters to be voted on are of minor importance. If the matters to be voted on are of major importance (e.g., merger or issuance of additional securities), the member may never vote the shares as it sees fit. In this case, if the proxy is not returned, the shares are not voted.

Member firms are reimbursed by issuers for all costs relating to the forwarding of proxy materials. Such costs include postage and related clerical expenses.

Shareholders may be asked to vote on an initiative that is strictly optional, such as a buy-back program.

2. 5. 4. 4   Buy-Back Program

A buy-back program is an offer by the company to its existing shareholders to repurchase the company's own shares. This reduces the number of outstanding shares.

2. 5. 4. 5   Dutch Auction

A Dutch auction offer stipulates a price range for which a fixed number of shares will eventually be purchased. Shareholders are asked to notify the company or its agent of the price they are willing to sell their shares. Once all shareholder instructions have been tallied up, the shares of stock of the shareholders who voted to sell at the lowest prices would be bought until a fixed number of shares is reached or the limit of the price range is reached.

2. 6 MARGIN AND STOCK LOAN/SECURITIES LENDING

Buying on margin is a common practice in the securities industry. It allows customers to increase their trading capital by borrowing from broker/dealers.

2. 6. 1   TYPES OF MARGIN ACCOUNTS

There are two types of margin accounts: long and short. In a long margin account, customers purchase securities and pay interest on the money borrowed until the loan is repaid. In a short margin account, stock is borrowed and then sold short, enabling the customer to profit if its value declines. All short sales must be executed through and accounted for in a margin account.

TAKE NOTE

In long margin accounts, customers borrow money; in short margin accounts, customers borrow securities.

Advantages of margin accounts for customers are that the customer can:

- purchase more securities with a lower initial cash outlay; and
- leverage the investment by borrowing a portion of the purchase price.

Leveraging magnifies the customer's rate of return, or rate of loss in adverse market conditions.

Cash/Margin Purchase

	Cash Purchase	Margin Purchase
Purchase of 1,000 shares of ABC for $20	Customer pays $20,000 for purchase	Customer borrows 50% ($10,000) from broker/dealer, deposits equity of $10,000
Return after increase from $20 to $30 per share	Customer experiences 50% return (gain/initial investment: $10,000 ÷ $20,000 = 50%)	Customer experiences 100% return (gain/initial investment: $10,000 ÷ $10,000 = 100%)
Return after decrease from $20 to $15 per share	Customer experiences 25% loss (loss/initial investment: – $5,000 ÷ $20,000 = – 25%)	Customer experiences 50% loss (loss/initial investment: – $5,000 ÷ $10,000 = – 50%)

The advantages of margin accounts for broker/dealers are:

- margin account loans generate interest income for the firm; and
- margin customers typically trade larger positions because of increased trading capital, generating higher commissions for the firm.

2. 6. 2   HYPOTHECATION

Hypothecation is the pledging of customer securities as collateral for margin loans.

When customers sign margin agreements, permission is given for this process to occur. After customers pledge their securities to the broker/dealer, the broker/dealer rehypothecates (repledges) them as collateral for a loan from the bank. Regulation U oversees the process of banks lending money to broker/dealers based on customer securities as collateral.

Broker/dealers are limited to pledging 140% of a customer's debit balance as collateral. Any customer securities in excess of this amount must be physically segregated. The firm cannot commingle customer securities with securities owned by the firm.

Firms can only commingle one customer's securities with another customer's securities for hypothecation if customers have given specific permission by signing the hypothecation agreement.

2. 6. 3   DOCUMENTATION AND DISCLOSURE REQUIREMENTS

Customers who open margin accounts must sign a margin agreement before trading can begin. The agreement consists of three parts: the credit agreement, the hypothecation agreement, and the loan consent form.

2. 6. 3. 1   Credit Agreement

The credit agreement discloses the terms of the credit extended by the broker/dealer, including the method of interest computation and situations under which interest rates may change.

2. 6. 3. 2   Hypothecation Agreement

The hypothecation agreement gives permission to the broker/dealer to pledge customer margin securities as collateral. The firm hypothecates customer securities to the bank, and the bank loans money to the broker/dealer on the basis of the loan value of these securities. All customer securities must be held in street name (registered in the name of the firm) to facilitate this process. When customer securities are held in street name, the broker/dealer is known as the nominal, or named, owner. The customer is the beneficial owner because he retains all rights of ownership.

2. 6. 3. 3   Loan Consent Form

If signed, the loan consent form gives permission to the firm to loan customer margin securities to other customers or broker/dealers, usually for short sales.

TAKE NOTE   It is mandatory that the customer signs the credit agreement and hypothecation agreement. The loan consent form is optional.

The interest paid by margin customers on money borrowed is a variable rate based on the broker call rate.

2. 6. 3. 4   Risk Disclosure

Before opening a margin account, you must provide customers with a risk disclosure document. This information must also be provided to margin customers on an annual basis. The document discusses the risks associated with margin trading, some of which are shown in the following.

- Customers are not entitled to choose which securities can be sold if a maintenance call is not met.
- Customers can lose more money than initially deposited.
- Customers are not entitled to an extension of time to meet a margin call.
- Firms can increase their in-house margin requirements without advance notice.

2. 6. 4   FEDERAL AND FINRA MARGIN REQUIREMENTS

The Securities Act of 1934 gives the Federal Reserve Board the authority to regulate the extension of credit in the securities industry. For margin accounts, Regulation T states that customers must deposit a minimum of 50% of the market value of the transaction within five business days. The minimum required is 50%; a customer can choose to pay a larger percentage of the purchase price.

Regulation T applies to both cash and margin accounts; customers have five business days to pay for the purchase, regardless of the account type. Firms, however, expect payment the regular way: within three business days of trade date.

2. 6. 4. 1   Marginable Securities

Regulation T also identifies which securities are eligible for purchase on margin and which may be used as collateral for loans for other purchases.

Differentiate between use of the terms margin and marginable.

- Margin is the amount of equity that must be deposited to buy securities in a margin account.
- Marginable refers to securities that can be used as collateral in a margin account.

The following may be purchased on margin and used as collateral:

- Exchange-listed stocks, bonds
- Nasdaq stocks
- Non-Nasdaq OTC issues approved by the FRB
- Warrants

The following cannot be purchased on margin and cannot be used as collateral:

- Put and call options
- Rights
- Non-Nasdaq OTC issues not approved by the FRB
- Insurance contracts

The following cannot be bought on margin but can be used as collateral after 30 days:

- Mutual funds
- New issues

2. 6. 4. 2   Exempt Securities

Certain securities are exempt from the Federal Reserve Board's Regulation T margin requirements.

If the securities are bought or sold in a margin account, they are subject to the firm's determination of an initial requirement. Firms may impose stricter requirements but at a minimum must follow maintenance requirements established by FINRA.

Securities exempt from Regulation T include:

- US Treasury bills, notes, and bonds;
- government agency issues; and
- municipal securities.

TAKE NOTE   The FRB can change Regulation T, but the current requirement has been in place since 1974. Assume Regulation T equals 50% in test questions.

2. 6. 4. 3   Initial Requirements

Customers are required to deposit a minimum amount of equity for their first purchase in a margin account. Although Regulation T states that a deposit of 50% of the market value of the purchase is required, FINRA rules require that this initial deposit cannot be less than $2,000.

Initial Requirements Example

Customer Purchase	Regulation T Requirement	FINRA Minimum Rule	Customer Deposit Required
100 shares at $50/share	$2,500	$2,000	$2,500
100 shares at $30/share	$1,500	$2,000	$2,000
100 shares at $15/share	$750	$1,500	$1,500

The customer is required to deposit the greater of the Regulation T requirement or the FINRA minimum. The exception occurs when the customer's initial purchase is less than $2,000; the customer is not required to deposit $2,000, only the full purchase price.

There is another way to look at this: if the customer's first purchase in a margin account is less than $2,000, deposit 100% of the purchase price. If the first purchase is between $2,000 and $4,000, deposit $2,000. If the first purchase is greater than $4,000, deposit 50%.

TAKE NOTE

The FINRA minimum rule also applies to short margin accounts. However, because short transactions are more speculative, the required deposit is still $2,000. Keep in mind that unlike the long position where it would be inappropriate to require more than the purchase amount, in shorting stock there is no purchase but rather the taking on of unlimited upside potential risk.

2. 6. 4. 4   Deadlines for Meeting Margin Calls

As previously discussed, Regulation T requires margin account customers to meet initial margin deposit requirements no more than five business days after the trade date. The deposit may be made in cash or in fully paid marginable securities valued at twice the amount of the Regulation T cash call.

If payment is late, the broker/dealer may apply to the designated examining authority (DEA) for an extension, as it may do on behalf of cash account customers. For introducing broker/dealers, who do not clear their own trades, the request is made by the clearing firm. For an amount less than $1,000, the broker/dealer can choose to take no action.

If no extension is requested on the morning of the sixth business day, the firm must sell out the securities purchased and freeze the account for 90 days.

If the customer wants to purchase securities in a frozen account, the customer must have good funds in the account before order entry.

2. 6. 5   SHORT SALES

A **short sale** involves the sale of a security that the customer does not own. To effect delivery to the buyer on settlement date, the customer must borrow stock. Essentially, a short sale is the sale of borrowed stock. The short seller profits if the stock declines in value and has potentially unlimited loss if the stock appreciates. As a supervisor, keep in mind that although short selling serves useful market purposes, selling short may also be done to drive down the price of a stock or to hasten a declining market in a stock. In some cases, short selling may be used to manipulate stock prices and subject the offender to criminal justice. Understanding short selling is of critical importance to a supervising principal and compliance officer.

TEST TOPIC ALERT   Short sales may only be done in a margin account.

2. 6. 5. 1   Borrowing

Stock can be borrowed from several sources: the member firm executing a short sale on behalf of the customer, margin customers of that member firm, other member firms, specialized companies known as stock lending firms and institutional investors. The most common source is another customer's margin account. (When opening a margin account, customers often sign a loan consent agreement that allows the member to loan out customer margin securities.)

2. 6. 5. 2   Privileges

The stock lender retains certain privileges, such as the right to cash dividends on the loaned stock. Dividends are paid by the issuer to the owner of record, the person who bought the shares from the short seller. However, the short seller must make good to the lender for the cash dividends the lender is no longer receiving. To ensure compliance, the member firm, on dividend payment date, will debit the short seller's account the amount of the cash dividend for credit to the stock lender.

Further, the lender retains the right to any stock dividends or stock splits. Again, these additional shares will be paid by the issuer to the owner of record. The short seller makes good to the lender when the stock is bought back for return to the lender. At this point, the short seller will return not only the number of shares originally borrowed, but the additional shares resulting from the distribution as well.

Whenever a customer effects a short sale, the member firm must make a determination that the stock can be borrowed (locate requirement). This determination must be noted on the order ticket. Member firms, rather than making a determination for each individual short sale, may rely on a blanket or standing assurance that the securities will be available for borrowing on settlement date.

The assurance generally takes the form of a list (paper or electronic) of securities available. Under FINRA rules, the list can be no more than 24 hours old (updated daily).

TEST TOPIC ALERT   Two important test points regarding short sales include the following.

■ A short seller is required to remit cash dividends paid by the issuer to the buyer of the stock to the stock lender.

■ The locate requirement for short sales can be made from an available securities list if the list is updated once per business day. This list is sometimes referred to as an easy-to-borrow list.

2. 6. 6   DAY TRADING AND BUYING POWER

A day trader is one who buys and sells the same security on the same day to try to take advantage of intraday price movements. A pattern day trader is one who executes four or more day trades in a five-business-day period.

Under FINRA rules, the minimum equity requirement for pattern day traders is $25,000 (pattern day traders must have on deposit in the account equity of at least $25,000 on any day on which day trading occurs). The minimum maintenance margin requirement for pattern day traders is 25%, the same as for regular customers.

Pattern day traders are also treated differently when it comes to buying power. Buying power for day traders is four times the maintenance margin excess. Maintenance margin excess is defined as the equity in the account above the 25% minimum requirement.

Margin rules also prohibit day trading accounts from using account guarantees, which are otherwise permitted.

A cross guarantee is one in which another customer agrees, in writing, to the use of money or securities in his account to carry the guaranteed accounts (e.g., to meet any margin calls).

2. 6. 7   MINIMUM MAINTENANCE MARGIN REQUIREMENT

As noted previously, the minimum maintenance margin requirement is 25% of the current market value of the securities in a long margin account.

Minimum maintenance requirements are set by a firm's SRO. Once a customer meets the initial Fed call of 50%, the percentage equity in the account can fall all the way to 25% without a maintenance margin call being sent. Once the percentage equity falls below 25%, the member will send the customer a maintenance call for an amount sufficient to bring the account back to minimum.

2. 7 SETTLEMENT

Settlement date is the date on which ownership changes between buyer and seller. It is the date on which broker/dealers are required to exchange the securities and funds involved in a transaction and customers are requested to pay for securities bought and to deliver securities sold.

The Uniform Practice Code (UPC) standardizes the dates and times for each type of settlement.

2. 7. 1   REGULAR WAY SETTLEMENT

Regular way settlement for most securities transactions is the third business day following the trade date, known as T+3.

EXAMPLE   If a trade occurs on a Tuesday (trade date), it will settle regular way on Friday. If a trade takes place on a Thursday, it will settle the following Tuesday.

Knowing that not all securities settle T+3 is equally important, and a summary of settlement rules is included later in this section. Briefly, corporate securities, municipals, and government agency securities settle T+3. US government T-bills, T-notes, T-bonds, and options settle next business day, T+1. Money market securities transactions settle the same day.

In trades between dealers, if the seller delivers before the settlement date, the buyer may either accept the security or refuse it without prejudice.

TAKE NOTE

Interdealer trades in government securities settle in federal funds. Interdealer trades in all other securities settle in clearinghouse funds.

2.7.2   CASH SETTLEMENT

Cash settlement, or same-day settlement, requires delivery of securities from the seller and payment from the buyer on the same day a trade is executed. Stocks or bonds sold for cash settlement must be available on the spot for delivery to the buyer.

Cash trade settlement occurs no later than 2:30 pm ET if the trade is executed before 2:00 pm. If the trade occurs after 2:00 pm, settlement is due within 30 minutes.

2.7.3   SELLER'S OPTION CONTRACTS

This form of settlement is available to customers who want to sell securities but cannot deliver the physical securities in time for regular way settlement.

A seller's option contract lets a customer lock in a selling price for securities without having to make delivery on the third business day. Instead, the seller can settle the trade as specified in the contract. Or, if the seller elects to settle earlier than originally specified, the trade can be settled on any date from the fourth business day through the contract date, provided the buyer is given a one-day written notice.

A buyer's option contract works the same way, with the buyer specifying when settlement will take place.

2.7.4   WHEN-, AS-, AND IF-ISSUED CONTRACTS (WHEN-ISSUED TRADES)

Typically, new municipal bond issues are sold to investors before the bonds are issued. An investor receives a when-issued confirmation describing the bonds. The confirmation does not include a total dollar amount or settlement date because, until the settlement date is known, the accrued interest cannot be calculated to determine the total dollar amount. Once the bonds are issued, the investor receives a new confirmation stating the purchase price and settlement date.

A when-issued transaction confirmation must include:

- a description of the security, with the contract price (yield); and
- the trade date.

Because the settlement date is unknown, a when-issued confirmation for municipal bonds cannot include accrued interest.

2. 7. 5   REGULATION T PAYMENT

Regulation T specifies the date customers are required to pay for purchase transactions. The settlement date, however, is the date customers are requested to deliver cash or securities involved in transactions. Under Regulation T, payment is due two business days after regular way settlement.

2. 7. 5. 1   Extensions

If a buyer cannot pay for a trade within five business days from the trade date, the broker/dealer may request an extension from its designated examining authority (DEA) before the fifth business day. In the case of introducing broker/dealers, those that do not clear their own trades, the extension request is made by the clearing firm. The broker/dealer has the option of ignoring amounts of $1,000 or less without violating Regulation T requirements.

If the customer cannot pay by the end of the extension, the broker/dealer has the option to either request an additional extension from its DEA or sell the securities in a closeout transaction. Broker/dealers are not likely to request too many extensions as a firm and are generally reluctant to request many for the same customer repeatedly unless severe circumstances warrant the request.

If the option to close out the position is chosen, the account is frozen for 90 days. A frozen account must have sufficient cash in it before a buy transaction can be executed.

✓ **TAKE NOTE**

Regulation T deals with the extension of credit for regular security trades. If a broker/dealer must close out a transaction and freeze the account, the customer may not be extended credit.

2. 7. 5. 2   Frozen Accounts

If a customer buys securities in a cash account and sells them before paying for the buy side by the fifth business day, the account is frozen. Any additional buy transactions require full payment in the account, and sell transactions need securities on deposit. Frozen account status continues for 90 calendar days. Frozen account status is lifted if the customer pays by the fifth business day.

❗ **TEST TOPIC ALERT**

The following table gives a summary of the trade settlements and delivery times for different securities and different types of settlement choices.

Summary of Settlement Rules

Equity	3 business days
Corporate and municipal bonds	3 business days
Equity options	Next business day
Index options	Next business day
T-bills, T-notes, and T-bonds	Next business day
US government agency	3 business days
Seller's option	No sooner than T + 4
Cash settlement	Same day
Regulation T	T + 5

Assume a question is asking about the normal customer settlement terms, regular way, unless the question specifically mentions Regulation T.

Also, here's a hint on municipal when-issued settlements. A probable question will ask either what is not included or what is included on a when-issued confirmation.

To discern the correct answer, remember SAT, which identifies what is not included:

■ Settlement date

■ Accrued interest

■ Total dollar amount due at settlement

If a question asks when customer confirmations must be sent, the answer is no later than the settlement date. But if the question asks when broker-to-broker confirmations must be sent, the answer is no later than the business day following the trade date (T+1).

2. 7. 6   COMPARISON OF TRADES

After trades have been executed, the two sides of the trade need to agree that the trade reported is accurate as to:

■ side (buy or sell);

■ security;

■ contra firm;

■ quantity;

■ price; and

■ accrued interest (if applicable).

This trade comparison is vital in ensuring that all trades are known by both parties to avoid trade breaks, such as DKs (discussed in the following). Trade comparison may be performed either electronically through a system such as ACT or manually, through a clearing firm's purchase and sales (P&S) department.

2. 7. 6. 1 Ex-Clearing Trades

As the majority of interdealer trades are confirmed and settled electronically, the need for paper confirmations has diminished. Nonetheless, there are trades, such as when-issued contracts, that are settled outside the scope of ACT and NSCC. The rules for these ex-clearing trades follow.

- Interdealer paper confirmations must be sent no later than T+1.

- When one party to a trade (the confirming member) sends a confirmation but does not receive one in return, the confirming member must send a don't know (DK) notice to the nonconfirming member after four business days from trade date.

- After receipt of the DK notice, the nonconfirming member has four business days to either confirm or DK the trade.

- If no response is received from the nonconfirming member, the confirming member can consider the nonresponse as a DK and can drop the trade or pursue remedies under the Code of Arbitration.

2. 7. 7 SETTLEMENT SERVICE PROVIDERS AND METHODS OF SETTLEMENT

Many years ago, Wall Street operations were grinding to a halt due to the crush of paper. Old stock certificates needed to be voided and replacements registered to the new owners typed up. To solve this problem, a new clearing company and process was created to automate, centralize, standardize, and streamline the entire process with the ultimate goal to do away with paper. The Depository Trust & Clearing Corp. (DTCC), along with its subsidiary the National Securities Clearing Corp., was established in 1976 to provide clearing, settlement, and a guarantee of completion for certain transactions for broker-to-broker trades involving equities, ADRs, ETFs, UITs, and corporate and municipal debt. Today, literally quadrillions of dollars of securities transactions settle through the DTC and its subsidiaries.

The DTCC, which is regulated by the SEC, has 10 subsidiaries, each of which serves a specific segment within the securities industry:

- National Securities Clearing Corporation (NSCC)
- The depository trust company (DTC)
- Fixed Income Clearing Corporation (FICC)
- DTCC Deriv/SERV LLC
- The Warehouse Trust Company LLC
- DTCC Derivatives Repository Ltd.
- DTCC Solutions LLC
- DTCC Loan/SERV LLC
- EuroCCP Ltd.
- Avox Ltd.

Services available through the DTCC include:

- Automated Customer Account Transfer Service (ACATS)
- Continuous Net Settlement (CNS)
- Trade Comparison and Reporting

- Settlement Services
- Stock Borrow Program

The billions of shares of stock that trade and settle so easily today was unimaginable just a few decades ago due to the services provided by the DTCC. Companies are no longer required to provide paper certificates, and an increasing number are opting out. Publicly traded securities such as Intel; Visa, Inc.; Tupperware; Tiffany; and Sears no longer trade as paper stock certificates but solely in the settlement cloud instead.

2. 7. 8   REPURCHASE AGREEMENTS

In a repurchase agreement (repo), a financial institution, such as a bank or broker/dealer, raises cash by temporarily selling some of the securities it holds with an agreement to buy back the securities at a later date. Thus, a repo is an agreement between a buyer and a seller to conduct a transaction (sale) and then reverse that transaction (repurchase) in the future.

A repo contract includes both a repurchase price and a maturity date. If the agreement sets a specific date, the repo is considered a fixed agreement.

If the maturity date is left to the initial buyer's discretion, the repo is known as an open repo and becomes a demand obligation callable at any time.

Though technically a sale of securities, a repo is similar to a fully collateralized loan. Instead of borrowing money and putting up securities as collateral for the loan, the dealer sells the securities and agrees to buy them back later at a higher price. The interest on the loan is the difference between the sale price and the repurchase price. The loan's interest rate (called the repo rate) is negotiated between the two parties and is generally lower than bank loan rates.

2. 7. 8. 1   Settlement for Repurchase Agreements

Settlement of repurchase agreements occur between the two contraparties using the FICC as an intermediary. The FICC allows the repo to be settled on a net basis and permits confidentiality between the ultimate buyer and seller. Delivery of repos must occur by 3:30 pm ET of the trade date over the securities FedWire, an electronic transfer service of the Federal Reserve.

2. 7. 9   CONTINUOUS NET SETTLEMENT (CNS)

Continuous net settlement (CNS) is an automated book-entry (no certificates) accounting system. The system provides clearance for equities, corporate and municipal bonds, UITs, and more. Interdealer trades are reported to the Automated Confirmation Transaction (ACT) system and submitted to National Securities Clearing Corp. (NSCC) for clearance and settlement. NSCC works on a continuous net settlement (CNS) basis; that is, interdealer buys and sells, per security, are netted each day for delivery and money settlement purposes.

Delivery for many securities is accomplished through bookkeeping entries at a securities depository such as the depository trust company (DTC). DTC provides securities certificate safekeeping for member firms, and changes in ownership are made by computerized entries rather than physical delivery.

To clear transactions, firms must be members of NSCC or clearing corporations associated with an exchange such as Midwest Clearing Corp. DTC itself is involved in custody and safekeeping, not in clearance. DTC also processes dividend and interest payments on securities it holds in safekeeping.

There is an SEC requirement for participants in NSCC's Continuous Net Settlement System to close out any fails that exists on the settlement date (T+3) for an equity security if the closeout does not take place at or before the opening of trading on T+4 (in the case of short sales). Fails relating to long sales or bona fide market making activity have two additional settlement days (T+6) before they must be closed out.

TAKE NOTE

BDs must track all fails to deliver from both long and short sales and then borrow or buy in a sufficient amount of stock to close out the fails at the beginning of regular trading on T+4 (in the case of short sales) and T+6 (in the case of long sales).

2. 7. 10 DON'T KNOW (DK) TRADE

In an interdealer trade, each side electronically submits its version of the transaction to the ACT system. If one side does not recognize the other side's details of the transaction (e.g., the number of shares is wrong or the price is wrong), it will electronically DK (Don't Know) the trade.

TAKE NOTE

DKs are used in interdealer trades for which one party to the transaction does not recognize the trade or, if it does, disagrees with the terms of the trade as submitted by the other party.

The term can also be used within a broker/dealer when an order or wire room does not recognize the account number or other information on an order ticket.

2. 7. 11 CLOSEOUTS

2. 7. 11. 1 Buy-Ins

In trades between members, failure to deliver securities sold does not result in cancellation of the trade. If securities are not delivered to the buying member on settlement, the buyer may close out the position no earlier than the third business day following settlement date. Prior to buying in the position, the member must provide written notice of the proposed buy-in to the seller by 12:00 noon, two business days prior to executing the buy-in. This means that written notice may be delivered to the seller as early as the day after settlement.

TAKE NOTE

The seller is permitted to make a partial delivery prior to the proposed buy-in date as long as the amount remaining to be delivered is not an odd lot or does not contain an odd lot. If the buy-in results in a loss (the stock price at buy-in was higher than the contract price), the loss is borne by the contra broker (i.e., the member that failed to deliver on settlement date).

Upon receiving the written notice of a proposed buy-in, the selling member can claim no fault, which means the selling member cannot deliver because another member (a third party) is not delivering to the selling member. In this case, the seller will retransmit the written notice to the third party. This retransmittal extends the proposed buy-in date by seven calendar days.

2. 7. 11. 2 Sellouts

A sellout will occur if a member sells securities to another member (the buyer) and the buying member fails to pay when the securities are delivered on settlement date. Sellouts can be executed any time after settlement. No prior written notice is required. As before, any loss resulting from the sellout (the sale price at sellout was lower than the contract price) will be borne by the contra broker (i.e., the member that failed to pay on settlement date).

2. 7. 12 AGED SECURITIES FAILS

A customer fail to deliver can arise when a customer sells stock and fails to deliver the securities by settlement date. At that point, the member sets up on its books a fail to deliver in the amount of the sales proceeds. It is an allowable asset for capital purposes. However, the longer it remains, the greater the risk to the member.

On the fifth business day after settlement, the fail to deliver must be aged for the firm's capital computation purposes. The position is marked to the market, and a 15% haircut is taken on its current market value. This has the effect of reducing its value for capital purposes. After being aged, it is still an allowable asset.

2. 8 ACCOUNT STATEMENTS AND CONFIRMATIONS

2. 8. 1   CUSTOMER ACCOUNT STATEMENTS

Members are required, under FINRA rules, to send statements to customers at least quarterly. If there is activity in the account in any given month, a statement must be sent that month. Activity is defined as purchases, sales, interest or dividends received, or any funds flowing in or out of the account.

The SEC has a comparable rule regarding notification of free credit balances (cash balances) in customer accounts. Free credit balances are a rarity, as most firms provide automatic sweep into a money market fund of any cash balances in customer accounts. The money market fund must satisfy the dual objectives of a highly rated money market fund by providing liquidity and preserving capital. In other words, they must never "break the buck."

Nevertheless, the SEC (under Rule 15c-3-2) requires that customers be notified of any free credit balance in their accounts at least quarterly or whenever a statement is sent. This notification must state that:

- these balances are not segregated by the member firm;

- they may be used by the member in the conduct of its business; and

- they are available to the customer on demand.

Account statements must include a statement advising customers to promptly report any discrepancy or inaccuracy to their brokerage firms and clearing firms.

TEST TOPIC ALERT   Free credit balance notification is required monthly in active accounts and quarterly in inactive accounts.

In January of each year, members must send statements to customers showing a summary of all interest and dividends credited to the account as well as the gross proceeds of all sales made the prior year. The statement is sent to the account owner and to the IRS on Form 1099.

Joint Accounts. With respect to joint accounts, the statement is sent to the person whose Social Security number is on the account. While the member collects information on all parties in a joint account, each account has a primary Social Security number.

2. 8. 2   CONFIRMATIONS

A trade confirmation is a printed document that confirms a trade, its settlement date, and the amount of money due from or owed to the customer. For each transaction, a customer must be sent or given a written confirmation of the trade at or before the completion of the transaction, the settlement date.

The trade confirmation includes the following information:

- Trade date—day on which the transaction is executed (the settlement date is usually the third business day after the trade date)
- Account number—branch office number followed by an account number
- Registered representative internal ID number (or AE number)— account executive's identification number
- BOT (bought) or SLD (sold)—indicates a customer's role in a trade
- Number (or quantity)—number of shares of stock or the par value of bonds bought or sold for the customer
- Description—specific security bought or sold for the customer
- Yield—indicates that the yield for callable bonds may be affected by the exercise of a call provision
- CUSIP number—applicable Committee on Uniform Securities Identification Procedures (CUSIP) number, if any
- Price—price per share for stock or bonds before a charge or deduction
- Amount—price paid or received before commissions and other charges; also referred to as extended principal for municipal securities transactions
- Commission—added to buy transactions; subtracted from sell transactions completed on an agency basis; a commission will not appear on the confirmation if a markup has been charged in a principal transaction
- Net amount—obtained on purchases by adding expenses (commissions and postage) to the principal amount (whether the transaction is a purchase or sale, interest is always added whenever bonds are traded with accrued interest)

2. 8. 2. 1   Disclosure of Capacity

The confirmation must also show the capacity in which the broker/dealer acts (agency or principal) and the commission in cases where the broker/dealer acts as an agent. Markups or markdowns are disclosed for Nasdaq securities.

TAKE NOTE

All firms can act in one of two capacities in a customer transaction. If the firm acts as an agent, it is the broker between the buying and selling parties. Agents receive commissions for transactions they perform, and commissions must be disclosed on confirmations.

If the firm acts as a dealer and transacts business for or from its inventory, it acts in a principal capacity and is compensated by a markup or markdown.

Additionally, confirmations must disclose markups or markdowns for Nasdaq securities, and a firm can never act as both agent and principal in the same transaction.

2. 8. 2. 2   Timely Mailing of Confirmations

Customer confirmations must be sent no later than at or before the completion of the transaction.

2. 8. 3   ELECTRONIC DELIVERY

FINRA allows members to electronically send documents, such as confirmations and account statements, to customers as long as certain conditions are met. To do so, the firm must have procedures in place to show that the information sent has been delivered as intended and that the confidentiality and security of personal information are protected. Furthermore, customers must provide written consent to electronic delivery.

In addition, a customer who consents to receive information and documents electronically must be provided with the information in paper form, upon request.

2. 8. 4   NON-TRADE CONFIRMATIONS/THIRD-PARTY ACTIVITY NOTICES

Customers with a foreign bank account may from time to time wire money from that country back to a brokerage account in the United States (or the reverse). When the funds are credited (or debited) to/from the account, a confirmation of the deposit/withdrawal is sent. It is a non-trade confirmation because there was activity in the account that had nothing to do with a securities transaction. Another example is when a deposit (or withdrawal) of a stock certificate is made. The customer receives a confirmation of the activity, but there is no trade.

A customer with an outside money manager handling some of the customer's money may execute through a broker/dealer where the customer has an account and the manager withdraws his fee quarterly in advance. Each time a fee is taken, a confirmation is sent from the broker/dealer indicating that specific "third-party activity" was logged.

2. 8. 5   PROSPECTUS DELIVERY REQUIREMENTS

In certain offerings, a final prospectus must be delivered by all members to buyers in the secondary market for a specified period following the effective date. This is termed the *prospectus delivery requirement period* and is summarized in the following.

2. 8. 5. 1   Prospectus Delivery Requirements for IPOs

Following an IPO, a prospectus must be delivered with any shares sold within:

■ 90 days if the security is to be quoted in OTC Pink Market or over the OTCBB (non-Nasdaq); or

■ 25 days if the security is to be listed or quoted over Nasdaq.

2. 8. 5. 2   Prospectus Delivery Requirements for Additional Issue Offerings

In an additional, or secondary, offering, a prospectus must be delivered with the shares.

■ If the security is listed or quoted over Nasdaq, a prospectus must be delivered only in connection with purchases at the public offering price, and once the distribution is complete, there is no obligation to deliver a prospectus in secondary market transactions.

■ If the security is non-Nasdaq, the prospectus delivery requirement period is 40 days.

TAKE NOTE   If a prospectus delivery requirement period exists in the secondary market, a prospectus must be delivered by all dealers—including those that did not participate in the distribution.

If there is a prospectus delivery requirement period and the information in the prospectus becomes misleading due to a material development (e.g., a patent approval, the loss of a major customer), the issuer has the obligation to update the information. This can be done by stickering the outside cover page with the updated information. Stickering a prospectus can be done as soon as the new information is filed with the SEC—it is effective immediately with the SEC.

2. 8. 6   TAX REPORTING

2. 8. 6. 1   Cost Basis

The sale of securities can result in a capital gain or a capital loss. A capital gain occurs when a security is sold for a price higher than the cost basis; if the selling price is lower than the cost basis, a capital loss occurs.

An investment's cost basis is used to determine whether a taxable gain or a tax-deductible loss occurs when an asset is sold. Because many events affect an asset's cost basis, the IRS allows the cost basis to be adjusted for such occurrences as stock splits and stock dividends.

2. 8. 6. 1. 1   Capital Gains

A capital gain occurs when capital assets (securities, real estate, and tangible property) are sold at prices that exceed the adjusted cost basis. Usually, computing the capital gain or loss on an asset involves comparing the purchase price with the selling price.

E X A M P L E

A customer bought 100 shares of ABC at $90 plus commission of $100. The payment due was $9,100. The customer's cost basis was $91 per share. The customer sold the shares six months later at $96, less commission of $100. The customer's net proceeds were $9,500 ($9,600 – $100).

The customer's capital gain is calculated by comparing the cost basis to the sales proceeds as follows.

Cost basis	$9,100	or	$91 per share
Sales proceeds	$9,500	or	$95 per share
Total	$ 400	or	$4 per share

Because the customer sold the shares after holding them for six months, the customer has a short-term capital gain taxable as ordinary income.

2. 8. 6. 1. 2   Capital Losses

A capital loss occurs when capital assets are sold at prices that are lower than the adjusted cost basis.

2. 8. 6. 1. 3   Net Capital Gains and Losses

To calculate tax liability, a taxpayer must first add all short-term capital gains and losses for the year. Then he separately adds all long-term capital gains and losses. Finally, the taxpayer offsets the totals to determine his net capital gain or loss for the year. If the result is a net capital gain, it is included in gross income and taxed.

Net capital losses are deductible against earned income to a maximum of $3,000 per year. Any capital losses not deducted in a taxable year may be carried forward indefinitely to be used in future years.

Member firms must report the sale proceeds of a trade and the cost basis in the security sold on Form 1099-B used to report proceeds from broker transactions. It must also disclose whether the capital gain or loss is long term (over one year) or short term. This does not remove the requirement to submit Form 1099 reporting interest and dividends.

2. 8. 6. 2   Tax Withholding

2. 8. 6. 2. 1   TEFRA Withholding

The Tax Equity and Fiscal Responsibility Act of 1982 (TEFRA) created a withholding tax of 10% of all dividends received in accounts that do not have a valid tax ID. If the account holder is a foreigner, and therefore no tax ID exists, the account holder must supply a W8-BEN in order to avoid TEFRA withholding.

2. 8. 6. 2. 2   Mutual Fund Tax Withholding

If an investor neglects or fails to include a Social Security number or tax ID number when purchasing mutual fund shares, the fund must withhold 31% of the distributions to the investor as a withholding tax.

2. 8. 6. 2. 3   *Rollover IRA Withholding*

If an individual receives a distribution of assets from an employer-sponsored qualified plan, the payor of the distribution must retain 20% of the distribution as a withholding tax. The option to forgo withholding is not available to the participant. This 20% withholding tax does not apply to rollovers made from individual IRAs. In the event that 20% of a rollover is withheld, the taxpayer must apply to the IRS for a refund.

If the individual elects a direct transfer, there is no withholding on the amount directly transferred.

2. 8. 7   PROHIBITED ACTIVITIES RELATED TO PRICING SECURITIES ON ACCOUNT STATEMENTS AND CONFIRMATIONS

2. 8. 7. 1   Falsifying or Withholding Documents

FINRA requires that "A member, in the conduct of his business, shall observe high standards of commercial honor and just and equitable principles of trade." It is well established that forgery and falsification of documents is not consistent with the high standards of commercial honor and just and equitable principles of trade required of registered representatives. Someone found in violation of the rule may be sanctioned, that is, fined; censured; suspended; and, in egregious cases, barred.

2. 8. 7. 2   Holding Mail Beyond the Permissible Time Frames

FINRA member firms may, upon written request, hold customer mail (statements, confirmations, and so forth) for up to two months if the customer will be traveling domestically and for up to three months if traveling abroad.

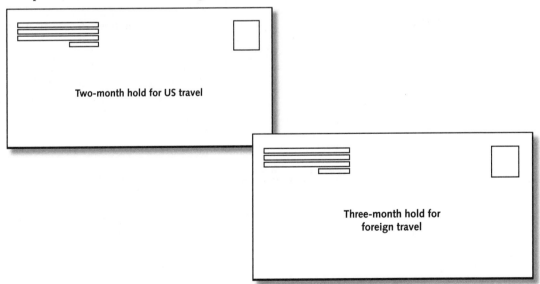

2. 9 BOOKS AND RECORDS

2. 9. 1   RECONCILIATIONS

A cash general ledger account is a record of the transactions (checks written, receipts from the company's customers, etc.) that involve its checking account. The company's bank also creates a record of the company's checking account when it processes the company's checks and deposits. After each month ends, the bank sends a bank statement to the company. The bank statement lists company activity in the account during the most recent month as well as the balance in the bank account.

When the company receives its bank statement, the company must verify that the amounts on the bank statement are consistent with the amounts in the company's cash account in its general ledger and vice versa. This process of confirming amounts is known as reconciliation or doing a "bank rec." The benefit of reconciling the bank statement is knowing that the amount of cash on the company's books is the same as the amount of cash shown in the bank's records.

2. 9. 2   TIMELINE OF POSTING ENTRIES

The SEC has established regulations for the timeliness of posting transactions for certain records. The following table identifies the transaction posting requirements.

Transaction Record	Posting/Recording Requirement
General ledger	Monthly; not later than 10 business days from month's end
Stock record	Not later than one business day following settlement
Blotters	Not later than one business day after activity
Customer ledger	Not later than settlement date
Transfer records	Not later than the second business day after securities are forwarded to a transfer agent
Stock borrowed/loaned	Not later than two business days after activity
Cash borrowed/loaned	Not later than two business days after activity
Fails to receive/deliver	Not later than two business days past settlement
Long/short securities differences	Not later than seven business days from discovery

2. 9. 3   RECORDKEEPING AND RECORD RETENTION

SEC Rules 17a-3 and 17a-4 deal with which records must be prepared by members, when such records must be prepared, and for how long such records must be retained. For retention purposes, records are generally either lifetime records, six-year records, or three-year records.

TAKE NOTE

In lieu of maintaining paper records, firms may use digital storage media such as CD-ROMs. Such media must have the capability to maintain records in non-rewriteable and non-erasable format.

2. 9. 3. 1   Lifetime Records

Records that must be kept for the life of the firm are partnership articles if a partnership, articles of incorporation if a corporation, minute books (records of directors' or partners' meetings), stock certificate books, and organizational documents such as Form BD and amendments.

2. 9. 3. 2   Six-Year Records

There are five primary records that must be retained for six years.

- **Blotters**. A blotter is a record of original entry. A member generally maintains blotters relating to the purchase and sale of securities, the receipt and delivery of securities, and the receipt and disbursement of cash. Blotters must reflect transactions as of trade date (or event date) and must be prepared no later than the following business day.

- **General Ledger**. The general ledger contains accounting records of the firm's assets, liabilities, and net worth accounts. From the general ledger, a firm prepares its financial statements. The general ledger must be prepared as frequently as necessary to determine compliance with the net capital rule, but in no event less frequently than monthly.

- **Stock Record**. The stock record shows all securities held by the firm, the ownership of those securities, and where the securities are held. The stock record must be posted no later than the business day after settlement date.

- **Customer Ledgers**. Customer ledgers are customer statements. Cash accounts and margin accounts are shown on separate ledgers. These ledgers must be posted no later than settlement date.

- **Customer Account Records**. Customer account records might include the new account form and margin agreement, if appropriate.

In addition, the principal designation record must be retained for six years.

2. 9. 3. 3   Three-Year Records

Most other records are three-year records. Examples of these records include the following:

- Advertising
- FOCUS reports
- Trial balances
- Form U-4, U-5, and fingerprint cards for terminated personnel
- Customer confirmations
- Order tickets
- Subsidiary ledgers such as securities borrowed and securities loaned, monies borrowed and monies loaned, securities failed to receive and failed to deliver, long and short securities differences, and dividends and interest received
- A list of every office where each associated person regularly conducts business
- Associated persons' compensation records
- The firm's Compliance and Procedures manual

TAKE NOTE

Whether a record retention requirement is six years or three years, the most recent two years must be in a readily accessible location.

Three records for which there is a five-year retention period include:

■ Form 104 filings;

■ SAR filings; and

■ information obtained to verify a customer's identity.

Exception reports must be retained for 18 months. These are reports generated daily to review for unusual activity in customer accounts.

UNIT TEST

1. A carrying firm must conduct a securities count at least
   A. monthly
   B. quarterly
   C. semiannually
   D. annually

2. A customer who makes 3 deposits of $9,000 on the same day
   I. is in the placement stage
   II. is in the layering stage
   III. should be reported to the Treasury Department
   IV. should be reported to the Justice Department
   A. I and III
   B. I and IV
   C. II and III
   D. II and IV

3. Customer account information must be verified at least
   A. annually
   B. every 2 years
   C. every 3 years
   D. every 5 years

4. Additional risk disclosures must be provided to customers for all the following products EXCEPT
   A. margin
   B. options
   C. penny stocks
   D. high-value stocks

5. Distributions in traditional IRAs must be made when the account holder is
   A. 59½
   B. 65
   C. 70½
   D. never

6. All the following must be obtained from a new individual customer EXCEPT
   A. full name
   B. address
   C. signature
   D. tax ID

7. Deposits available same day include
   I. cash
   II. check
   III. wire transfer
   IV. ACH transfer
   A. I and III
   B. I and IV
   C. II and III
   D. II and IV

8. A 2-for-1 stock split is declared on XYZ, which is currently trading at $25.00. What will the price be adjusted to after the split?
   A. $12.50
   B. $25.00
   C. $37.50
   D. $50.00

9. If a customer wishes to purchase $2,000 worth of marginable securities in a margin account, a deposit must be made of
   A. $1,000
   B. $1,500
   C. $1,750
   D. $2,000

10. Stock certificates must be signed by
    I. the owner
    II. a registered principal
    III. the notary public
    IV. the NYSE medallion guarantor
    A. I and III
    B. I and IV
    C. II and III
    D. II and IV

ANSWERS AND RATIONALES

1. **B.** SEC Rule 17a-13 requires that carrying firms conduct a count of securities at least quarterly.

2. **A.** When a customer makes multiple deposits that together would exceed $10,000, a FinCEN Form 104 (or Currency Transaction Report) needs to be submitted to the Treasury Department by the 15th calendar day after the transaction.

3. **C.** Customer account information, such as address and investing objectives, must be verified and updated no less than every 36 months.

4. **D.** Prior to trading, risk disclosures must be given for options, margin, and penny stocks. There is no required disclosure for trading in securities with a high price.

5. **C.** Distributions must be made from a traditional IRA once the account holder turns 70½ to avoid a tax penalty. This requirement does not exist for a Roth IRA. Distributions may begin without penalty at 59½.

6. **C.** While individual firms may choose to require a customer signature on new account forms, there is no stated regulatory rule for such. Full name, address, and tax ID are all required as part of the new account process.

7. **A.** Funds that are available for same-day use include cash and wire transfers. Check and ACH transfers both take up to three days to clear, before the funds are received.

8. **A.** Once the stock split occurs, the number of shares outstanding will double, decreasing the value of each share to half its original value. The new price per share will be $12.50.

9. **D.** When a purchase is made on margin, before the 50% Regulation T requirement is used, FINRA requires the lesser of the total market value of the purchase or $2,000 be deposited. In this case, those two are equal, resulting in a required initial deposit of $2,000.

10. **B.** To be deliverable, stock certificates must be signed by the certificate's owner and guaranteed by a clearing firm or bank that participates in the NYSE Medallion Signature Guarantee Program.

QUICK QUIZ ANSWERS

Quick Quiz 2.A

1. **C**

2. **E**

3. **D**

4. **B**

5. **A**

Quick Quiz 2.B

1. **D.**   All of the persons listed have fiduciary responsibilities because of the authority with which they are entrusted.

2. **B.**   The donor may name himself the custodian of an UGMA or UTMA account. No documentation of custodial status is required to open a custodial account, and the custodian is not required to be the minor's legal guardian.

3. **D.**   Trading on margin is prohibited in fiduciary accounts except with the appropriate documentation.

4. **D.**   A minor may not be a party in a joint account because a minor cannot legally exercise control over the account. A custodial account should be set up for the minor.

5. **C.**   Transfer of securities into the custodial account completes the gift. At that time, the minor becomes the owner of the securities.

Quick Quiz 2.C

1. **A.**   Any individual with earned income who is younger than age 70½ may contribute to a traditional IRA. Deductibility of the contribution is determined by that person's coverage under other qualified plans and by their income level.

2. **B.**   All withdrawals from IRAs are taxed at the individual's ordinary income tax rate at the time of withdrawal. Distributions taken before age 59½ will incur an additional 10% penalty.

3. **C.**   The penalty for premature withdrawals from an IRA or a Keogh account is 10% plus normal income tax. Excess contribution penalty is 6%, while the 50% penalty applies after age 70½.

4. **A.**   Early withdrawals without penalty are permitted only in certain situations, such as death or qualifying disability.

5. **B.**   Life insurance contracts may not be purchased in an IRA.

6. **C.**   The common factor for both traditional and Roth IRAs is that investment earnings are not taxed when earned. Traditional IRAs offer tax-deductible contributions, but withdrawals are generally taxed. Roth IRAs do not offer tax-deductible contributions, but qualified withdrawals are tax free. Traditional IRAs require distributions to begin in the year after the year an owner reaches age 70½, but this is not true for Roth IRAs.

Quick Quiz 2.D

1. **D.**

2. **A.**

3. **C.**

4. **E.**

5. **B.**

6. **H.**

7. **F.**

8. **G.**

9. **I.**

Quick Quiz 2.E

1. **D.**

2. **A.**

3. **G.**

4. **B.**

5. **E.**

6. **F.**

7. **H.**

8. **I.**

9. **F.**

Quick Quiz 2.F

1. **D.**

2. **A.**

3. **C.**

4. **B.**

5. **F.** A shareholder must own the stock on the record date to receive the dividend.

6. **F.** The ex-date is 2 business days before the record date.

7. **F.** The customer may still do securities sales and may make purchases if he deposits the full purchase price in his account first.

8. **F.** The payable date is usually 3 to 4 weeks after the record date.

3

Professional Conduct and Ethics

T he securities industry in the United States is among the most heav-
ily regulated in the world. Firms and representatives must comply
with SEC rules, the rules of the SROs, and house rules developed by
the firm internally. The intent of these rules is to protect the public, and
your career depends on your ability to follow the rules and regulations of the
industry.

This unit reviews the various rules and procedures on dealing with customers, the FINRA Code of Conduct, customer privacy, and broker-dealer
supervision and internal controls.

This unit will cover information that will account for 20 questions on
the Series 99 exam.

When you have completed this unit, you should be able to:

- **describe** the process of FINRA registration for broker/dealers and associated persons;

- **describe** the FINRA Code of Conduct;

- **list** the methods of communications with the public;

- **list** potential red flags;

- **describe** the controls used to segregate information and resources in a broker/dealer;

- **explain** and **describe** the use of written supervisory procedures; and

- **describe** a firm's business continuity plan.

3. 1 EMPLOYEE CONDUCT

3. 1. 1   REGISTRATION, CONTINUING EDUCATION, AND TERMINATION OF ASSOCIATED PERSONS

3. 1. 1. 1   Form U-4

A **representative** is defined as any person, other than a principal, who solicits or conducts business in securities for the member.

A **principal** is defined as any person associated with a member who is actively engaged in the management of the member's investment banking or securities business, including supervision, solicitation, the conduct of business, or the training of associated persons. These persons include sole proprietors, officers, partners, and managers of offices of supervisory jurisdiction.

To register an associated person of a member firm with FINRA, the member fills out and submits Form U-4, but registration is not effective until the person passes the appropriate qualification exam(s). If a person fails, 30 days must elapse before a second attempt can be made. If a person fails an exam three straight times, the person must wait six months before making a fourth attempt.

Information required on Form U-4 is extensive and includes:

- name, address, and any aliases;
- five-year residency history;
- 10-year employment history; and
- information on any charges, arrests, or convictions relating to the investment business.
    - A Yes answer to any of these questions requires a detailed explanation. This information must be provided on the Disclosure Reporting Page (DRP) on Form U-4.

Any changes to this information require filing an amended form with the CRD no later than 30 days after the member becomes aware of these changes. If the amendment involved a statutory disqualification, an amended form must be filed within 10 business days.

In addition to registering with FINRA, a representative must satisfy the registration requirements of each state he does business in. The Form U-4 must be check marked for each state and the accompanying fee and qualification exam if any must be satisfied. If a representative's firm is also a member of an exchange, such as the NYSE or the CBOE, this must be noted on the Form U-4, and once again, applicable fees must be paid and qualification exams passed.

TAKE NOTE   Information on marital status or educational background is not required on Form U-4.

FINRA will deny membership to a broker/dealer or any of its associated persons who:

- have been expelled, denied registration, or suspended by another SRO;
- are subject to an SEC order denying, suspending, or revoking registration as a broker/dealer;

- have willfully filed a false or misleading application or have failed to disclose material facts; or
- have been convicted of any securities- or money-related misdemeanor or any felony within the past 10 years.

3. 1. 1. 2   License and Jurisdictional Retention

If a registered person leaves the industry and reaffiliates with a member firm within two years, that person's license remains valid. If reaffiliation occurs after two years, that person must requalify by passing the appropriate exam.

Similarly, when a registered person leaves the business, FINRA retains jurisdiction over that person for two years. If that person becomes subject to a customer complaint or charges are brought against that person by FINRA, that person is still subject to FINRA rules for the two-year period following termination.

To avoid having a securities registration lapse, it may be tempting for former registered representatives to park their registrations with a member as the end of the two-year period nears. However, parking a securities license will subject the registered representative and the member firm to FINRA sanctions.

3. 1. 1. 3   Continuing Education

Registered persons must participate in continuing education (CE) programs. The CE requirement has two components: regulatory element and firm element.

The regulatory element requires that all registered persons complete a computer-based training session within 120 days of the person's second registration anniversary and every three years thereafter (i.e., within 120 days of the person's 5th, 8th, 11th registration anniversary, and so forth). The content of the regulatory element is determined by FINRA and is appropriate to either the registered representative or principal status of the person.

If a person fails to complete the regulatory element within the prescribed period, FINRA will inactivate that person's registration until the requirements of the program have been met.

The firm element requires member firms to prepare an annual training plan that takes into account such factors as recent regulatory developments, the scope of the member's business activities, the performance of its personnel in the regulatory element, and its supervisory needs. This annual in-house training must be given to all registered persons who have direct contact with the public.

Under FINRA's continuing education requirements, every person registered as an Operations Professional will be subject to firm element continuing education. If you hold only an Operations Professional registration, you will be subject to the S901 Regulatory Element Program. If you registered as an Operations Professional by using an eligible registration, you will take the Regulatory Element Program appropriate for the eligible registration. For example, if you registered as an Operations Professional by holding a Series 6 license, you will be subject to the S101 Regulatory Element Program instead of the S901. The S901 Regulatory Element Program will become available during the fourth quarter of 2013.

3. 1. 1. 4   Form U-5

Should a person registered with a member resign or be terminated, the member must file Form U-5 with the CRD within 30 days of termination date. The member must also provide a copy of the form to their former employee within the same time frame. Failure to do so within 30 days will result in a late filing fee being assessed against the member. The form requires the member to indicate the reason for termination and provide an explanation where appropriate. Failure to provide accurate information could lead to severe disciplinary action.

If the member checks the Discharged or Permitted to Resign box, all of the details surrounding the termination must be disclosed.

In the event that the member, after filing the form, learns of facts or circumstances that would cause the information filed to be inaccurate or incomplete, the member must file an amended Form U-5 within 30 days of learning of facts giving rise to the amendment. A copy of the amended filing must be sent to the former employee. There is no time limit on how long after termination an amended Form U-5 is required.

If a registered person leaves one member to join another, the new employer, in addition to filing Form U-4, must get a copy of Form U-5 filed by the former employer within 60 days of the U-4 filing.

3. 1. 2   CODE OF CONDUCT

3. 1. 2. 1   Outside Business Activities and Outside Securities Accounts

Proper supervision involves knowing what registered representatives are doing even when they are not working for the member firm. There is a rule dealing with business activity away from the firm. This rule states that no person associated with a member in any registered capacity may be employed by, or accept compensation from, any other person as a result of any business activity (other than as an investor) outside the scope of his relationship with his employer firm, unless he has provided prompt written notice to the employing member.

A passive investment, such as the purchase of a limited partnership unit or mutual fund shares, is not considered an outside employment or business activity, even if the purchaser receives money as a result of the investment.

An associated person may make a passive investment for his own account without written notice to or receiving written approval from the employing broker/dealer.

3. 1. 2. 2   Prohibition Against Insider Trading

Although the Securities Exchange Act of 1934 prohibited the use of insider information in making trades, the Insider Trading and Securities Fraud Enforcement Act (ITSFEA) of 1988 expanded the penalties for insider trading and securities fraud. An insider is any person who has access to nonpublic information about a company. Inside information is any information that has not been disseminated to, or is not readily available to, the general public.

The act prohibits insider trading on or communicating nonpublic information. Both tippers (the person who gives a tip) and tippees (the person who receives a tip) are liable, as is anyone who trades on information that he knows or should know is not public or has control over the misuse of this information. No trade need be made for a violation to occur; even a personal benefit of a nonfinancial nature could lead to liability under the rules.

The key elements of liability under insider trading rules follow.

- Does the tipper owe a fiduciary duty to a company/its stockholders? Has he breached it?

- Does the tipper meet the personal benefits test (even something as simple as enhancing a friendship or reputation)?

- Does the tippee know or should the tippee have known that the information was inside or confidential?
- Is the information material and nonpublic?

TAKE NOTE

Even a slip of the tongue by a corporate insider could create liability under these rules. The SEC has a greatly broadened scope of authority for investigating and prosecuting the abuse of inside information.

3.1.2.2.1 Written Supervisory Procedures

All broker/dealers must establish written supervisory procedures specifically prohibiting the misuse of inside information. Additionally, they must establish policies that restrict the passing of potentially material, nonpublic information between a firm's departments. This barrier against the free flow of sensitive information is known as a Chinese wall or firewall.

3.1.2.2.2 Blue Sheets

In initiating an investigation into possible insider trading, the SEC will send Blue Sheets to member firms that have customers who may be involved. If, for instance, the commission is investigating unusual trading patterns regarding ABCD common stock, the Blue Sheets will require members to provide the SEC with information on the:

- identity of customers who bought or sold the common stock during a certain period;
- number of shares bought or sold;
- exact timing of these purchases or sales;
- transactions in derivative securities such as options; and
- home addresses and phone numbers of the customers making these transactions.

Failure to provide this information to the SEC on a timely basis will subject the member to serious disciplinary action.

3.1.2.2.3 Civil Liability

If the SEC determines that a person has violated the Insider Trading Act, it may seek a civil penalty against that person in a US district court. The maximum penalty is three times profits made or losses avoided (treble damages). If that person is an employee of a member firm, the member firm (which is supposed to have procedures in place to prevent this) could be fined up to treble damages or $1 million, whichever is greater.

Criminal penalties can be up to $5 million and 20 years in prison.

TAKE NOTE

Any fines levied for insider-trading violations must be paid to the US Treasury.

3.1.2.2.4 Statute of Limitations

A lawsuit can be brought in court by anyone who, at the same time, bought (if the insider sold) or sold (if the insider bought) securities of the same class. The suit may be initiated up to five years after the violation, and the damages imposed under a lawsuit of this kind can go up to three times profits made or losses avoided by the insider.

The SEC, in its sole discretion, is permitted to pay bounties to informants in insider trading cases. The total amount of the bounty that may be paid from a civil penalty cannot exceed 10% of that penalty.

3. 1. 2. 3 Fiduciary Information

During the course of business, employees of member firms will have access to proprietary information regarding individual customers and securities issuers.

Such information must be treated with strict confidentiality.

3. 1. 2. 4 Confidentiality of Customer Information

Broker/dealer and investment adviser employees may not divulge any personal information about customers without a customer's express permission. This includes security positions, personal and financial details, and trading intentions.

3. 1. 2. 4. 1 Confidentiality of Issuer Information

When a member broker/dealer serves an issuer as a paying agent, a transfer agent, or an underwriter or in another similar capacity, the member has established a fiduciary relationship with that issuer and so may obtain confidential information. The member may not use the information it obtains through its fiduciary role unless the securities issuer specifically asks and authorizes the member to do so.

3. 1. 2. 4. 2 Artificial Transactions

Transactions intended to portray an artificial market for a stock are strictly prohibited. These transactions are sometimes called matching or matched buy-sell orders.

3. 1. 2. 5 Selling Away—Private Securities Transactions

FINRA defines a private securities transaction as any sale of securities outside an associated person's regular business and his employing member. Private securities transactions are known as selling away.

3. 1. 2. 5. 1 Notification

An associated person who wishes to enter into a private securities transaction must:

- provide prior written notice to his employer;
- describe in detail the proposed transaction;
- describe in detail his proposed role in the transaction; and
- disclose if he has or may receive compensation for the transaction.

If the associated person wishes to enter into the transaction or business activity for compensation, the employing member may approve or disapprove the associated person's participation. If the member approves the participation, it must treat the transaction as if it is being done on its own behalf by entering the transaction on its own books and supervising the associated person during the transaction. If the member disapproves the transaction, the associated person may not participate in it.

If the associated person has not or will not receive compensation for the private securities transaction, the employing member must acknowledge that it has received written notification and may require the associated person to adhere to specified conditions during his participation.

Transactions that the associated person enters into on behalf of immediate family members and for which the associated person receives no compensation are excluded from the definition of private securities transactions. Also excluded are personal transactions in investment company and variable annuity securities.

3. 1. 2. 6   Restrictions for Associated Persons Purchasing IPOs

FINRA prohibits member firms from selling a new issue to any account in which restricted persons are beneficial owners. Restricted persons are defined as:

- member firms;
- employees of members;
- finders and fiduciaries acting on behalf of the managing underwriter, including attorneys;
- accountants and financial consultants;
- portfolio managers, including any person who has the authority to buy or sell securities for a bank, savings and loan association, insurance company, investment adviser or collective investment partnership, investment corporation, venture capital funds, or any other vehicle engaged primarily in the purchase or sale of securities; and
- any person owning 10% or more of a member firm.

Any immediate family member of any person listed here is also restricted. Immediate family includes parents, in-laws, spouses, siblings, children, or any other individual to whom the person provides material support.

EXAMPLE   Aunts, uncles, and grandparents are not considered immediate family. If, however, one of these individuals lives in the same household as a restricted person, that individual is a restricted person.

There is an exemption granted to employees of a limited business broker/dealer, which is defined as a firm engaged solely in the purchase and sale of investment company/variable contract securities, direct participation program securities, or both.

 TAKE NOTE   This exemption only applies to employees of a limited business firm, not the firm itself.

3. 1. 2. 7   Use of Manipulative, Deceptive, or Other Fraudulent Devices

The Conduct Rules and the laws of most states require broker/dealers, registered representatives, and investment advisers to inquire into a customer's financial situation before making any recommendation to buy, sell, or exchange securities. This includes determining the client's other security holdings, income, expenses, and financial goals and objectives.

The following activities violate the fair dealing rules:

- Recommending any investment unsuitable for the customer's financial situation and risk tolerance
- Short-term trading of mutual funds
- Setting up fictitious accounts to transact business that otherwise would be prohibited
- Making unauthorized transactions or use of funds
- Recommending purchases that are inconsistent with the customer's ability to pay
- Committing fraudulent acts, such as forgery or the omission or misstatement of material facts

FINRA member firms are strictly prohibited from using manipulative, deceptive, or other fraudulent tactics or methods to induce a security's sale or purchase. The statute of limitations under the Securities Exchange Act of 1934 is three years from the alleged violation and within one year of its discovery. No dollar limit is placed on damages in lawsuits based on allegations of manipulation.

QUICK QUIZ 3.A

1. Regarding the civil penalties that may be imposed for insider trading violations under the Securities Exchange Act of 1934, which of the following statements is NOT true?

   A. A civil penalty may be imposed only on a person who is registered under a securities act.

   B. The violation for which a penalty may be imposed is defined as buying or selling securities while in possession of material, nonpublic information.

   C. The SEC may ask a court to impose a penalty of up to 3 times the loss avoided or profit gained on an illegal transaction.

   D. Improper supervision may cause a broker/dealer firm to be liable for a penalty payment if one of its representatives commits an insider trading violation.

2. For purposes of insider trading, which of the following are considered insiders?

   I. Attorney who writes an offering circular for a company

   II. Bookkeeper in a company's accounting department

   III. Wife of a company's president

   IV. Brother of a company's president

   A. I and II

   B. I and III

   C. III and IV

   D. I, II, III and IV

Quick Quiz answers can be found at the end of the unit.

3. 1. 2. 8 Prohibitions Against Improper Use of Customer's Securities or Funds

An example of improper use of a customer's funds is when funds are not used as intended by a customer of the firm. Improper use of a customer's funds often includes conversion (i.e., when a registered representative uses the funds for his own use without authorization and fails to repay the customer). FINRA has consistently held that failing to return a customer's funds constitutes misuse of funds and violates the rule requiring high standards of commercial honor.

This may happen when a representative has a personal relationship with a customer. Failing to make earnest, timely efforts to return any customer's funds because of a personal relationship is a serious infraction of the high standards rule. All customers need to receive equal treatment. Friendship is no excuse for not using funds as the customer intended.

3. 1. 2. 9 Guarantees and Sharing in Customer Accounts

Broker/dealers, investment advisers, and registered representatives may not guarantee any customer against a loss or guarantee a gain. Members, advisers, and representatives are also prohibited from sharing in profits or losses in a customer's account. An exception is made if a joint account has received the member firm's prior written approval and the registered representative shares in the profits and losses only to the extent of his proportionate contribution to the joint account. The firm may share in a loss if the loss was due to an error by the firm.

If the member firm authorizes such a shared account, any such sharing must be directly proportionate to the financial contributions each party makes. If a member or an associated person shares an account with a member of that person's immediate family, directly proportionate sharing of profits and losses is not mandatory.

Immediate family members include parents, mother-in-law or father-in-law, husband or wife, children, and any relative to whom the officer or employee in question contributes financial support.

TAKE NOTE

An agent may share in an account with a customer if the agent has written consent from both the customer and the employing firm and shares in profits and losses proportionate to his contribution. In this situation, it is permissible to commingle agent and customer funds. A firm and a customer may never have a joint account.

3. 1. 2. 10 Prohibition Against Paying Commissions to Unregistered Persons

Member firms can only grant concessions, discounts, and other allowances to other members. Nonmember firms, including suspended members, always buy at the public price, never at a discount. In general, nonmembers are treated as members of the general public. However there is one exception: foreign nonmember firms, which, for whatever reason, are ineligible for membership, may be granted concessions, discounts, or other allowances, provided they agree to abide by FINRA.

Similarly, members may not pay a commission to a nonmember for executing an over-the-counter trade in a nonexempt security. Commissions, however, may be paid to nonmembers for executing trades in exempt securities or to nonmembers executing trades on an exchange floor.

Also, member firms, when organizing a group to underwrite nonexempt securities, can only invite other members into the syndicate or selling group. However, when it comes to exempt securities such as municipal bonds, nonmembers such as banks can be part of the underwriting group.

A suspended member cannot be part of a group underwriting nonexempt securities.

TAKE NOTE   Suspended members cannot be a part of an underwriting syndicate for nonexempt securities, even if the member's suspension period would end before the effective date of the offering.

3. 1. 2. 11 Continuing Commissions

A registered person who leaves a member firm (e.g., upon retirement) may continue to receive commissions on business placed while employed. There must, however, be a contract to this effect before the representative leaves the firm. Heirs of a deceased representative may receive continuing commissions if this is part of the written agreement.

There is no requirement for members to pay continuing commissions. Continuing commissions may never be paid on business referred or introduced by an employee after that person ceases to be registered with the member.

3. 2 RELATIONSHIPS AND DEALINGS WITH CUSTOMERS, VENDORS, AND ASSOCIATED PERSONS

3. 2. 1   METHODS OF COMMUNICATIONS

In addition to any written or electronic communication prepared for a single customer, the definition of correspondence also includes group correspondence, which is form letters and group email sent to fewer than 25 prospective or existing retail customers within any 30-calendar-day period.

Prior principal approval is not required for correspondence, including group correspondence, although firms may elect to review and approve all correspondence before distribution. Member firms that do not preapprove correspondence must educate and train their representatives as to FINRA rules on public communications and document this training in writing. Firms must have procedures in place for a postdistribution review of at least some of each representative's correspondence to ensure adherence to FINRA rules.

With regard to incoming correspondence, firms can elect to do a predistribution review or a postdistribution review. If a firm elects the latter, it must take steps to ensure that proper procedures are followed if any incoming mail contains either a customer complaint or customer funds or securities.

TEST TOPIC ALERT Prior principal approval is not required for incoming or outgoing customer correspondence. If a firm does not review correspondence before distribution, it must have procedures in place to perform a postdistribution review. A file of all correspondence must be retained for three years.

3. 2. 1. 1 Advertising and Sales Literature

Advertising includes copy and support graphics intended for use in public media. Examples include the following:

- Website operated by the member
- Newspapers, magazines, or other periodicals
- Radio or television
- Prerecorded telephone marketing messages and tape recordings
- Videotape displays
- Signs or billboards
- Motion pictures and filmstrips
- Telephone directories (other than routine listings)
- Any other use of the public media

Sales literature is any written or electronic communication, not using public media, that is distributed to customers or to the general public. Examples include the following:

- Performance reports or summaries
- Circulars
- Research reports
- Market letters
- Form letters and group email sent to 25 or more prospective or existing retail customers within any 30-calendar-day period
- Text prepared and used for educational seminars
- Telemarketing scripts
- Reprints or excerpts from any advertisement, sales literature, or published news item or article that are not independently prepared

3. 2. 1. 2 Approval and Recordkeeping

Advertising and sales literature must be approved by a principal before use. With the exception of options communications, a general securities principal must review all public communications.

Copies of any advertising or sales literature must be retained for three years from last use. The file must include the name of the principal who approved the communication and the date approval was given.

3. 2. 1. 3   Filing Requirements

Advertising and sales literature relating to investment companies, direct participation programs, and government securities must be filed with FINRA within 10 days of first use (postfiling).

Options advertising is limited to:

- a general description of the security being offered and its issuer, the Options Clearing Corporation;
- a description of the nature and functions of the options markets; and
- the name and address of the person at the member firm placing the advertisement from whom a current OCC Disclosure Booklet may be obtained.

For member firms that have not filed advertisements with FINRA, prefiling is required for the initial advertisement, and prefiling must continue for one year. Once a year has elapsed since the initial filing, prefiling is not required except for options and certain investment company material.

All advertisements and sales literature for investment companies that include a ranking or comparison that is generally not published, or is the creation of the investment company or the member, must be filed at least 10 days before first use. If the ranking or comparison is generally published or is the creation of an independent entity (e.g., Lipper, Morningstar®), the basic filing rules for investment companies apply (within 10 days of first use [postfiling]).

All advertisements and sales literature for investment companies that contain bond fund volatility rating must be prefiled.

Any advertising or sales literature provided to a member by an investment company is not subject to filing by the member. In this case, it is the investment company's responsibility to see that a proper filing has been made.

If FINRA believes that a member's advertising or sales literature has departed from acceptable standards, it can mandate prefiling of any communications with the public.

TAKE NOTE   All filings with FINRA's Advertising Regulation Department must include the actual or anticipated date of first use, the name and title of the principal who approved the advertising or sales literature, and the date the approval was given.

TEST TOPIC ALERT   Questions may require you to distinguish between prefiling and postfiling of advertising and sales literature.

3. 2. 1. 4   Advertising and Sales Literature Filing Requirements

Advertisements and sales literature filed 10 days before use	Advertisements and sales literature filed within 10 days of use
CMOs; options	Investment company material
Security futures	DPPs
Investment company material that includes rankings created by the member or rankings that are not generally recognized	Government securities

3. 2. 1. 4. 1   Exceptions to Filing Requirements

The following types of advertisements or sales literature are excluded from filing requirements:

- Those relating solely to changes in a member's name, personnel, location, ownership, business structure, officers or partners, phone, fax, or teletype numbers, or to mergers involving and/or acquisitions by another member
- Those identifying only a member's Nasdaq symbol or the Nasdaq symbol and security in which the member makes a market
- Those identifying only the member and/or offering a security at a stated price
- Those for internal distribution only and not distributed to the public
- Those prepared by mutual fund underwriters and used without material change

Also excluded from the filing requirements are prospectuses, preliminary prospectuses, tombstones, offering circulars, and similar documents used in connection with an offering of securities filed with the SEC.

3. 2. 1. 5   Institutional Material

Communications that are distributed only to institutional investors are not subject to preuse approval by a principal or any filing requirements with FINRA. Institutional sales material is subject to the same supervision and review requirements applicable to correspondence (i.e., it can be reviewed by a principal after distribution). However, there is one exception: if a member has reason to believe that any institutional sales material will be made available to retail customers, it must be treated as sales literature subject to preuse approval.

 EXAMPLE   A member distributes sales material to a 401(k) plan administrator (an institution). If the firm believes that the material will be distributed to participants in the plan (retail customers), it must treat the material as sales literature.

3. 2. 1. 6   Public Appearance

Public appearances include participation in a seminar, forum (including an interactive electronic forum such as an Internet chat room), radio or TV interview, or other public appearance or public speaking activity in which a research analyst offers an opinion on an equity security.

Scripted presentation used in a public appearance, as well as the appearance itself, requires prior principal approval. Copies of these scripts, including the names of the persons who prepared and approved the material, must be maintained for three years.

3. 2. 1. 7 Independently Prepared Reports

As noted earlier, reprints or excerpts from any advertisement, sales literature, or published news items or articles are considered sales literature and are subject to preuse approval by a principal and, if applicable, filing with FINRA. An independently prepared reprint is any article reprint prepared by an independent publisher and not materially altered by the member firm (other than to correct factual errors). An independent publisher is one who is not an affiliate of the member firm or is not an underwriter of any security mentioned in the reprint. Independently prepared reprints require preuse approval by a principal to ensure accuracy of the reprint but are not subject to any filing requirements with FINRA.

3. 2. 1. 8 Instant Messaging

A form of electronic communication with the public is instant messaging. Depending on its use, it can be considered individual correspondence or group correspondence, neither of which requires prior principal approval. It can also be considered sales literature, which does require prior principal approval. FINRA requires that if firms permit instant messaging, they must use a platform that enables members to monitor, archive, and retrieve message traffic. Copies of message traffic must be kept for three years.

3. 2. 2 GIFTS AND GRATUITIES

Persons associated with a member are prohibited from giving or accepting gifts or gratuities in excess of $100 per person per year, where the gift or gratuity is related to services provided by the member. This prohibition pertains to gifts given to or received from customers as well as to or from employees of other member firms.

The prohibitions in Rule 3220 do not apply to personal gifts, such as wedding gifts, or to promotional items of de minimis value, such as pens or modest desk ornaments. Furthermore, FINRA does not apply this rule to Lucite tombstones given to commemorate business transactions, such as an underwriting, even when the cost of such items exceeds $100.

Members are required to have systems and procedures in place to ensure that gifts given in relation to the business of the member are reported to the firm, are reviewed for compliance with the rule, and are maintained in the firm's records.

TAKE NOTE   Gifts given by a member to its employees are not covered by this rule.

3. 2. 2. 1 Contracts

The limitations of FINRA Rule 3220 do not apply to contracts of employment in which compensation is paid. For instance, a member could hire, on a temporary basis, administrative employees of another member firm as long as a written agreement that spells out the nature of the employment and the compensation arrangement is in place between the member firm and the persons to be employed.

The written consent of each person's employing firm is also required. Permission of FINRA to enter into contracts with employees of another member is not required. Records of these contracts, as well as of gifts made or received, must be retained for three years.

3. 2. 2. 2   Media

Similarly, FINRA prohibits member firms from giving anything of value to any person to influence the publication in any media of information intended to affect the market price of any security.

3. 2. 2. 3   Noncash Compensation

FINRA is concerned about the potential conflicts of interest created when program sponsors, such as investment companies, provide incentives or rewards to representatives for selling the sponsor's products. These incentives are in the form of noncash compensation; an occasional meal or a ticket to a sporting event or the theatre is acceptable as long as it is not conditioned on the achievement of a sales target. Payment or reimbursement by sponsors in connection with meetings held to train or educate representatives is acceptable as long as:

- the representative obtains the member's permission to attend;
- the location of the meeting is appropriate to the purpose of the meeting (e.g., an office of the sponsor or the member would be appropriate; a meeting held at the Atlantis Hotel in the Bahamas is not);
- there is no payment or reimbursement for a guest (e.g., a spouse) of the representative attending the meeting;
- payment or reimbursement is not conditioned on the achievement of a sales target;
- there is no payment or reimbursement for certain expenses incurred in connection with meetings such as golf outings, cruises, tours, and similar types of entertainment; and
- the member firm creates a record of all noncash compensation received by its representatives as well as the details of the meeting.

3. 2. 3   POLITICAL CONTRIBUTIONS

The **Municipal Securities Rulemaking Board (MSRB)** was established as an SRO to enact and interpret rules relating to the underwriting and trading of municipal securities as well as advising municipal issuers. The MSRB has no enforcement capability. The SRO that enforces MSRB rules for virtually all municipal brokers or dealers is FINRA.

One MSRB rule that FINRA, in auditing member firms, will always review is **Rule G-37**. This rule, called the play for pay rule, deals with the influence of political contributions on the selection of underwriters. The rule focuses on:

- negotiated underwritings in which a municipal issuer selects an underwriter and negotiates a deal; and
- financial advisory work in which a municipal issuer selects a municipal firm to help it structure a new issue.

The rule does not apply to competitive underwritings in which syndicates bid on a proposed new issue. In this instance, the winning bid is the one that provides the issuer with the lowest net interest cost. Competitive underwritings cannot be influenced by political contributions made by municipal firms to officials of an issuer.

Rule G-37 prohibits municipal firms from engaging in municipal securities business (negotiated underwritings/financial advisory work) with an issuer for two years after a contribution is made to an official of that issuer by:

- the municipal firm;
- a municipal finance professional (MFP) associated with the firm; or
- any political action committee (PAC) controlled by the firm.

An MFP is an associated person of a FINRA member firm engaged in municipal securities underwriting, trading, sales, financial advisory, research, investment advice, or any other activities that involve communication with public investors. Associated persons whose activities are limited solely to sales with natural persons and clerical or ministerial functions are not MFPs.

Contributions of up to $250 per election are permitted to be made by municipal finance professionals (registered persons) eligible to vote for that official. The $250 de minimis exemption does not apply to contributions made by municipal firms.

FORM G-37

 MSRB

Name of dealer: _____

Report period: _____

I. CONTRIBUTIONS made to issuer officials (list by state)

State

Complete name, title (including any city/county/state or other political subdivision) of issuer official

Contributions by each contributor category (*i.e.,* dealer, dealer controlled PAC, municipal finance professional controlled PAC, municipal finance professionals and non-MFP executive officers). For each contribution, list contribution amount and contributor category (For example, $500 contribution by non-MFP executive officer)

If any contribution is the subject of an automatic exemption pursuant to Rule G-37(j), list amount of contribution and date of such automatic exemption.

II. PAYMENTS made to political parties of states or political subdivisions (list by state)

State

Complete name (including any city/county/state or other political subdivision) of political party

Payments by each contributor category (*i.e.,* dealer, dealer controlled PAC, municipal finance professional controlled PAC, municipal finance professionals and non-MFP executive officers). For each payment, list payment amount and contributor category (For example, $500 payment by non-MFP executive officer)

TAKE ✓ NOTE

If a municipal finance professional makes a contribution that triggers a two-year prohibition and then leaves to join another firm, the time remaining on the prohibition carries over to the new firm. Both firms would serve out the balance of the prohibition time remaining.

Quarterly reports must be filed with the MSRB on Form G-37 detailing all contributions made by the dealer and its professionals during the preceding quarter. These reports must be filed by the last day of the month following the end of each calendar quarter.

Once an election is over, an incumbent may solicit contributions to extinguish campaign debt. If the incumbent has lost the election and is out of office, that person is no longer an issuer official. Therefore, G-37 does not apply. An MFP, in this case, may contribute an unlimited amount.

3. 3 CUSTOMER PRIVACY

Regulation SP, mandated by the Gramm-Leach-Bliley Act, requires that firms have adequate safeguards in the form of privacy policies to protect nonpublic personal information from unauthorized access or use. Member firms must provide an initial privacy notice to new customers when an account is opened and must provide an annual privacy notice to all customers. Regulation SP permits firms to disclose nonpublic personal information to unaffiliated third parties unless the customer has elected to opt out of the disclosure. Examples of nonpublic personal information include a customer's Social Security number, account balances, transaction history, and any information collected through an Internet cookie.

Regulation SP distinguishes between a consumer and a customer. A **consumer** is an individual who obtains a financial product or service from a firm and has no further contact with the firm. A **customer** is an individual who has an ongoing relationship with a firm. Consumers are given an initial privacy notice only, while customers must be given both an initial and annual privacy notice.

Regulation SP also requires members to adopt policies and procedures that address the protection of customer information and records. Recent technological advancements, such as Wireless Fidelity (Wi-Fi), present confidentiality issues for firms. The first is that data are broadcast out into the airwaves, making interception easier. Another issue raised by the use of Wi-Fi is that wireless connections present an attractive mechanism for hackers to tap into the user's workstation to gain access to the corporate network. Before permitting brokers to access customer information remotely, members must implement appropriate measures to secure customer information.

3. 4 ESCALATING COMPLAINTS AND/OR POTENTIAL RED FLAGS

Whenever a customer complaint is received or a potential red flag for a customer or account is identified, it is essential that the proper personnel are notified. Persons who should be notified may include the account's representative, the account's principal, the branch manager, or a member of the compliance department. Generally, a principal will need to address these concerns.

3. 4. 1 COMPLAINTS

A complaint is defined as a written statement by a customer (or a person acting on behalf of a customer) alleging a grievance arising out of, or in connection with, a securities transaction.

TAKE NOTE   Under NYSE rules, a complaint can be either written or verbal.

If a complaint is resolved to the satisfaction of both the member firm and the customer, no further action is needed.

If it cannot be resolved, it must be referred to FINRA's director of arbitration. If the complaint involves allegations of theft, misappropriation of funds or securities, or forgery, the member must immediately report this to FINRA within 10 business days.

3. 4. 1. 1   Recordkeeping

Copies of all customer complaints must be maintained in a file at the supervising OSJ. Each complaint in the file must be accompanied by a statement of its resolution and be endorsed by a principal. Member firms must electronically file information on all customer complaints with FINRA. These filings must be made within 15 days of the end of each calendar quarter.

TEST TOPIC ALERT   Copies of customer complaints, as well as the quarterly filings, must be retained for three years.

---

3. 4. 2   RED FLAGS

FINRA expects member firms to detect or investigate "red flags" that alert the firm to improper use of customer funds. Exception reports may be generated to indicate red flags, such as conflicting information in new account applications and suspicious transfers of funds between unrelated accounts. The broker/dealer is expected to implement reasonable systems and controls regarding the supervisory review of customer accounts to thwart, among other things, the falsification of new account applications and other records to take advantage of vulnerable customers.

3. 4. 2. 1   Examples of Red Flags

There is no end to the number of red flags and combinations of red flags, but just a very small sampling might include:

- suspicious activity involving transfers and disbursements in customer accounts;
- activity in the account of a deceased person; and
- excessive customer complaints.

An additional example of a red flag would be an exception report that highlights two address discrepancies in the customer's account documents, where the street address does not correspond to the city and zip code provided for the address and the telephone prefix does not match the zip code of the address.

TAKE NOTE

> Red flags are generally detected through exception reports. These reports can be either manually or automatically generated using predefined criteria the firm uses as a red flag (such as the examples listed previously). Exception reports are frequently used by managers and the compliance department to assess potential risks.

3. 5 BROKER-DEALER SUPERVISION AND CONTROL

3. 5. 1   KEY CONTROLS AND THE SEPARATION/SEGREGATION OF DUTIES

3. 5. 1. 1   Segregation of Functions and Supervision Among Departments

While departments may need to work together in order to effectively accomplish their duties, segregation occasionally needs to be enforced between departments, especially in connection with supervision. For instance, an employee or manager of the investment banking department may not supervise anyone from the research department because the supervisor would be in a position to penalize a research analyst for publishing a negative research report on a client of the investment banking department.

3. 5. 1. 2   Information Barriers

Information barriers, or Chinese walls, are frequently implemented between departments, occasionally due to regulatory requirements. For example, an information barrier must be implemented between a firm's investment banking and research departments. Collaboration between the two may cause a conflict where the research analyst is exposed to material, nonpublic information from an investment banker, or a research analyst may receive pressure to give a company a positive review simply because the company is a client of the investment banking department.

3. 5. 1. 3   Access to Facilities, Files, and Systems

Access to the firm's facilities, files, databases, and systems must be controlled to ensure data privacy. This includes restricting access for potential thieves as well as unauthorized firm employees. Access can be controlled through entitlement policies, such as entitlements linked to a login username and password, as well as security keys for access to the firm's physical facilities.

While the means of preventing the unauthorized access to firm's information and equipment may differ among firms, all firms have the responsibility of securing these items and documenting the methods to ensure the security in its written supervisory procedures.

3. 5. 2   WRITTEN SUPERVISORY PROCEDURES (WSPs)

Each member firm must adopt written supervisory procedures to ensure that the firm and its employees are in compliance with its SRO (Self Regulatory Organization) and SEC rules. Further, each member must attest annually to FINRA, by April 1 of each year, that it has adopted and implemented these procedures. The annual attestation must be made by a senior officer of the member and must specifically address compliance with all rules appertaining to the business lines of that particular broker/dealer.

Although the WSPs must be attested to annually, they are updated as often as needed to account for new rules, interpretations of rules, added or removed lines of business, or alterations to the membership agreement with FINRA.

A copy of the member's written supervisory procedures and a copy of the *FINRA Manual* must be kept in each office of supervisory jurisdiction and at each location where supervisory activities are conducted. Further, a copy of the *FINRA Manual* must be made available to customers on request. Electronic access to the *FINRA Manual* will also satisfy the requirement.

3. 5. 3   BUSINESS CONTINUITY PLAN (BCP)

FINRA requires each member to create and maintain a business continuity plan to deal with the possibility of a significant business disruption. Firms must designate a member of senior management who is also a principal to approve the plan and be responsible for updating the plan where appropriate and, at a minimum, conducting an annual review of the plan.

The plan must address, at a minimum, the following:

- Data backup and recovery (hard copy and electronic)
- Alternate communications between the firm and its customers
- Alternate communications between the firm and its employees
- Alternate physical location of employees
- Communications with regulators
- How the firm will ensure customers prompt access to their funds and securities in the event the firm is unable to continue its business

Further, a firm must disclose to its customers how it will respond to events of varying scope. This disclosure must be made, in writing, to customers at account opening, posted on the firm's Website, and mailed to customers on request.

FINRA requires firms to provide FINRA with the names of two emergency contact persons whom FINRA may contact in the event of a significant business disruption. Each person must be a principal and a member of senior management.

The rules require firms to update the contact information promptly but in no event later than 30 days following any change. Further, firms must review and, if necessary, update the information within 17 business days after the end of each calendar year.

UNIT TEST

1. Registered persons must undergo firm element continuing education at least
   A. annually
   B. every 2 years
   C. every 3 years
   D. every 5 years

2. A registered representative makes a one-time $200 donation to a mayoral candidate in the city where he lives and underwrites the city's bonds. This activity is
   A. not allowed because the donation exceeds $100
   B. not allowed because it is a political donation in a municipality where the firm conducts underwriting business
   C. is allowed with notice to the SEC
   D. is allowed with notice to the MSRB

3. A registered person engages in conversation concerning a stock on an open Internet chat room. This communication is considered
   A. advertizing
   B. sales literature
   C. public appearance
   D. private communications

4. Privacy disclosures must be sent to customers at least
   A. monthly
   B. semiannually
   C. annually
   D. every 2 years

5. Which of the following is a potential red flag?
   A. A customer requests a check for his account's balance
   B. A customer received a wire of $3,000
   C. A customer sends a foreign 3rd-party wire of $4,000
   D. A customer asks the broker/dealer to hold his mail for 2 months

6. A firm's business continuity plan (BCP) must address all the following EXCEPT
   A. data recovery
   B. death of an owner
   C. communication with regulators
   D. communication with inactive customers

7. When a firm receives a complaint, the complaint must be
   I. resolved internally or sent to the director of arbitration
   II. resolved within 10 days
   III. retained for 3 years
   IV. retained for 6 years
   A. I and III
   B. I and IV
   C. II and III
   D. II and IV

8. All the following are restricted from purchasing IPOs EXCEPT
   A. registered persons from an uninterested broker/dealer
   B. an independent grandparent of a registered representative
   C. 25% passive owner of a broker/dealer
   D. a spouse of the underwriter's accountant

9. A manager in the underwriting department may NOT
   A. supervise a research analyst who covers a firm unaffiliated with the investment banking department
   B. review a research report for factual errors
   C. sit on the firm's board of directors
   D. be paid commission on investment banking business

10. During a lunch, XYZ Inc's CEO states to a registered representative that the company is in secret negotiations to triple sales with a new client. If the registered representative then purchases shares of XYZ stock, who has broken insider trading laws?

   I. The registered representative
   II. The CEO
   III. The registered representative's principal
   IV. The registered representative's member firm
   A. I only
   B. I and II
   C. I, II and III
   D. I, II, III and IV

ANSWERS AND RATIONALES

1. **A.** Registered persons must undergo an in-house (firm element) continuing education course at least annually. Regulatory element continuing education is required 3 years after their initial registration and every subsequent 2 years.

2. **D.** The registered representative is permitted to make political contributions of up to $250 to a candidate in a municipality where the representative is eligible to vote. This de minimis contribution is available only available to the representative and must be included on a quarterly report of contributions to the MSRB.

3. **C.** When a registered person engages in a public discussion regarding a security on an open chat room, the communication is considered a public appearance under FINRA rules and must be approved in advance by a principal.

4. **C.** A privacy statement must be sent to each customer at least annually.

5. **C.** Sending foreign 3rd-party wires triggers a red flag for potential money laundering. While the transaction does not require the filing of a CTR or SAR, it should be flagged for review.

6. **B.** Business continuity plans need not address the death of an owner. They must, however, address communication with all customers (regardless of activity), employees, and regulators. Additionally, they must address back-up operations and recovery of data.

7. **A.** All customer complaints need to first attempt to be resolved internally. If resolution is not possible, the complaint is required to be sent to the FINRA Director of Arbitration. Complaints are retained at an OSJ for 3 years.

8. **B.** Grandparents who are not supported by a restricted person do not constitute immediate family and may participate in an IPO. Restricted persons include registered persons, 10% owners of a member firm, member firms, accountants, and finders for the lead underwriter.

9. **A.** To maintain the objectivity of research analysts, members of the investment banking department may never supervise a research analyst. They may, however, review a research report for factual errors so long as all communication is made either through or in the presence of the compliance department.

10. **B.** Both the tipper (the CEO) and the tippee (the registered representative) have violated insider trading laws. The principal and member firm have not, so long as they were not informed of the inside information.

QUICK QUIZ ANSWERS

Quick Quiz 3.A

1. **A.** The penalty may be imposed on anyone who trades on inside information, not just persons registered under the act. The other statements are correct: Choice B defines insider trading, the penalty is up to three times the profit gained or loss avoided (Choice C), and an advisory firm may face a penalty for the actions of its representatives (Choice D).

2. **D.** While the Securities Exchange Act of 1934 defines an insider as an officer, a director, or a 10% stockholder of a company, the courts have broadened the definition to include anyone who has inside information.

Common Abbreviations

ADR/ADS American depository receipt (share)
AML anti-money laundering
AP associated person
BD broker/dealer
CA confidentiality agreement
CAGR compound annual growth rate
CAPM capital asset pricing model
CF cash flow
COGS cost of goods sold
DDM dividend discount model
DIP debtor in possession
DPP direct participation program
EBIT earnings before interest and taxes
EBITDA earnings before interest, taxes, depreciation, and amortization
EPS earnings per share
ESOP employee stock option plan
EV enterprise value
Fed Federal Reserve System
FINRA Financial Industry Regulatory Authority
GARP growth at a reasonable price
IPO initial public offering
IRR internal rate of return
LBO leveraged buyout
LTM last twelve months
M&A merger and acquisition
MPO member private offering

Nasdaq National Association of Securities Dealers Automated Quotation system
NAV net asset value
NYSE New York Stock Exchange, Inc.
OSJ office of supervisory jurisdiction
OTC over the counter
OTCBB Over-the-Counter Bulletin Board
P/E (price-to-earnings) ratio
PEG ratio (price-to-earnings/growth ratio)
PIPE private investment in public equity
POP public offering price
PP&E property, plant, and equipment
QIB qualified institutional buyer
REIT real estate investment trust
ROA return on assets
ROE return on equity
ROI return on investment
SEC Securities and Exchange Commission
SG&A sales, general, and admin expenses
STRIPS Separate Trading of Registered Interest and Principal of Securities
TO tender offer
TTM trailing twelve months
VC venture capital
WACC weighted average cost of capital
WKSI well-known, seasoned issuer

Glossary

Numerical

30-second update requirement Requires that market makers update their quotes to reflect customer limit orders. This must be done within 30 seconds of receiving an order under normal market conditions.

9:30X 9:30X is the time at which the primary market disseminates the first print after the 9:30 am ET market open.

12(b)-1 Fee Fee assessed shareholders by an open-ended management company for promotional expenses. The fee must be registered as such with the SEC and be disclosed to investors.

A

accredited investor As defined in Rule 502 of Regulation D, any institution or individual meeting minimum net worth requirements for the purchase of securities qualifying under the Regulation D registration exemption.

An accredited investor is generally one who:

- has a net worth of $1 million or more, excluding home equity;

- has had an annual income of $200,000 or more in each of the two most recent years (or $300,000 jointly with a spouse) and who has a reasonable expectation of reaching the same income level in the current year;

- is an officer or director of the issuer; or

- is an institutional investor.

accrued interest The interest that has accumulated since the last interest payment up to, but not including, the settlement date and that is added to the contract price of a bond transaction.

ACES *See* Advanced Computerized Execution Service.

Act of 1933 *See* Securities Act of 1933.

Act of 1934 *See* Securities Exchange Act of 1934.

active, competitive market A market where no market maker dominates trading activity and where interdealer trades occur at competitive prices.

ADF *See* alternative display facility.

administrator An official or agency that administers the securities laws of a state.

ADR (American Depositary Receipt) A security created by a US bank that evidences ownership to a specified number of shares of a foreign security held in a depositary in the country of the issuing company. ADRs are nearly identical to US securities and facilitate lower transaction costs as well as dividend distribution. Similar to GDR (Global Depositary Receipt), which is traded outside the United States.

Advanced Computerized Execution Service (ACES) A subscription service that allows order entry firms to route orders to their preferred market makers' internal trading systems.

ADTV The average daily trading volume of a security as calculated over the preceding four calendar weeks.

advertisement Any promotional material designed for use by newspapers, magazines, billboards, radio, television, telephone recording, or other public medium where the firm has little control over the type of individuals being exposed to the material.

Advertising Regulation Electronic Files (AREF) The Web-based system for filing advertising materials with FINRA is called Advertising Regulation Electronic Files (AREF).

affiliate (1) A person who directly or indirectly owns, controls, or holds with power to vote 10% or more of the outstanding voting securities of a company. (2) With respect to a direct participation program, any person who controls, is controlled by, or is under common control with the program's sponsor and includes any person who beneficially owns 50% or more of the equity interest in the sponsor. (3) Under the Investment Company Act of 1940, a person who has any type of control over an investment company's operations, which includes anyone with 5% or more of the outstanding voting securities of the investment company or any corporation of which the investment company holds 5% or more of outstanding securities. *See also* control person; insider.

agency basis *See* agency transaction.

agency transaction A transaction in which a broker/dealer acts for the accounts of others by buying or selling securities on behalf of customers. *Syn.* agency basis.

agent (1) An individual or firm that effects securities transactions for the accounts of others. (2) A person licensed by a state as a life insurance agent. (3) A securities salesperson who represents a broker/dealer or issuer when selling or trying to sell securities to the investing public.

algorithmic trading Algorithmic trading is making use of computer programs for entering orders. The algorithm, usually proprietary, has a set of automatic responses to many complex market conditions. Depending on the circumstances, the algorithm will generate low latency orders. *Syn.* algo trading, black-box trading.

alternative display facility (ADF) A display-only facility that is operated by FINRA. The ADF provides FINRA members with a facility for the display of quotes (best bid and offer), trade reports, and the comparison of trades. CQS-listed securities, as well as Nasdaq-listed securities, are eligible for posting quotations through the ADF. ADF does not provide automated order routing functionality, execution facilities, or linkages between ADF trading centers.

annuity A contract between an insurance company and an individual; it generally guarantees lifetime income to the individual on whose life the contract is based in return for either a lump sum or a periodic payment to the insurance company. The contract holder's objective is usually retirement income.

Anti-Internalization Qualifier (AIQ) A modifier that allows market makers to execute only against the quotes of other market makers, not against their own quotes.

appreciation The increase in value of an asset.

arbitrage The simultaneous purchase and sale of the same or related securities to take advantage of a market inefficiency.

arbitrageur One who engages in arbitrage.

arbitration The arrangement whereby an SRO, or a designated arbitration association, hears and settles disagreements between members. Unresolved disputes with customers are also submitted to binding arbitration.

artificial transactions Attempts to stage a hot market for a stock; such transactions are strictly prohibited. Sometimes referred to as *wash trading* or *painting the tape*.

ask An indication by a trader or a dealer of a willingness to sell a security or a commodity; the price at which an investor can buy from a broker/dealer. *Syn.* offer.

assignee A person who has acquired a beneficial interest in a limited partnership from a third party but who is neither a substitute limited partner nor an assignee of record.

assignee of record A person who has acquired a beneficial interest in a limited partnership and whose interest has been recorded on the books of the partnership and is the subject of a written instrument of assignment.

assignment (1) A document accompanying or part of a stock certificate that is signed by the person named on the certificate for the purpose of transferring the certificate's title to another person's name. (2) The act of identifying and notifying an account holder that the option owner has exercised an option held short in that account. Related item(s): stock power.

assistant representative–order processing *See* Series 11.

associated person of a member Any employee, manager, director, officer or partner of a member broker/dealer or other entity (issuer, bank, etc.), or any person controlling, controlled by, or in common control with that member.

auction market A market in which buyers enter competitive bids and sellers enter competitive offers simultaneously. The NYSE is an auction market. *Syn.* double auction market.

Automated Confirmation Transaction Service (ACT) Compares trade information provided by market participants and submits locked-in trades for clearance and settlement. Also disseminates last sale information to the public. The FINRA/Nasdaq TRF operates on the ACT technology platform. Upload functionality for the ACT platform is available through the Nasdaq Workstation/Weblink ACT.

Automated Quotation System (Nasdaq) The Nasdaq Stock Market is a US registered stock exchange providing an automatic execution venue. Trade reporting for Nasdaq trades goes through the FINRA/Nasdaq Trade Reporting Facility (TRF).

B

back away The failure of an over-the-counter market maker to honor a firm bid and asked price; this violates Conduct Rules. *Syn.* backing away.

Bank Secrecy Act The act establishing the US Treasury Department as the lead agency for developing regulation in connection with anti-money laundering programs, which require broker/dealers to establish internal compliance procedures to detect abuses.

best execution The responsibility of the broker/dealer to seek the most favorable terms for the execution of client transactions.

bid An indication by an investor, a trader, or a dealer of a willingness to buy a security or commodity; the price at which an investor can sell to a broker/dealer.

blank-check company A company with no business plan. Investors have no knowledge as to how cash assets in the firm are to be spent. A highly speculative company that has the view to merge with or acquire another company. *See* SPAC.

blockbuster A trade that exceeds the single trade limit of a correspondent firm in the ACT system. Currently, this limit is $1,000,000. The clearing firm has 15 minutes to accept or decline the trade. If no indication is made, the clearing firm is obligated to accept the trade.

block positioners Firms defined under the SEC Rule 3b-8 as firms that purchase long or short blocks of stock worth $200,000 or more.

blue-chip stock The equity issues of financially stable, well-established companies that have demonstrated their ability to pay dividends in both good and bad times.

blue-sky To register a securities offering in a particular state.

blue-sky laws Nickname for state regulations governing the securities industry coined in the early 1900s by a Kansas Supreme Court justice who wanted regulation to protect against "speculative schemes that have no more basis than so many feet of blue sky."

bona fide quote A bid or an offer from a broker/dealer to buy or sell securities; it indicates a willingness to execute a trade under the terms and conditions accompanying the quote.

bond A legal obligation of an issuing company or government to repay the principal of a loan to bond investors at a specified future date. Corporate bonds are often issued with a par or face value of $1,000, representing the principal amount of money borrowed. The issuer promises to pay a percentage of the par value as interest on the borrowed funds.

bond quote One of a number of quotations listed in the financial press and most daily newspapers that provide representative bid prices from the previous day's bond market. Quotes for corporate and government bonds are percentages of the bonds' face values (usually $1,000). Corporate bonds are quoted in increments of 1/8, where a quote of 99 1/8 represents 99.125% of par ($1,000) or $991.25. Government bonds are quoted in 32nds. Municipal bonds may be quoted on a dollar basis or on a yield-to-maturity basis.

bond rating An evaluation of the possibility of a bond issuer's default, based on an analysis of the issuer's financial condition and likelihood of meeting all obligations. Standard & Poor's, Moody's Investors Service, and Fitch Investors Service, among others, provide bond rating services. Ratings of municipal bonds may be found on the EMMA System operated by the Municipal Securities Rulemaking Board.

book-entry security A security sold without delivery of a certificate. Evidence of ownership is maintained on records kept by a central agency; for example, the Treasury keeps records of Treasury bill purchasers. Transfer of ownership is recorded by entering the change on the books or electronic files.

bookrunning manager The investment bank responsible for the order book including the allocation of securities. The bookrunning manager's name appears above all other members of the syndicate on a tombstone advertisement. *Syn.* book runner.

branch office Any location identified by any means to the public as a place where a registered broker/dealer conducts business.

breaking the buck (or break the buck) Jargon used to describe the disturbing event of net asset value (NAV) of a money market fund falling below $1. Breaking the buck may happen if a fund leverages assets. Without outside emergency help the investors would lose money. Those investors needing added security may choose investment grade money market funds (e.g., Moody's Aaa-mf, Aa-mf), which have demonstrated a strong ability to meet the dual objectives of a money market fund of providing liquidity and preserving capital.

breakpoint The schedule of sales charge discounts offered by a mutual fund for lump-sum or cumulative investments.

breakpoint sale The sale of mutual fund shares in an amount just below the level at which the purchaser would qualify for reduced sales charges; this violates the Conduct Rules.

broker (1) An individual or firm that charges a fee or commission for executing buy and sell orders submitted by another individual or firm. (2) The role of a firm when it acts as an agent for a customer and charges the customer a commission for its services.

broker/dealer Person or firm in the business of buying and selling securities. A firm may act as both broker (agent) or dealer (principal) but not in the same transaction. Broker/dealers normally must register with the SEC, the appropriate SROs, and any state in which they do business.

bulge bracket (1) Members of an underwriting syndicate who appear on a tombstone advertisement. (2) The largest full-service broker/dealers in the world.

bulletin board *See* OTC Bulletin Board.

buy-in The procedure that the buying firm of a security follows when the selling firm fails to complete the contract by delivering the security. The buying firm closes the contract by buying the security in the open market and charging the account of the selling firm for transaction fees and any loss caused by changes in the markets.

buying power The amount of securities a margin client can buy using the special memorandum account balance and without depositing additional equity. Buying power is 2 × SMA. For pattern day traders, buying power is 4 × maintenance margin excess.

C

callable bond A type of bond issued with a provision allowing the issuer to redeem the bond prior to maturity at a predetermined price.

capping Placing selling pressure on a stock in an attempt to keep its price low or to move its price lower; this is manipulative.

cash account An account in which the customer is required by the SEC's Regulation T to pay in full for securities purchased not later than two days after the standard payment period. *Syn.* special cash account.

cashiering department Department within a brokerage firm that delivers and receives securities and money to and from other firms and clients of the firm. *Syn.* security cage.

cash settlement Requires delivery of securities from the seller and payment from the buyer on the same day the trade is executed.

cash transaction A settlement contract that calls for delivery and payment on the same day the trade is executed; payment is due by 2:30 pm ET (or within 30 minutes of the trade if made after 2:00 pm ET).

Chinese Wall A descriptive name for the division within a brokerage firm that prevents inside information from passing from corporate advisers to traders.

churning Excessive trading in a customer's account by a registered representative who ignores the customer's interests and seeks only to increase commissions.

circuit breaker halt Rule 80B of the NYSE calls for trading halts based on a decline in the DJIA.

class A share A class of mutual fund share issued with a front-end sales load. A mutual fund offers different classes of shares to allow investors to choose the type of sales charge they will pay.

class B share A class of mutual fund share issued with a back-end load. A mutual fund offers different classes of shares to allow investors to choose the type of sales charge they will pay.

class C share A class of mutual fund share issued with a level load. A mutual fund offers different classes of shares to allow investors to choose the type of sales charge they will pay.

clearing agency An intermediary (third party) between the buy and sell sides in a securities transaction that receives and delivers payments and securities. Any organization that fills this function, including a securities depository, such as the National Securities Clearing Corporation.

clearing broker/dealer A broker/dealer that clears its own trades as well as those of introducing (correspondent) brokers. A clearing broker/dealer can hold customers' securities and cash. *Syn.* carrying broker.

clearly erroneous trades Transactions in which an obvious error has occurred in the security's price, number of shares, identification, or other relevant terms. Under FINRA Rule 11890, such trades may be submitted to FINRA for review. FINRA may subsequently declare the transaction null and void, adjust the terms, or decline to act on the complaint. If a party to the trade wishes to appeal the staff determination, it may seek review by the Market Operations Review Committee (MORC).

close (1) The price of the last transaction for a particular security on a particular day. (2) The midprice of a closing trading range.

closed-end management company An investment company that issues a fixed number of shares in an actively managed portfolio of securities. The shares may be of several classes, and they are traded in the secondary marketplace, either on an exchange or over the counter. The market price of the shares is determined by supply and demand and not by NAV. *Syn.* publicly traded fund.

closing range The relatively narrow range of prices at which transactions take place in the final minutes of the trading day.

CNS *See* Continuous Net Settlement.

Code of Arbitration FINRA's formal method of handling securities-related disputes or clearing controversies between members, public customers, clearing corporations, or associated persons.

Code of Procedure (COP) FINRA's formal procedure for handling trade practice complaints involving violations of the Member Conduct Rules.

collateral Certain assets set aside and pledged to a lender for the duration of a loan. If the borrower fails to meet obligations to pay principal or interest, the lender has claim to the assets.

collateralized mortgage obligation (CMO) A mortgage-backed corporate security. Unlike pass-through obligations issued by FNMA and GNMA, its yield is not guaranteed and it does not have the backing of any agency of the federal government. These issues attempt to return interest and principal at a predetermined rate. *See also* tranche.

collect on delivery (COD) *See* delivery vs. payment.

colocation Colocation exists when a high-frequency trader sets up a trading platform (computer servers) on an exchange or in very close proximity to a market center to save a small amount of time on order execution. This small savings in time, measured in sub-milliseconds, gives the trader an advantage over those traders whose servers are in distant locations. *See* low latency.

combined account A customer account that has long and short margin positions in different securities. *Syn.* mixed account.

commercial bank An institution that is in the business of accepting deposits and making business loans. Commercial banks may not underwrite corporate securities or most municipal bonds. Related item(s): investment banker.

commercial paper An unsecured, short-term promissory note issued by a corporation for financing accounts receivable and inventories. It is usually issued at a discount reflecting prevailing market interest rates. Maturities range up to 270 days.

commingling The combining by a brokerage firm of one customer's securities with another customer's securities and pledging them as joint collateral for a bank loan; unless authorized by the customers, this violates SEC Rule 15c2-1.

commission A service charge assessed by an agent in return for arranging the purchase or sale of a security. A commission must be fair and reasonable, considering all the relevant factors of the transaction. *Syn.* sales charge.

Commodities Futures Trading Commission (CFTC) A federal government agency that regulates commodity futures and option markets.

common stock A security that represents ownership in a corporation. Holders of common stock exercise some control by electing a board of directors and voting on changes in capital structure such as a stock split.

competitive inactive markets Occurs when there are two or three nondominant market makers in a security with low trading activity. Contemporaneous sales to and purchases from other dealers are used to establish a prevailing price for markups and markdowns.

completion of the transaction The point at which a customer pays any part of the purchase price to the broker/dealer for a security he has purchased or delivers a security that he has sold. If the customer makes payment to the broker/dealer before the payment is due, the completion of the transaction occurs when the broker/dealer delivers the security into the customer's account, which is the settlement date.

compliance department The department within a brokerage firm that oversees the trading and market-making activities of the firm. It ensures that the employees and officers of the firm are abiding by the rules and regulations of the SEC, exchanges, and SROs.

confirmation A printed document that states the trade, settlement date, and money due from or owed to a customer; it is sent or given to the customer on or before the settlement date.

Consolidated Quotation System (CQS) A quotation system only providing last-sale reporting service for exchange-listed equity securities. Newly registered CQS market makers must begin entering quotes within five days.

Consolidated Tape A service of the New York Stock Exchange that delivers real-time market data to subscribers as they occur on the various exchanges. The Tape distributes reports to subscribers over two different networks that the subscribers can tap into through either the high-speed electronic or the low-speed ticker lines. Network A reports transactions in NYSE-listed securities. Network B reports AMEX-listed securities transactions and reports of transactions in regional exchange issues.

contemporaneous trader A person who enters a trade at or near the same time and in the same security as a person who has acted on inside information. The contemporaneous trader may bring suit against the inside trader.

continuing education Firm element is required for all registered persons who have direct contact with the public; it is conducted annually. Regulatory element is required for all registered persons within 120 days of second registration anniversary and every three years thereafter.

Continuous Net Settlement (CNS) An automated book-entry (no certificates) accounting system. The system provides clearance for equities, corporate and municipal bonds, UITs, and more.

control (controlling, controlled by, under common control with) The power to direct or affect the direction of the management and policies of a company, whether through the ownership of voting securities, by contract, or otherwise. Control is presumed to exist if a person, directly or indirectly, owns, controls, holds with the power to vote, or holds proxies representing more than 10% of a company's voting securities.

control of securities A term used to indicate the responsibilities of a broker/dealer with regard to securities in its possession. Under the SEC's customer protection rule, broker/dealers must maintain control over customer funds and securities. Securities are considered under the control of, or in the possession of, a broker/dealer if they are in the broker/dealer's physical possession or are in an alternative location acceptable to the SEC.

control person (1) A director, officer, or other affiliate of an issuer. (2) A stockholder who owns at least 10% of any class of a corporation's voting securities.

control security Any security owned by a director, officer, or other affiliate of the issuer or by a stockholder who owns at least 10% of any class of a corporation's outstanding securities. Who owns a security, not the security itself, determines whether it is a control security.

convertible bond A debt security, usually in the form of a debenture, that can be exchanged for equity securities of the issuing corporation at specified prices or rates.

COP *See* Code of Procedure.

coordination *See* registration by coordination.

corporate account An account held in the name of a corporation. The corporate agreement, signed when the account is opened, specifies which officers are authorized to trade in the account. In addition, a corporation must provide a copy of its charter and bylaws authorizing a margin account.

corporate securities limited representative *See* Series 62.

correspondence Communication to a single customer, to existing retail customers, or to fewer than 25 prospective retail customers in any 30-calendar-day period. Can be reviewed by a principal after use.

covenant A component of a debt issue's trust indenture that identifies bondholders' rights and other provisions. Examples include rate covenants that establish a minimum revenue coverage for a bond, insurance covenants that require insurance on a project, and maintenance covenants that require maintenance on a facility constructed by the proceeds of a bond issue.

CQS *See* Consolidated Quotation System.

credit agreement A component of a customer's margin account agreement, outlining the conditions of the credit arrangement between broker and customer.

crossed market Occurs when one market maker bids for stock at a higher price than another market maker asks for the stock.

cumulative preferred stock An equity security that offers the holder any unpaid dividends in arrears. These dividends accumulate and must be paid to the cumulative preferred stockholder before any dividends may be paid to the common stockholders. Related item(s): convertible preferred stock; noncumulative preferred stock; preferred stock.

cumulative voting A voting procedure that permits stockholders either to cast all of their votes for any one candidate or to cast their total number of votes in any proportion they choose. This results in greater representation for minority stockholders. Related item(s): statutory voting.

current market value (CMV) The worth of the securities in an account. The market value of listed and Nasdaq securities is based on the closing prices on the previous business day. *Syn.* long market value.

current report *See* Form 8K.

custodial account An account in which a custodian enters trades on behalf of the beneficial owner, often a minor.

custodian An institution or person responsible for making all investment, management, and distribution decisions in an account maintained in the best interests of another. Mutual funds have custodians responsible for safeguarding certificates and performing clerical duties.

customer Any person who opens a trading account with a broker/dealer. A customer may be classified in terms of account ownership, trading authorization, payment method, or types of securities traded.

customer agreement (margin agreement) A document that a customer must sign when opening a margin account with a broker/dealer; it allows the firm to liquidate all or a portion of the account if the customer fails to meet a margin call.

customer ledger The accounting record that lists separately all customer cash and margin accounts carried by a firm.

customer limit order protection *See* Manning Rule.

customer protection rule *See* Rule 15c3-3.

customer statement A document showing a customer's trading activity, positions, and account balance. The SEC requires that customer statements be sent at least quarterly.

D

dated date The date on which interest on a new bond issue begins to accrue.

dealer (1) An individual or firm that is engaged in the business of buying and selling securities for its own account. (2) The role of a firm when it acts as a principal and charges the customer a markup or markdown. *Syn.* principal.

debit balance The amount of money a customer owes a brokerage firm.

debt security A security representing a loan by an investor to an issuer such as a corporation, municipality, the federal government, or a federal agency. In return for the loan, the issuer promises to repay the debt on a specified date and to pay interest.

declaration date The date on which a corporation announces the amount, payment date, and record date of an upcoming dividend.

decrementation The process by which a market maker's published quote size is automatically reduced due to executions.

defined benefit plan A qualified retirement plan that specifies the total amount of money that the employee will receive at retirement.

defined contribution plan A qualified retirement plan that specifies the amount of money that the employer will contribute annually to the plan.

delivery The change in ownership or control of a security in exchange for cash. Delivery takes place on the settlement date.

delivery versus payment (DVP) A transaction settlement procedure in which securities are delivered to the buying institution's bank in exchange for payment of the amount due. *Syn.* collect on delivery (COD).

derivative An investment vehicle, the value of which is based on the value of another security. Futures, forwards, swaps, and options are among the most common types of derivatives. Derivatives are generally used by institutional investors to increase overall portfolio return or to hedge portfolio risk.

designated market maker (DMM) A member of the NYSE or NYSE Amex that is held accountable for maintaining a fair and orderly market. They must, among other things, quote at the NBBO a certain percentage of the time and facilitate price discovery through the trading day, at the open and close and during periods of significant order imbalance.

direct participation program (DPP) A business organized so as to pass all income, gains, losses, and tax benefits to its owners (partners), the investors; the business is usually structured as a limited partnership. Examples include oil and gas programs, real estate programs, agricultural programs, motion pictures, and cattle programs. *Syn.* program.

discretion Authority given to someone other than the beneficial owner of an account to make investment decisions for the account concerning the security, the number of shares or units, and whether to buy or sell. The authority to decide only timing or price does not constitute discretion.

discretionary account An account in which the customer has given the registered representative authority to enter transactions at the representative's discretion.

display rule SEC rule that requires that a market maker immediately publish and display in its quotation the price and full size of certain customer limit orders that improve its size or price.

dividend A distribution of the earnings of a corporation. Dividends may be in the form of cash, stock, or property. All dividends must be declared by the board of directors. *Syn.* stock dividend.

DJIA *See* Dow Jones Industrial Average.

DK *See* don't know.

DMM *See* designated market maker.

dominated or controlled markets A market that is strongly influenced by one or two market makers.

do not reduce order (DNR) An order that stipulates that the limit or stop price should not be reduced.

don't know (DK) A response to a comparison received from a broker/dealer indicating a lack of information about, or record of, the transaction.

Dow Jones averages The most widely quoted and oldest measures of change in stock prices. Each of the four averages is based on the prices of a limited number of stocks in a particular category.

Dow Jones Industrial Average (DJIA) The most widely used market indicator, composed of 30 large, actively traded issues of industrial stocks.

Dow Jones Transportation Average (DJTA) A market indicator composed of 20 transportation stocks.

Dow Jones Utilities Average (DJUA) A market indicator composed of 15 utilities stocks.

down tick *See* minus tick.

due bill A printed statement showing the obligation of a seller to deliver cash dividends to a purchaser used when a transaction settles late and after the record date.

due diligence The careful investigation by the underwriters that is necessary to ensure that all material information pertinent to an issue has been disclosed to prospective investors.

due diligence meeting A meeting at which an issuing corporation's officials and representatives of the underwriting group present information on and answer questions about a pending issue of securities. The meeting is held for the benefit of brokers, securities analysts, and institutional investors.

duplicate confirmation A copy of a customer's confirmation that a brokerage firm sends to an agent or an attorney if the customer requests it in writing. In addition, if the customer is an employee of another broker/dealer, SRO regulations may require a duplicate confirmation to be sent to the employing broker/dealer.

duration of tender offers The period for which tender offers are held open following the first publication of the offer. SEC rules require that this period be at least 20 business days.

DVP *See* delivery versus payment.

E

ECN *See* Electronic Communications Network.

effective date The date the registration of an issue of securities becomes effective, allowing the underwriters to sell the newly issued securities to the public and confirm sales to investors.

Electronic Communications Network (ECN) Any electronic trading system that widely disseminates to third parties orders entered by market makers, institutional investors, and so forth. ECNs are agency broker/dealers.

Employee Retirement Income Security Act of 1974 (ERISA) The law that governs the operation of most corporate pension and benefit plans. The law eased pension eligibility rules, set up the Pension Benefit Guaranty Corporation, and established guidelines for the management of pension funds. Corporate retirement plans established under ERISA qualify for favorable tax treatment for employers and participants. *Syn.* Pension Reform Act.

equity In a margin account, equity equals what is owned minus what is owed. Alternatively, ownership in a company.

escrow agreement The certificate provided by an approved bank that guarantees that the indicated securities are on deposit at that bank.

excess equity The value of securities in a margin account that is in excess of the federal requirement. *Syn.* margin excess; Regulation T excess.

excess margin securities The securities in a margin account that are in excess of 140% of the account's debit balance.

exchange Any organization, association, or group of persons that maintains or provides a marketplace in which securities can be bought and sold. An exchange does not have to be a physical place, and several strictly electronic exchanges do business around the world.

Exchange Act *See* Securities Exchange Act of 1934.

ex-date The first date on which a security is traded without entitling the buyer to receive distributions previously declared.

executor A person given fiduciary authorization to manage the affairs of a decedent's estate.

exempt security A security exempt from the registration requirements (although not from the antifraud requirements) of the Securities Act of 1933. Examples include US government securities and municipal securities.

exempt transaction (federal) Transactions that do not trigger a federal registration. Examples include: Regulation A offerings; Regulation S offerings; Regulation D offerings; and Rule 147 offerings.

F

fail to deliver Following a transaction the seller, whether a long sale or a short sale, is unable to deliver the securities. The fail-to-deliver is an allowable asset on the carrying broker/dealer's books subject to a haircut if aged more than four business days.

fast market An exchange or stock market experiencing extreme volatility and high share volume. This condition may be the result of positive or negative news. Not to be confused with high frequency trading (HFT).

Federal Deposit Insurance Corporation (FDIC) A federal government agency that insures deposits in banks and thrifts for $250,000 per depositor.

Federal Reserve The central bank of the United States, it regulates the monetary system. Strives for price stability and economic growth.

fictitious quotation A bid or an offer published before being identified by source and verified as legitimate. A fictitious quote may create the appearance of trading activity where none exists; this violates the Conduct Rules.

fidelity bond Insurance coverage required by self-regulatory organizations for all employees, officers, and partners of firms to protect members from employee theft. Generally, 120% times capital requirement.

fiduciary A person legally appointed and authorized to hold assets in trust for another person and manage those assets for the benefit of that person.

final prospectus The legal document that states the price of a new issue security, the delivery date, the underwriting spread, and other material information. It must be given to every investor who purchases a new issue of registered securities. *Syn.* prospectus.

Financial Industry Regulatory Authority (FINRA) The largest regulator for securities firms doing business in the United States. It oversees approximately 635,000 registered representatives. Overseen by the SEC, its primary role is to maintain the fairness of US capital markets. FINRA was preceded by NASD, which merged with most of NYSE Regulation in 2007 to form a new regulatory authority.

FINRA Rule 5130 Deals with IPOs of common stock. Defines restricted persons as member firms, employees of member firms and their immediate families, finders and fiduciaries, portfolio managers, and 10% or more owners of member firms.

firm quote The actual price at which a trading unit of a security (such as 100 shares of stock or five bonds) may be bought or sold. All quotes are firm quotes unless otherwise indicated.

5% markup policy General guideline for the percentage markup, markdown, and commissions on OTC securities transactions. The policy is intended to ensure fair and reasonable treatment of the investing public.

five-minute window The period between the time when market makers may re-enter quotations and the time when the security will be released for trading as indicated by Nasdaq Market Watch through a T3 code.

fixed annuity An insurance contract in which the insurance company makes fixed dollar payments to the annuitant for the term of the contract, usually until the annuitant dies. The insurance company guarantees both earnings and principal.

fixing Trading in a new security for the purpose of stabilizing its price above the established public offering price; this practice is prohibited. *Syn.* pegging.

foreign associate A non-US citizen employed by a FINRA member firm. Foreign associates are subject to registration but are exempt from having to pass a qualifying licensing exam.

Form 3 A legal document used by officers, directors, and principal stockholders of a corporation to file an initial statement of beneficial ownership of equity securities. The form is filed with the SEC.

Form 4 A legal document used to update Form 3 when there are changes in the beneficial ownership of a corporation. Filed within two business days of any change.

Form 8K A legal document used to report events of consequence that occur in a corporation; such events include changes in control of the corporation or in its name, address, financial standing, board of directors, or auditors. *Syn.* current report.

Form 10C A legal document used by an issuer of securities quoted on Nasdaq to report a change of more than 5% in the amount of securities it has outstanding.

Form 10K An annual audited report. A Form 10K is due within 90 days of year-end.

Form 10Q A quarterly report containing a corporation's unaudited financial data. A Form 10Q is due 45 days after the end of each of the first three fiscal quarters.

Form 13F SEC required form for investment managers who in the course of its business exercises discretion over $100 million.

Form BD The Uniform Application for Broker-Dealer Registration. Broker/dealers must file this form to register with the SEC, SROs, and states through the Central Registration Depository (CRD) system, operated by FINRA. BDs are required to promptly update Form BD whenever the form becomes inaccurate or incomplete.

Form F-6 SEC required form to register American Depositary Receipts.

Form NMA FINRA's electronic New Membership Application.

401(k) plan A tax-deferred defined contribution retirement plan offered by an employer.

403(b) plan A tax-deferred annuity retirement plan available to employees of public schools and certain nonprofit organizations.

fourth market The market where securities are traded directly from one institutional investor to another without the services of a brokerage firm. Also called the ECN market.

fraud The deliberate concealment, misrepresentation, or omission of material information or the truth, so as to deceive or manipulate another party for unlawful or unfair gain.

free credit balance The unencumbered cash funds in customer accounts. Broker/dealers are required to notify customers of their free credit balances at least quarterly and carry the credit as a liability on the broker/dealer's books.

freeriding Buying and immediately selling securities without making payment. This practice violates the SEC's Regulation T.

front running A situation in which a broker/dealer holds an unexecuted customer order to buy or sell and buys or sells for the firm's own account before placing the customer's order.

frozen account An account requiring cash in advance before a buy order is executed.

full power of attorney A written authorization for someone other than the beneficial owner of an account to make deposits and withdrawals and execute trades in the account.

fully disclosed broker *See* introducing broker.

G

general securities principal *See* Series 24.

general securities representative *See* Series 7.

give-up A process whereby an executing broker/dealer credits a trade to another broker/dealer.

good delivery A term describing a security that is negotiable, in compliance with the contract of the sale, and ready to be transferred from seller to purchaser.

green shoe option A provision of an issue's registration statement that allows an underwriter to buy extra shares from the issuer (thus increasing the size of the offering) if public demand proves exceptionally strong. The term derives from the Green Shoe Manufacturing Company, which first used the technique. The maximum number for new shares that can be purchased is 15% of the total amount of shares covered by the issuer's registration statement.

guardian A fiduciary who manages the assets of a minor or incompetent for the benefit of that person.

H

haircut The reduction in the value of securities in a broker/dealer's trading/investment account used in calculating net capital. It is a conservative asset valuation practice required by the SEC to provide a cushion against investment losses.

highest current independent bid A bid from a market maker that is not participating in the distribution.

high frequency trading (HFT) High-frequency trading is executing algorithmic, ultra-low latency computerized trading strategies. HFT may respond to tiny changes in market inefficiencies. Each algorithmic trading program is proprietary.

HR-10 plan *See* Keogh plan.

hypothecation Pledging to a broker/dealer securities bought on margin as collateral for the margin loan.

I

immediate family A parent, mother-in-law or father-in-law, husband or wife, child, sibling, or other relative supported financially by a person associated with the securities industry.

independently prepared reprints A form of public communication that requires principal approval prior to use. Does not have to be filed with FINRA.

indication of interest An investor's expression of conditional interest in buying an upcoming securities issue after the investor has reviewed a preliminary prospectus. An indication of interest is not a commitment to buy.

individual retirement account (IRA) A retirement investing tool for employed individuals that allows an annual contribution of 100% of earned income up to a maximum of $5,000. Some or all of the contribution may be deductible from current taxes, depending on the individual's adjusted gross income and coverage by employer-sponsored qualified retirement plans.

inducements Techniques that are used to persuade customers to buy or sell securities, such as claims of no commission or commission rebate. Any action of this sort is prohibited by the Act of 1934.

initial margin requirement The amount of equity a customer must deposit when making a new purchase in a margin account. The SEC's Regulation T requirement for equity securities is currently 50% of the purchase price.

initial public offering (IPO) The first sale of common stock by a corporation to the public.

in-part call Redemption of a certain portion of a bond issue.

inside information Material information that has not been disseminated to, or is not readily available to, the general public.

inside market The best (highest) bid price at which an OTC stock can be sold, and the best (lowest) ask price at which the same stock can be bought in the inter-dealer market.

insider Any person who has or has access to material, nonpublic information about a corporation.

Insider Trading Act *See* Insider Trading and Securities Fraud Enforcement Act of 1988.

Insider Trading and Securities Fraud Enforcement Act of 1988 Legislation that defines what constitutes the illicit use of nonpublic information in making securities trades and the liabilities and penalties that apply.

institutional sales material A form of public communication that does not require prior principal approval. Does not have to be filed with FINRA.

intermarket sweep order (ISO) A limit order submitted for automatic execution in a specific market center even when the other market center (exchange) is posting a better price. This appears to be a trade-through but when sending an ISO, the sender fulfills Regulation NMS order-protection obligations by simultaneously sending orders to market centers with better prices. These orders are not auto-routed and are marked with an "F" trade indicator.

interpositioning Placing a third party in the middle of a trade between a broker/dealer and the best available market. The practice violates FINRA Rules unless it results in a lower cost to the customer or higher sales proceeds.

interstate offering An issue of securities registered with the SEC and sold to residents of states other than that in which the issuer does business.

intrastate offering An issue of securities exempt from SEC registration, available to companies that do business in one state, and sell their securities only to residents of that same state.

introducing broker (IB) A broker/dealer that does not hold customers' money or securities; instead, it introduces customer accounts to a clearing broker/dealer, which holds all cash and securities for those accounts. *Syn.* fully disclosed broker.

investment adviser (1) Any person who makes investment recommendations in return for a flat fee or percentage of assets managed. (2) For investment companies, the individual who has the day-to-day responsibility of investing the cash and securities held in the fund's portfolio in accordance with the objectives stated in the fund's prospectus.

investment banker An institution in the business of raising capital for corporations and municipalities.

Investment Grade Debt securities in the following credit categories are "Investment Grade": AAA/Aaa, AA/Aa, A/A, and BBB/Baa.

in-whole call The redemption of a bond issue in its entirety at the option of the issuer, as opposed to its redemption based on a lottery held by an independent trustee.

IPO *See* initial public offering.

IRA *See* individual retirement account.

IRA rollover The reinvestment of assets that an individual receives as a distribution from a qualified tax-deferred retirement plan into an individual retirement account within 60 days of receiving the distribution. The individual may reinvest either the entire sum or a portion of the sum, although any portion not reinvested is taxed as ordinary income.

IRA transfer The direct reinvestment of retirement assets from one qualified tax-deferred retirement plan to an individual retirement account. The account owner never takes possession of the assets, but directs that they be transferred directly from the existing plan custodian to the new plan custodian.

K

Keogh plan A qualified tax-deferred retirement plan for persons who are self-employed and unincorporated or who earn extra income through personal services aside from their regular employment. Also known as an H.R. 10 plan.

L

legal list The selection of securities determined by a state agency (usually a state banking or insurance commission) to be appropriate investments for fiduciary accounts.

Level 1 The basic level of Nasdaq service; through a desktop quotation machine, it provides registered representatives and public subscribers with up-to-the-minute inside bid and ask quotations on hundreds of over-thecounter stocks.

Level 2 A level of Nasdaq data service; providing real time bid and ask quotations by market marker of each Nasdaq-, NYSE-, Amex-, and regional exchange-listed security.

Level 3 The highest level of Nasdaq service; through a desktop quotation machine, it provides real time inside bid and ask quotations, supplies the bids and asks of each market maker for a security, and allows each market maker to enter new and updated quotations.

limited power of attorney A written authorization for someone other than the beneficial owner of an account to make certain investment decisions regarding transactions in the account.

limited principal A person who has passed an examination attesting to the knowledge and qualifications necessary to supervise the business of a broker/dealer in a limited area of expertise. A limited principal is not qualified in the general fields of expertise reserved for a general securities principal; these include supervision of underwriting and market making and approval of advertising.

limited representative A person who has passed an examination attesting to the knowledge and qualifications necessary to sell certain specified investment products.

loan consent agreement Optional contract between a brokerage firm and a margin customer that permits the firm to lend the margined securities to other brokers; the contract is part of the margin agreement.

locate requirement SEC rule requiring firms to locate securities for borrowing prior to the short sale of any equity security. *See* Regulation SHO.

locked market The situation created when there is no spread between the bid and the ask on the same security; that is, one market maker bids for a stock at the same price that another market maker quotes its ask price.

low latency Low latency refers to very short time periods (faster than human perception) for investors to connect to exchanges and ECNs to effect transactions. The lower the latency, the greater the trading advantage for high frequency traders. *Syn.* ultra-low latency.

M

make a market To stand ready to buy or sell a particular security as a dealer for its own account. A market maker accepts the risk of holding the position in the security.

managed underwriting An arrangement between the issuer of a security and an investment banker in which the banker agrees to form an underwriting syndicate to bring the security to the public. The syndicate manager then directs the entire underwriting process.

Manning Rule Rule that bans member trading ahead of customer orders. *Syn.* customer limit order protection.

margin The amount of equity contributed by a customer as a percentage of the current market value of the securities held in a margin account.

margin account A customer account in which a brokerage firm lends the customer part of the purchase price of securities.

margin call The Federal Reserve Board's demand that a customer deposit a specified amount of money or securities when a purchase is made in a margin account; the amount is expressed as a percentage of the market value of the securities at the time of purchase. The deposit must be made within one payment period. *Syn.* Fed call; federal call; federal margin; Reg T call; T call.

margin maintenance call A demand that a margin customer deposit money or securities when the customer's equity falls below the margin maintenance requirement.

margin maintenance requirement The minimum equity that must be held in a margin account, determined by the broker/dealer and by the SRO. The amount of equity required varies with the type of security bought on margin, and the broker/dealer's house requirement is usually higher than that set by the SRO.

markdown The difference between the highest current bid price among dealers and the lower price that a dealer pays to a customer.

market letter A publication that comments on securities, investing, the economy, or other related topics and is distributed to an organization's clients or to the public.

market maker A dealer willing to accept the risk of holding a particular security in its own account to facilitate trading in that security.

Market Participant Identity (MPID) An MPID is obtained from FINRA and serves as a unique indentifier for member firms to report trades and to satisfy audit requirements.

mark to the market To adjust the value of the securities in an account to the current market value of those securities; used to calculate the market value and equity in a margin account.

markup The difference between the lowest current offering price among dealers and the higher price a dealer charges a customer.

markup policy *See* 5% markup policy.

material information Any fact that could affect an investor's decision to trade a security.

minimum margin requirement *See* margin maintenance requirement.

minus tick A security transaction's execution price that is below the previous execution price, by a minimum amount.

modifier *See* trade modifiers.

municipal finance professional (MFP) An associated person of a FINRA member firm engaged in municipal securities underwriting, trading, sales, financial advisory, research, investment advice, or any other activities that involve communication with public investors. APs whose activities are limited solely to sales with natural persons and clerical or ministerial functions are not MFPs.

municipal securities principal *See* Series 53.

Municipal Securities Rulemaking Board (MSRB) A self-regulatory organization that regulates the issuance and trading of municipal securities. The Board functions under the supervision of the Securities and Exchange Commission; it has no enforcement powers.

N

naked short selling Selling a stock short without first borrowing the stock or confirming that the stock can be borrowed. Sellers who cannot deliver the shares sold by settlement will cause a fail-to-deliver transaction. Naked short selling is a violation.

Nasdaq Composite Index The Nasdaq Composite Index measures all (over 5,000) Nasdaq domestic and non-US based common stocks listed on the Nasdaq Stock Exchange.

Nasdaq Execution Services Nasdaq's broker/dealer.

Nasdaq Global Market Companies The Nasdaq Global Market consists of companies that meet and continue to meet stringent financial and liquidity requirements and agree to meet specific corporate governance standards.

Nasdaq Global Select Market Companies The Nasdaq Global Select Market demands the highest initial listing standards. Issuers of Global Select securities are well known by regulatory authorities and investors around the world as companies that provide market participants with a high degree of transparency, liquidity, and strict corporate governance. Considered the top tier of Nasdaq-listed securities.

NASD Rule 2711 Deals with research analyst conflict of interest rules.

National Association of Securities Dealers Automated Quotation System (Nasdaq) A US-based cash equities stock exchange. Companies wishing to list their publicly traded shares on Nasdaq must qualify by having at least three broker-dealers committing to act as market makers, the company's stock must be registered under the 1933 Act and meet minimum number of public shares, assets, and capital.

National Association of Securities Dealers, Inc. (NASD) The self-regulatory organization for the over-the-counter markets. NASD was organized under the provisions of the 1938 Maloney Act. NASD was dissolved with the formation of FINRA in 2007. *See* FINRA.

National Securities Clearing Corporation (NSCC) An organization that acts as a medium through which member brokerage firms and exchanges reconcile accounts with each other. Provides clearance and settlement functions. *See* qualified service representative.

net asset value (NAV) The value of a mutual fund share calculated once a day, based on the closing market price for each security in the fund's portfolio. It is computed by deducting the fund's liabilities from the total assets of the portfolio and dividing this amount by the number of shares outstanding.

net capital The amount of cash and SEC-approved assets readily convertible into cash that a broker/dealer owns in excess of its liabilities. The SEC sets net capital requirements to ensure that broker/dealers have enough capital to deal responsibly with the investing public.

Net Order Imbalance Indicator (NOII) Nasdaq disseminates imbalance information every five seconds:

- Opening Cross: 9:28 to 9:30 am ET;
- Closing Cross: 3:50 to 4:00 pm ET; and
- IPO and Halt Crosses: beginning with the quote-only period of the IPO of halt resumption.

net transaction A principal transaction in which a market maker, after having received an order to buy (or sell) a stock, buys (or sells) the stock at one price and then sells to (or buys from) the customer at a different price.

new account form The form that must be filled out for each new account opened with a brokerage firm. The form specifies, at a minimum, the account owner, trading authorization, payment method, and types of securities appropriate for the customer.

new issue market The securities market for shares in privately owned businesses that are raising capital by selling common stock to the public for the first time. *Syn.* primary market. *See also* initial public offering (IPO).

New York Stock Exchange (NYSE) The largest stock floor-based exchange in the United States. It is one of several equities and derivative exchanges comprising NYSE Euronext, a holding company.

New York Stock Exchange Composite Index An index of the common stocks, ADRs, REITs, and tracking stock listed on the NYSE.

nominal owner The person in whose name securities are registered if that person is other than the beneficial owner. This is the role of a brokerage firm when customer securities are registered in street name.

nominal quote A quotation on an inactively traded security that does not represent an actual offer to buy or sell but is given for informational purposes only.

nonaccredited investor An investor not meeting the income or net worth requirements of Regulation D. Nonaccredited investors are counted for purposes of the 35-investor limitation for Regulation D private placements.

nonallowable asset An asset that a broker/dealer may not include when computing its net capital.

nonissuer transaction A securities trade that does not directly or indirectly benefit the issuer. Under the Uniform Securities Act, the proceeds of a nonissuer transaction go to the selling stockholder. Most nonissuer transactions are secondary transactions.

non-Nasdaq registration In accordance with SEC 15c2-11, firms that wish to make market in OTC Pink or OTC Bulletin Board securities must file Form 211 with FINRA.

non-Nasdaq three call rule Requires that any trader performing a riskless principal or agency trade for a client in a non-Nasdaq security contact a minimum of three market makers to obtain the best interdealer market in the security.

nonqualified retirement plan A corporate retirement plan that does not meet the standards set by the Employee Retirement Income Security Act of 1974. Contributions to a nonqualified plan are not tax deductible.

normal trading hours The hours during which market makers must be open for business (9:30 am ET–4:00 pm ET, Monday–Friday).

numbered account An account titled with something other than the customer's name; the title might be a number, symbol, or special title. The customer must sign a form designating ownership of the account.

O

offering circular An abbreviated prospectus used by corporations issuing less than $5 million of stock. The SEC's Regulation A allows these offerings an exemption from the full registration requirements of the 1933 Act.

office of supervisory jurisdiction (OSJ) The broker/dealer office responsible for supervising the activities of registered representatives and associated persons housed in that office and in other offices within the same region.

Office of the Comptroller of the Currency (OCC) A federal government agency of the US Treasury. It regulates national banks.

Office of Thrift Supervision (OTS) An independent federal government agency of the US Treasury that regulates thrifts.

omnibus account A master account in the name of a carrying broker/dealer that holds customer securities.

order memorandum The ticket completed by a registered representative that contains customer instructions regarding the placement of an order. The memorandum contains such information as the customer's name and account number, a description of the security, the type of transaction (buy, sell, sell short, etc.) and any special instructions (such as time or price limits).

OTC Bulletin Board An electronic quotation system for equity securities that are not listed on a national exchange or included in the Nasdaq system.

P

painting the tape The practice by a broker/dealer of creating a false appearance of active trading to induce customers to either buy or sell.

partnership account An account that empowers the individual members of a partnership to act on behalf of the partnership as a whole.

passive market making In accordance with Rule 103 of Regulation M, market-making firms that are also underwriters may enter quotes and execute trades as a market maker as long as their bids do not exceed the highest independent bid. Net daily purchase limit is 30% of ADTV.

pattern day trader Someone who executes four or more day trades in a five-business-day period. Minimum equity for such accounts is $25,000.

payable date Day on which a declared dividend is paid to all stockholders owning shares on the record date.

penalty bid Used to minimize sellbacks of public offering stock to the underwriters at the stabilizing bid. The bid may be entered by the book-running managing underwriter to reclaim a selling concession from a syndicate member in connection with an offering when the securities originally sold by the syndicate member are purchased in syndicate covering transactions.

pension plan A contract between an individual and an employer, labor union, government entity, or other institution, that provides for the distribution of pension benefits at retirement.

person As defined in securities law, an individual, corporation, partnership, association, fund, joint stock company, unincorporated organization, trust, government or political subdivision of a government.

piggyback exception An exception from the market maker filing requirements under Rule 15c2-11 exists if the security has been quoted on at least 12 business days over the past 30 calendar days and there have been no more than four consecutive business days without a quotation during this period.

Pink Sheets OTC Pink Market, formerly known as Pink Sheets, is an e-quotation system that displays bids and asks from market makers for thousands of OTC stocks. The name *Pink Sheets* comes from the color of paper they were printed on many years ago.

possession of securities *See* control of securities.

power of substitution *See* stock power.

preemptive right The legal right of stockholders to maintain their proportionate ownership by purchasing newly issued shares before the new stock is offered to the public.

preliminary prospectus An abbreviated prospectus that is distributed while an issuer's registration statement is being reviewed by the SEC. It contains the essential facts about the forthcoming offering (except the underwriting spread, final public offering price, and date on which the shares will be delivered). *Syn.* red herring.

prime broker Provides custody and financing of securities while other firms (called executing brokers) handle all trades placed by the customer.

primary distribution *See* primary offering.

primary market makers Firms registered as market makers in Global Market stocks who satisfy at least two of the following:

- quotes are maintained at the inside market at least 35% of the time;

- the dealer maintains a spread of no greater than 102% of the average dealer spread;

- no more than 50% of the quotes are updated without being accompanied by an execution; or

- a volume of 1½ times the proportionate volume in the stock is executed.

primary offering An offering in which the proceeds of the underwriting go to the issuing corporation.

principal transaction A transaction in which a broker/dealer either buys securities from customers and takes them into its own inventory or sells securities to customers from its inventory.

profit-sharing plan An employee benefit plan established and maintained by an employer whereby the employees receive a share of the profits of the business. The money may be paid directly to the employee, deferred until retirement, or a combination of both approaches.

prospectus *See* final prospectus.

proxy A limited power of attorney from a stockholder authorizing another person to vote on stockholder issues according to the stockholder's instructions. To vote on corporate matters, a stockholder must either attend the annual meeting or must vote by proxy.

proxy department The department within a brokerage firm that is responsible for sending proxy statements to customers whose securities are held in the firm's name and for mailing financial reports received from issuers to their stockholders.

prudent man rule A legal maxim that restricts trades in a fiduciary account to only those investments that a reasonable and prudent person might make.

public appearance A form of public communication that requires principal approval. Does not have to be filed with FINRA.

public offering price (POP) The price of new shares disclosed in the issuing corporation's final prospectus.

Q

qualification *See* registration by qualification.

qualified retirement plan A corporate retirement plan that meets the standards set by the Employee Retirement Income Security Act of 1974. Contributions to a qualified plan are tax deductible.

Qualified Special Representative (QSR) An NSCC full-service member (NSCC member) who has been granted status as a QSR for the purposes of locking-in trades for other NSCC members and/or their correspondents.

qualified third-market maker An OTC dealer that makes a market in an exchange-listed stock and that meets minimum net capital requirements.

quarterly securities count The counting of securities under its possession or control that a broker/dealer must conduct each calendar quarter. The procedure includes verifying securities in transit, comparing the count with its records, and recording all unresolved differences.

quotation The price being offered or bid by a market maker or broker/dealer for a particular security.

R

reclamation Reclamation occurs when a buyer, after accepting securities as good delivery, later discovers that the certificates were not in good deliverable form. The securities can be sent back to the selling dealer with a Uniform Reclamation Form attached.

record date The date established by a corporation's board of directors that determines which of its stockholders are entitled to receive dividends.

red herring *See* preliminary prospectus.

reference security A security into which a subject security may be converted, exercised, or exchanged that may influence significantly the subject security's value in accordance with Regulation M.

registered Term that describes a security that prints the name of the owner on the certificate. The owner's name is stored in records kept by the issuer or a transfer agent.

registered options principal (ROP) The officer or partner of a brokerage firm who approves, in writing, accounts in which options transactions are permitted.

registered principal An associated person of a member firm who manages or supervises the firm's investment banking or securities business. This includes persons who train associated persons. Unless the member firm is a sole proprietorship, it must employ at least two registered principals.

registered representative (RR) An associated person engaged in the investment banking or securities business who solicits or conducts business in securities. Anyone employed by a brokerage firm who is not a principal and who is not engaged in clerical or brokerage administration is subject to registration and exam licensing as a registered representative. *Syn.* account executive; stockbroker of a member.

registrar The independent organization or part of a corporation responsible for accounting for all of the issuer's outstanding stock and certifying that its bonds constitute legal debt.

registration by coordination A process that allows a security to be sold in a state. It is available to an issuer who files for registration of the security under the Securities Act of 1933 and files duplicates of the registration documents with the state Administrator. State registration becomes effective at the same time the federal registration statement becomes effective.

registration by filing A process that allows a security to be sold in a state. Previously referred to as "registration by notification," it is available to an issuer who files for registration of the security under the Securities Act of 1933, meets minimum net worth and certain other requirements, and notifies the state of this eligibility by filing certain documents with the state Administrator. The state registration becomes effective at the same time the federal registration statement becomes effective.

registration by qualification A process that allows a security to be sold in a state. It is available to an issuer who files for registration of the security with the state Administrator, meets minimum net worth, disclosure and other requirements, and files appropriate registration fees. The state registration becomes effective when the administrator so orders.

registration statement The legal document that discloses all pertinent information concerning an offering of a security and its issuer. It is submitted to the SEC in accordance with the requirements of the Securities Act of 1933 and forms the basis of the final prospectus that is distributed to investors.

regular way A settlement contract that calls for delivery and payment within a standard payment period from the date of the trade.

Regulation A The provision of the Securities Act of 1933 that exempts from registration small public offerings valued at no more than $5 million worth of securities issued during a 12-month period.

Regulation D The provision of the Securities Act of 1933 that exempts from registration offerings sold to a maximum of 35 nonaccredited investors.

Regulation M SEC regulation that addresses market maker activities during syndication.

Regulation NMS An SEC regulation that fosters competition between markets/exchanges and competition among individual orders through four initiatives. (1) The "Order Protection Rule" requires trading centers to enforce written policies designed to prevent tradethroughs. (2) The "Access Rule" requires fair access to quotations, establishes a limit on access fees to harmonize the pricing of quotations across different trading centers, and requires every exchange to enforce written rules that prohibit their members from engaging in a pattern or practice of displaying quotations that lock or cross automated quotations. (3) The "Sub-Penny Rule" prohibits market participant from accepting, ranking, or displaying orders, quotations, or indications of interest in a pricing increment smaller than a penny, except for orders, quotations, or indications of interest that are priced at less than $1.00 per share. (4) "Market Data Rules" amendments that update the requirements for consolidating, distributing, and displaying market information.

Regulation S-AM An SEC regulation that allows a consumer, in certain limited situations, to block affiliates of brokers/dealers, investment companies, investment advisers, and transfer agents registered with the Commission from soliciting the consumer based on eligibility information.

Regulation SHO Mandates a locate requirement with regard to short sales. Before entering a short sale order, members are required to locate the security to be assured that delivery can be made on the settlement date. The locate requirement applies to short sales in all equity securities.

Regulation SP An SEC regulation covering privacy rules promulgated under the Gramm-Leach-Bliley Act. A broker/dealer must provide customers with a notice of its privacy policies and practices and must not disclose nonpublic personal information about a consumer to nonaffiliated third parties unless it provides certain information to the consumer and the consumer has not opted out of the disclosure. Rigorous standards to protect privacy are also required under the regulation.

Regulation T The Federal Reserve Board regulation that governs customer cash accounts and the amount of credit that brokerage firms may extend to customers for the purchase of securities. Reg T currently sets the loan value of marginable securities at 50% and the payment deadline at two days beyond regular way settlement.

Regulation U The Federal Reserve Board regulation that governs loans by banks to broker/dealers for the purchase of securities. Also deals with loans from banks to customers.

rehypothecation The pledging of a client's securities as collateral for a bank loan. Brokerage firms may rehypothecate up to 140% of a customer's debit balance.

rejection Right of the buyer of a security to refuse to accept delivery to complete a trade because the security does not meet the requirements of good delivery.

restricted account A margin account in which the equity is less than the Regulation T initial requirement.

restricted security An unregistered, nonexempt security acquired either directly or indirectly from the issuer, or an affiliate of the issuer, in a transaction that does not involve a public offering.

retention requirement The provision of Regulation T that applies to the withdrawal of securities from a restricted account. The customer must deposit an amount equal to the unpaid portion of the securities being withdrawn in order to reduce the debit balance. The retention requirement is the reciprocal of the initial margin requirement. *Related item(s)*: restricted account.

reverse split A reduction in the number of a corporation's shares outstanding that increases the par value of its stock or its earnings per share. The market value of the total number of shares remains the same. Related item(s): stock split.

right (1) A legal guarantee. (2) A security representing a stockholder's entitlement to the first opportunity to purchase new shares issued by the corporation at a predetermined price (normally less than the current market price) in proportion to the number of shares already owned. Rights are issued for a short time only, after which they expire. *Syn.* subscription right; subscription right certificate.

rights offering An issue of additional shares of stock accompanied by the opportunity for each current stockholder to maintain a proportionate ownership by purchasing additional shares before the stock is offered to the non-shareholders.

riskless and simultaneous transaction The buying or selling by a broker/dealer of a security for its own account so as to fill an order previously received from a customer. Although the firm is technically acting as a principal in the trade, the transaction is relatively riskless because the purchase and sale are consummated almost simultaneously.

Rule 10b-21 SEC rule that is targeted at short sellers who purposely mislead a broker/dealer about their ability or intention to deliver securities by the settlement date causing a fail to deliver. In addition, it targets short sellers who deceive broker/dealers about their source of borrowable securities to satisfy the locate requirement of Regulation SHO as well as long sellers who falsify to their broker/dealers that they actually own the shares being sold.

Rule 101 Restricts the activities of distribution participants during new offerings of securities under Regulation M.

Rule 102 Identifies restrictions on issuers and selling security holders and is intended to prevent market manipulation by these persons before a distribution under Regulation M.

Rule 103 Allows market makers (who are also syndicate members) to engage in passive market making during a restricted period.

Rule 104 Regulates the prices at which stabilizing bids may be made under Regulation M.

Rule 105 Prohibits manipulative short sales in anticipation of an offering under Regulation M.

Rule 144 SEC rule requiring that persons who hold control or restricted securities may sell them only in limited quantities, and that all sales of restricted stock by control persons must be reported to the SEC by filing a Form 144, "Notice of Proposed Sale of Securities."

Rule 144a Allows nonregistered foreign and domestic securities to be sold to certain qualified institutional investors in the US, without holding period requirements.

Rule 145 SEC rule that excepts stock splits and stock dividends from the registration requirements of the Act of 1933.

Rule 147 SEC rule that provides exemption from the registration statement and prospectus requirements of the Act of 1933 for securities offered and sold exclusively intrastate.

Rule 15c2-1 SEC rule that prohibits broker/dealers from using customer securities as collateral for a loan in excess of loans made to customers.

Rule 15c2-11 SEC rule requiring prospective market makers in non-Nasdaq stocks to file Form 211 with FINRA at least three business days prior to quotation entry. In signing Form 211, the firm agrees to maintain a file on the issuer that contains financial and operations information.

Rule 15c3-1 The SEC Net Capital rule governing the net capital requirements of broker/dealers.

Rule 15c3-2 SEC rule requiring broker/dealers to inform customers of their free credit balances at least quarterly.

Rule 15c3-3 The SEC Customer Protection rule that requires (1) that carrying firms have the daily requirement to reduce to possession or control all fully paid-for securities and all excess margin securities, and (2) that carrying firms must, each week, compute monies owed to the BD by customers (debits) and monies owed by the BD to customers (credits). If credits exceed debits, the excess must be on deposit in a special reserve account within one hour after banks open on the second business day following computation.

Rule 17a-3 SEC rule governing the maintaining of records by a broker/dealer and the posting of such records.

Rule 17a-4 SEC rule governing the retention time and storage by a broker/dealer of records and reports.

Rule 17a-5 SEC rule governing the filing by a broker/dealer of certain FOCUS reports.

Rule 17a-11 SEC rule governing violations of the net capital rule and setting out early warning rules.

Rule 17f-2 SEC rule requiring the fingerprinting of all associated persons and others who handle cash or securities, and the keeping of such fingerprint records.

Rule 204 Regulation SHO requirement for participants in NSCC's Continuous Net Settlement System (CNS) to close out any fails that exists on the settlement date (T+3) for an equity security.

Rule 405 Defunct NYSE rule requiring the exercise due diligence to learn the essential facts about every customer. *Syn.* know your customer rule. *See* FINRA Rule 2111 and 2090.

Rule 415 SEC rule governing shelf offerings. The rule allows an issuer to sell limited portions of a new issue over a two-year period.

Rule 504 SEC rule providing that an offering of less than $1 million during any 12-month period may be exempt from full registration. The rule does not restrict the number of accredited or nonaccredited purchasers.

Rule 505 SEC rule providing that an offering of $1 million to $5 million may be exempt from full registration. The rule restricts the number of nonaccredited purchasers to 35 but does not restrict the number of accredited purchasers.

Rule 506 SEC rule providing that an offering of more than $5 million may be exempt from full registration. The rule restricts the number of nonaccredited purchasers to 35 but does not restrict the number of accredited purchasers.

Rule 611—Order Protection Rule The rule states that a trading center, such as Nasdaq or the NYSE, enforce written policies and procedures that are reasonably designed to prevent trade-throughs on that trading center of protected quotations in NMS stocks. *See* trade-through, Regulation NMS.

Rule 1014 An NASD rule, which sets the standards for admission as a member of FINRA. The rule seeks to ascertain whether an applicant is qualified by exam, free of any criminal or civil actions, and that past infractions, if any, have been disclosed. FINRA will also look to see whether the applicant has made proper contractual agreements with a clearing firm(s), banks, and service bureaus; has sufficient capital; and in all ways is ready to perform its lines of business and duties of a broker/dealer.

Rule 6434 This FINRA rule prohibits market participants from displaying, ranking, and accepting quotations, orders, or indications of interest in OTC Equity Securities priced in an increment smaller than $0.01 if the order is priced at $1.00 per share or greater. If the quotation, order, or indications of interest is priced less than $1.00 per share, the minimum pricing increment is $0.0001.

Rule G-37 If a municipal dealer makes a political contribution to an issuer official, it is prohibited from engaging in a negotiated underwriting of municipal securities with that issuer on a negotiated basis for two years. Municipal finance professionals are permitted to make contributions of $250 or less per election without triggering a two-year prohibition if they are eligible to vote for that official.

S

sale *See* sell.

sales literature Any written material distributed to customers or the public by a firm. Examples include circulars, research reports, speeches, market letters, performance reports, and text used for seminars.

Schedule 13D The form that must be filed by an individual (or individuals acting in concert) after acquiring beneficial ownership of 5% or more of any nonexempt equity security. It must be sent within 10 business days to the issuing company, the exchange where the stock is trading, and the SEC.

Schedule 13G An abbreviated Schedule 13D used principally by an investment company, bank, or insurance company if it acquires a 5% position in the normal course of business and not for the purpose of changing or influencing control of the company. The schedule must be filed 45 days after the first calendar year-end when the firm becomes subject to the requirement.

SEC Rule 203 A broker/dealer effecting a short sale in any equity security must "locate" the security being borrowed and document the location prior to the trade entry. The rule effectively prohibits a broker/dealer from accepting a short sale order unless the broker/dealer has borrowed the security so that it can be delivered on the settlement date. The rule provides for some limited exceptions, such as shorts effected in connection with bona-fide market making.

Securities Act of 1933 Federal legislation requiring the full and fair disclosure of all material information about the issuance of new securities. *Syn.* Act of 1933; Full Disclosure Act; New Issues Act; Prospectus Act; Trust in Securities Act; Truth in Securities Act.

Securities and Exchange Commission (SEC) Commission created by Congress to regulate the securities markets and protect investors. It is composed of five commissioners appointed by the president of the United States and approved by the Senate. The SEC enforces, among other acts, the Securities Act of 1933, the Securities Exchange Act of 1934, the Trust Indenture Act of 1939, the Investment Company Act of 1940, and the Investment Advisers Act of 1940.

Securities Exchange Act of 1934 Federal legislation that established the Securities and Exchange Commission. The act aims to protect investors by regulating the exchanges, the over-the-counter market, extension of credit by the Federal Reserve Board, broker/dealers, insider transactions, trading activities, client accounts, and net capital. *Syn.* Act of 1934; Exchange Act.

Securities Information Center (SIC) The organization designated by the SEC to act as a central data bank for reports of lost and stolen securities.

Securities Investor Protection Corporation (SIPC) A nonprofit membership corporation created by an act of Congress to protect clients of brokerage firms that are forced into bankruptcy. Membership is composed of all brokers and dealers registered under the Securities Exchange Act of 1934, all members of national securities exchanges, and most FINRA members. SIPC provides customers of these firms up to $500,000 coverage for cash and securities held by the firms (coverage of cash is limited to $250,000).

segregation Holding customer-owned securities separate from securities owned by other customers and securities owned by the brokerage firm.

self-regulatory organization (SRO) An organization accountable to the SEC for the enforcement of federal securities laws and the supervision of securities practices within an assigned field of jurisdiction (e.g., FINRA, NYSE, CBOE, MSRB).

seller's option A settlement contract that calls for delivery and payment according to a number of days agreed to by the buyer. The earliest delivery can be made is settlement date + 1.

selling away An associated person engaging in private securities transactions without the knowledge and consent of the employing broker/dealer. This violates FINRA rules.

selling dividends Inducing customers to buy mutual fund shares by implying that an upcoming distribution will benefit them; this practice is prohibited.

sellout Procedure that the seller of a security follows when the buyer fails to complete the contract by accepting delivery of the security. The seller closes the contract by selling the security in the open market and charging the account of the buyer for transaction fees and any loss caused by changes in the market.

separate account The account that holds funds paid by variable annuity contract holders. The funds are kept separate from the insurer's general account and are invested in a portfolio of securities that matches the contract holders' objectives.

Series 3 The national commodity futures exam. Passing this exam serves to meet the requirements for the National Futures Association to issue the license that is needed to do futures business with the public.

Series 4 The registered options principal license, which qualifies the holder to supervise the sale and trading of options. A Series 7 qualification is a prerequisite for this license. Every FINRA member firm engaged in trading options must employ at least one registered options principal.

Series 6 The investment company/variable contract products limited representative license, which entitles the holder to sell mutual funds and variable annuities and is used by many firms that sell primarily insurance-related products. The Series 6 can serve as the prerequisite for the Series 26 license.

Series 7 The general securities registered representative license, which entitles the holder to sell all types of securities products with the exception of commodities futures (requires a Series 3 license).

Series 9/10 The NYSE branch office manager (BOM) or general securities sales supervisor limited principal license, which entitles the holder to supervise the sale of all types of securities products except most futures (comprised of Series 9 (options) and Series 10 (general securities)). Cannot supervise investment banking or market making. Cannot approve advertising.

Series 11 The assistant representative–order processing license, which entitles the holder to accept unsolicited orders, enter order tickets, update client information, fill out client new account forms, and provide to customers quotes and other pro forma information relating to securities. The license does not permit the holder to determine suitability, recommend transactions, or provide advice to customers. An assistant representative–order processing may be compensated on a salary or hourly wage basis only.

Series 14 The NYSE Compliance Official examination for those individuals designated as having day-to-day compliance responsibilities for a NYSE-member firms or who supervise 10 or more people engaged in compliance activities.

Series 23 The General Securities Principal—Sales Supervisor Module, which offers an alternative to persons associated with FINRA members who are registered as Series 9/10 to complete the Series 24. The Series 23 examination covers material from the Series 24 not otherwise covered under the Series 9/10.

Series 24 The general securities principal license entitles the holder to supervise the business of a broker/dealer. A Series 7 or a Series 62 is a prerequisite. The Series 24 can serve as the prerequisite for the Series 51 license.

Series 26 The investment company/variable contract products limited principal license, which entitles the holder to supervise the sale of investment company and variable annuity products. A Series 6 or a Series 7 qualification is a prerequisite. The Series 26 can serve as the prerequisite for the Series 51 license.

Series 27 The financial and operations limited principal license, which entitles the holder to supervise the financial administration of a brokerage firm.

Series 51 The municipal fund securities principal license, which entitles the holder to supervise the activities of registered representatives effecting municipal fund securities transactions (e.g., 529 college savings plans and Local Government Investment Pools [LGIPs]).

Series 53 The municipal securities principal license, which entitles the holder to supervise the municipal securities business of a brokerage firm. A Series 7 or a Series 52 qualification is a prerequisite.

Series 62 The corporate securities limited representative license, which entitles the holder to sell all types of corporate securities but not municipal securities, options, DPPs, or certain other products.

settlement The completion of a trade through the delivery of a security and the payment of cash or other consideration.

settlement date The business day on which delivery of a security and payment of money is to be made through the facilities of a registered clearing agency in connection with the sale of a security. Settlement provisions are standardized by the Uniform Practice Code.

shelf offering An SEC provision allowing well-known, seasoned issuers (WKSIs) to register a new issue security without selling the entire issue at once. The issuer can sell limited portions of the issue over a two-year period without reregistering the security. *See* Rule 415.

short The term used to describe the selling of a security not owned by the seller. For example, an investor who borrows shares of stock from a broker/dealer and sells them on the open market is said to have a short position in the stock.

short against the box The term used to describe the selling of a security, contract, or commodity that the seller owns but prefers not to deliver; frequently this is done to defer taxation.

short interest The total number of shares in the stock that are reflected on the books and records of a reporting firm as short as of the current reporting period's settlement date.

short sale The sale of a security that the seller does not own, or any sale consummated by the delivery of a security borrowed by or for the account of the seller.

short securities difference A shortfall between the number of shares identified in a broker/dealer's accounting records and the number of shares in a physical count of its securities.

SIC *See* Securities Information Center.

simplified arbitration An expedient method of settling disputes involving claims not exceeding $25,000, whereby a panel of arbitrators reviews the evidence and renders a decision. All awards are made within 30 business days.

SLP *See* supplemental liquidity provider.

SPAC A special purpose acquisition corporation is a type of blank-check company. Owners of SPAC shares expect the SPAC to be acquired by or merged with another company within a certain time period.

special memorandum account (SMA) A notation on a customer's general or margin account indicating that funds are credited to the account on a memo basis; the account is used much like a line of credit with a bank.

special reserve bank account A separate account maintained by a broker/dealer for the exclusive benefit of customers.

spread In a quotation, the difference between the bid and the ask prices of a security. In a new issue, the difference between the POP and proceeds to the issuer.

stabilizing Bidding at or below the public offering price of a new issue security. Underwriting managers may enter stabilizing bids during the offering period to prevent the price from dropping sharply. *See also* fixing.

standby underwriter An investment banker that agrees to buy any part of an issue that has not been purchased by current stockholders through a rights offering. The firm exercises the remaining rights, maintains a trading market in the rights, and offers the stock acquired to the public.

statutory disqualification Prohibiting a person from associating with a self-regulatory organization because the person has been expelled, barred, or suspended from association with a member of a self-regulatory organization; has had his registration suspended, denied, or revoked by the SEC; has been the cause of someone else's suspension, barment, or revocation; has been convicted of certain crimes; or has falsified an application or report that he is required to file with or on behalf of a membership organization.

statutory voting A voting procedure that permits stockholders to cast one vote per share owned for each position. The procedure tends to benefit majority stockholders. Related item(s): cumulative voting.

sticky offering An offering of new shares of stock that are difficult to sell. This may be as a result of bad news about the company whose stock is being sold or the overall economy.

stock power A standard form that duplicates the back of a stock certificate and is used for transferring the stock to the new owner's name. A separate stock power is used if the registered owner of a security does not have the certificate available for signature endorsement. *Syn.* irrevocable stock power; power of substitution.

stock record A broker/dealer's accounting system that shows separately for each security all long and short positions, as well as the location of each security, the holdings of all customers, and all securities due from or owed to other broker/dealers. *Syn.* securities record.

stock record break A discrepancy between the number of shares reported in a broker/dealer's accounting records and the number of shares in a physical count of its securities. The discrepancy can be due to a counting error or to missing securities.

stopping stock A member agrees to hold the price (or better) of a security for a short time for another party.

stop stock price The specific price at which a member agrees to execute an order.

stub quote Order placed far from a stock's market price. Used by market makers when they want to be sure no trades occur. *Syn.* placeholder quote.

subject quote A tentative quote the market maker must reconfirm.

subordinated debenture A debt obligation backed by the general credit of the issuing corporation that has claims to interest and principal subordinated to ordinary debentures and all other liabilities. Related item(s): debenture.

subordinated debt financing A form of long-term capitalization used by broker/dealers in which the claims of lenders are subordinated to the claims of other creditors. Subordinated financing is considered part of the broker/dealer's capital structure and is added to net worth when computing its net capital.

subordinated loan A loan to a broker/dealer in which the lender agrees to subordinate its claim to the claims of the firm's other creditors.

suitability A determination made by a registered representative as to whether a particular security matches a customer's objectives and financial capability. The representative must have enough information about each customer to make this judgment.

Super Display Book (SDBK) The electronic order entry and processing system used by the New York Stock Exchange. SDBK replaced SuperDOT.

supplemental liquidity provider (SLP) An off-floor (upstairs), electronic member of the NYSE or NYSE Amex who is compensated for adding liquidity to the market on specifically assigned stocks.

switching Redeeming shares in a mutual fund in order to purchase shares in a different fund. Although not a violation per se it is a supervisory concern due to possible additional sales charges and tax liabilities.

SYND Nasdaq quote montage symbol for a non-penalty stabilizing bid.

syndicate A group of investment bankers formed to handle the distribution and sale of a security on behalf of the issuer. Each syndicate member is responsible for the sale and distribution of a portion of the issue. *Syn.* underwriting syndicate.

systematic risk Undiversifiable risk associated with a downturn in the market generally. Common stock that is fundamentally sound may lose market value due to a downturn in overall market conditions.

systemic risk The risk associated with the failure of entire financial markets. A single financial institution collapse leading to another and another cascading throughout a region or the world is an example of systemic risk, not to be confused with systematic risk.

T

tender offer An offer to buy securities for cash or for cash plus securities.

tentative net capital A broker/dealer's total available capital minus all nonallowable assets. It is capital before haircuts are taken.

testimonial An endorsement of an investment or service by a celebrity or public opinion influencer. The use of testimonials in public communications is regulated by FINRA.

third market A trading market in which exchange-listed securities are traded over-the-counter (also called the Nasdaq Intermarket).

third-party account (1) A customer account for which the owner has given power of attorney to a third party. (2) A customer account opened by an adult naming a minor as beneficial owner. (3) A customer account opened for another adult. This type of account is prohibited.

tick A minimum upward or downward movement in the price of a security.

time value The amount an investor pays for an option above its intrinsic value; it reflects the amount of time left until expiration. The amount is calculated by subtracting the intrinsic value from the premium paid. Related item(s): intrinsic value.

tombstone A printed advertisement that is limited to basic information about the offering, such as the name of the issuer, type of security, names of the underwriters, and where a prospectus is available.

TotalView A data feed operated by the Nasdaq Stock Exchange. It provides information about every quote and order at every price level in Nasdaq-, NYSE-, Amex-, and regional-listed securities on Nasdaq and supplies the Net Order Imbalance Indicator (NOII).

trade-by-trade match Occurs when both parties to the trade submit transaction data, and the ACT system performs an online match.

trade comparison The memorandum sent by both broker/dealers engaged on either side of a trade; it confirms the details of the transaction.

trade confirmation A printed document that contains details of a transaction, including the settlement date and amount of money due from or owed to a customer. It must be sent to the customer on or before the settlement date.

trade date The date on which a securities transaction is executed.

Trade Reporting and Comparison Service (TRACS) Used to report trades executed through the ADF, including Nasdaq Global Market, Nasdaq Capital, Nasdaq Convertible Debt, and CQS securities.

Trade Reporting Facility (TRF) FINRA/Nasdaq's Trade Reporting Facility (TRF) provides FINRA members with a service for the reporting and reconciliation of transactions effected away from an exchange floor. Nasdaq operates the TRF, but it is subject to FINRA rules. Trades by FINRA members on Nasdaq, NYSE, and other exchange-listed securities executed off an exchange floor may be reported to FINRA/Nasdaq's TRF.

trade shredding A prohibited practice that involves splitting a large single order into smaller orders in order to maximize payment for order flow.

trade-through The execution of trades at prices inferior to protected quotations displayed by other trading centers.

trading ahead Engaging in trading activity in anticipation of the issuance of research reports is a prohibited practice.

trading along Buying or selling at the same time and at the same price as an institutional customer. Need order by order agreement with the institution (no blanket approvals).

trading halt codes Indicate the status of trading halts, suspensions, and cease trade orders (CTOs) in Nasdaq and Consolidated Quotation System (CQS) securities.

tranche One of the classes of securities that forms an issue of collateralized mortgage obligations. Each tranche is characterized by its interest rate, average maturity, risk level, and sensitivity to mortgage prepayments. Neither the rate of return nor the maturity date of a CMO tranche is guaranteed. *See also* collateralized mortgage obligation.

transfer agent A person or corporation responsible for recording the names and holdings of registered security owners, seeing that certificates are signed by the appropriate corporate officers, affixing the corporate seal, and delivering securities to the new owners.

transfer and hold in safekeeping A securities buy order settlement and delivery procedure whereby the securities bought are transferred to the customer's name but are held by the broker/dealer. Related item(s): hold in street name; transfer and ship.

transfer and ship A securities buy order settlement and delivery procedure whereby the securities bought are transferred to the customer's name and sent to the customer. Related item(s): hold in street name; transfer and hold in safekeeping.

Treasury bill A marketable US government debt security with a maturity of less than one year. Treasury bills are issued through a competitive bidding process at a discount from par; they have no fixed interest rate. *Syn.* T bill.

Treasury bond A marketable, fixed-interest US government debt security with a maturity of more than 10 years. *Syn.* T bond.

treasury stock Equity securities that the issuing corporation has issued and repurchased from the public at the current market price. Related item(s): issued stock; outstanding stock.

Trust Indenture Act of 1939 The legislation requiring that all publicly offered, nonexempt debt securities be registered under the Securities Act of 1933 and be issued under a trust indenture that protects the bondholders. Applies to bond issues of $5 million or more.

two-dollar broker An exchange member that executes orders for other member firms when their floor brokers are especially busy. Two-dollar brokers charge a commission for their services; the amount of the commission is negotiated.

U

UGMA *See* Uniform Gifts to Minors Act.

UIT *See* unit investment trust.

underlying securities The securities that are bought or sold when an option, right, or warrant is exercised.

underwriter An investment banker who works with an issuer to help bring a security to the market and sell it to the public.

underwriting The procedure by which investment bankers channel investment capital from investors to corporations and municipalities that are issuing securities.

underwriting compensation The amount paid to a broker/dealer firm for its involvement in offering and selling securities.

underwriting discount *See* underwriting spread.

underwriting manager The brokerage firm responsible for organizing a syndicate, preparing the issue, negotiating with the issuer and underwriters, and allocating stock to the selling group. *Syn.* manager of the syndicate; managing underwriter; syndicate manager, book running manager. *Related item(s)*: agreement among underwriters; syndicate.

underwriting spread The difference in price between the public offering price and the price an underwriter pays to the issuing corporation. The difference represents the profit available to the syndicate or selling group. *Syn.* underwriting discount; underwriting split.

underwriting syndicate *See* syndicate.

unethical trading practices The use of any manipulative, fraudulent, or deceptive activity in selling securities. *See* front running, capping, painting the tape.

Uniform Gifts to Minors Act (UGMA) Legislation that permits a gift of money or securities to be given to a minor and held in a custodial account that is managed by an adult for the minor's benefit.

Uniform Practice Code (UPC) The FINRA policy that establishes guidelines for a brokerage firm's dealings with other brokerage firms.

Uniform Securities Act (USA) Model legislation for securities industry regulation at the state level. Each state may adopt the legislation in its entirety or it may adapt it (within limits) to suit its needs. *Related item(s)*: blue-sky laws; Series 63.

Uniform Transfers to Minors Act (UTMA) Legislation adopted in some states that permits a gift of money or securities to be given to a minor and held in a custodial account that an adult manages for the minor's benefit until the minor reaches a certain age (not necessarily the age of majority). *Related item(s)*: Uniform Gifts to Minors Act.

unit investment trust (UIT) An investment company that sells a fixed number of redeemable shares in a professionally selected portfolio of securities. It is organized under a trust indenture, not a corporate charter.

unlisted securities Securities that are not listed on any exchange.

Unlisted Trading Privilege (UTP) The right granted to exchange member firms to trade in stocks not listed on that exchange. The exchange granting the privilege must itself first receive clearance to do so by applying to the SEC.

UTP *See* Unlisted Trading Privilege.

V

variable annuity An insurance contract in which the insurance company guarantees a minimum total payment to the annuitant at the end of the accumulation stage. The performance of a separate account, generally invested in equity securities, determines the amount of this total payment.

VIX The volatility market index, known as the fear index, that measures investor expectation of implied volatility in the S&P 500.

volatility The magnitude and frequency of changes in the price of a security or commodity within a given time period.

Volume-Weighted Average Price (VWAP) The VWAP is the price at which the majority of trading in a stock took place in a given period. It is determined by multiplying the price by the shares traded for each transaction and dividing the total transaction value by the total number of shares traded for the period. Buy-side customers often judge the quality of a trade by its VWAP for the trading period.

voting right A stockholder's right to vote for members of the board of directors and on matters of corporate policy—particularly the issuance of senior securities, stock splits, and substantial changes in the corporation's business. A variation of this right is extended to variable annuity contract holders and mutual fund shareholders, who may vote on material policy issues.

W

warrant (1) A security that gives the holder the right to purchase securities from the warrant issuer at a stipulated subscription price. Warrants are usually long-term instruments with expiration dates years in the future. (2) A debt security issued in certain municipal jurisdictions issued in small amounts to pay project costs as they are incurred.

when-issued security (WI) A securities issue that has been authorized and is sold to investors before the certificates are ready for delivery. Typically, such securities include new issue municipal bonds, stock splits, and Treasury securities. *Syn.* when-, as-, and if-issued security.

Whistleblower Office The Whistleblower Office of the SEC's Division of Enforcement is responsible for handling whistleblower tips and complaints and setting awards for people who provide leads to successful enforcement actions.

WKSI A well-known, seasoned issuer is a company that is current in its 10K, 10Q, and 8K filings and has a greater than $700 million market capitalization or issued $1 billion in registered debt offerings over the past three years.

workout quote A qualified quotation whereby a broker/ dealer estimates the price on a trade that will require special handling owing to its size or to market conditions. *See also* bona fide quote; firm quote; nominal quote.

wrap account A managed account in which the customer pays one annual package price for all products and services for the account. Considered to be advisory accounts.

writer The seller of an option contract. An option writer takes on the obligation to buy or sell the underlying security if and when the option buyer exercises the option. *Syn.* seller.

Z

zero-coupon bond A corporate or municipal debt security traded at a deep discount from face value. The bond pays no interest; rather, it may be redeemed at maturity for its full face value. It may be issued at a discount, or it may be stripped of its coupons and repackaged.

zero-minus tick A security transaction's execution price that is equal to the price of the last sale but lower than the last different price.

zero-plus tick A security transaction's execution price that is equal to the price of the last sale but higher than the last different price.

Index